SALT : PROBLEMS & PROSPECTS

SALT:
PROBLEMS
&
PROSPECTS

Edited by Morton A. Kaplan
University of Chicago

GENERAL LEARNING PRESS
250 James Street
Morristown, N.J. 07960

© 1973 General Learning Corporation.

All rights reserved. No part of this publication may be reproduced or transmitted in any form or by any means, electronic or mechanical, including photocopy, xerography, recording, or any information storage and retrieval system, without written permission from the publisher.

Manufactured in the United States of America.

Published simultaneously in Canada.

Library of Congress Catalog Card Number 72-8184

Biographical Data on Contributors

Morton A. Kaplan, the director of the Arms Control and Foreign Policy Seminar, is professor of political science and chairman of the Committee on International Relations at the University of Chicago.

The late **Leonard Beaton** was a distinguished British journalist. Mr. Beaton was the author of *Must the Bomb Spread?,* a book which explores the possibilities of the proliferation of nuclear weapons. He wrote for the *Montreal Gazette,* Reuters, *The London Times* and *The Guardian* and served as editor of *Round Table,* a journal of Commonwealth affairs.

Hedley Bull is a former Director of the Arms Control and Disarmament Research Unit of the British Foreign Office and is now Professor of International Relations at the Australian National University at Canberra. *The Control of the Arms Race,* written by Mr. Bull in 1965, has been acclaimed both as a significant scholarly work and as the best work available for the layman who wishes to acquaint himself with arms control.

Freeman J. Dyson is professor of physics at the Institute for Advanced Study at Princeton University. Dyson, an internationally acclaimed physicist, has served as a consultant for numerous government agencies in such fields as disarmament, space exploration, and weapons development.

Richard L. Garwin is an IBM Fellow with the IBM Corporation, member of the IBM Corporate Technical Committee, and Adjunct Professor of Physics at Columbia University. Mr. Garwin has done major research on liquid helium, superconductors, fundamental particles of physics, and novel computer and communications elements and systems. He has also made substantial contributions in the design of nuclear weapons, instruments and electronics for research in nuclear and low-temperature physics, the non-conservation of parity and its consequences, properties of mu mesons, computer elements and systems, and military technology.

Harry G. Gelber is a Reader in Politics at Monash University in Australia. Dr. Gelber is a consultant to several Australian government agencies and author of several books. He had edited *Problems of Australian Defense,* published in 1970 by Oxford University Press. He has been an American Studies Fellow of the American Council of Learned Societies and Research Associate at the Harvard Center for International Affairs.

Johan J. Holst is director of the Norwegian Institute of International Affairs in Oslo. Mr. Holst is a member of the Advisory Commission on Arms Control and Disarmament for the Norwegian Government, and of the Institute of Strategic Studies. He has served on the research staff of the systems analysis division of the Norwegian Defence Research Establishment, where he directed research on arms control and long-range planning. He has also been a research associate at the Harvard University Center for International Affairs and a senior member of the professional staff of the Hudson Institute. He is co-author and co-editor of *Why ABM? Policy Issues in the Missile Defense Controversy.*

Richard N. Perle is a member of the professional staff of the U.S. Senate Sub-Committee on National Security and International Operations. Perle is an international strategic arms expert who has served as consultant and special assistant to the Secretary of Defense, as a member of the staff of the Committee to Maintain a Prudent Defense Policy, and as a Senior Political Scientist for the Advanced Studies Group of the Defense and Space Center of the Westinghouse Electric Corporation.

Frederick S. Wyle was formerly U.S. Deputy Assistant Secretary of Defense for European and NATO Affairs. Wyle is now engaged in the practice of law in New York City.

Preface

When President Nixon and Leonid Brezhnev, the leader of the Soviet Communist Party, initialed in Moscow in 1972 a treaty intended to limit the expansion of nuclear weapons, both of them pointed out that the agreement was only a first step and that the years of negotiations that led to it would be followed by more years of negotiations leading, they hoped, to more treaties. Nonetheless, people have the impression that the first treaty is a final step, a singular achievement, and a few even have the notion that it is a solution to the terrible problem troubling mankind since nuclear energy was first brought under control and then released in the form of bombs.

As Morton A. Kaplan points out in the first of the papers collected in this book, Strategic Arms Limitation talks are in fact continuing processes in the conduct of international diplomacy with wide and subtle effects on every aspect of relations among the many governments of the world. That SALT is so central is hardly surprising; the fact that a handful of governments own ultimate weapons, or that anyone owns them, has altered the conduct of foreign policy, its aims, and its timing. Foreign policy may be concerned with many things and diplomatic dealings between nations may turn on many events, but nuclear weapons and the means of delivering them are primary concerns of all governments. For many years, nothing one can foresee is likely to become more important in international affairs than are these weapons.

The chapters of this book are papers prepared for the Arms Control and Foreign Policy Seminar being conducted under the auspices of the Center for Policy Study at the University of Chicago. The seminar is funded by the Ford Foundation. Its director is Mr. Kaplan, who is Professor of Political Science and Chairman of the Committee on International Relations at the University.

Scholars from this country and abroad have been involved in the seminar, along with officials of government, business and industrial leaders, journalists and interested citizens. The basic purpose of the seminar is to clarify underlying issues related to arms control and foreign policy. The papers printed here, like all those presented during the seminar, were subjected to critical response by the participants in the different sessions. The papers in this volume were presented during the winter of 1970 and the early spring of 1971. They not only throw light on what we now know of the discussions leading to the first SALT agreement, but delineate the broad concerns upon which governments must reflect in their future negotiations. All the papers except Mr. Kaplan's have been printed previously in pamphlet form and widely disseminated by the Center.

D. J. R. Bruckner, *Director*
Center for Policy Study
Vice President for Public Affairs
The University of Chicago

CONTENTS

Introduction

The seminar *SALT: Problems and Prospects* was specifically designed for seminar participants who were not all expert in arms control problems. The papers for the seminar—and the chapters of this book—are intended to provide sufficient background in the kinds of strategic calculations required to understand arms control negotiations such as SALT and the political context in which they are likely to be conducted. Although the political factors involved in SALT, and the political consequences, have greater importance, we did not believe that they could be adequately understood by those who were unaware of, or insufficiently familiar with, the central strategic problems. Moreover, since the actual negotiations are conducted in secret and depend upon a degree of technical detail that would be neither interesting nor comprehensible to most of the participants, the papers assigned by the seminar were designed to cope more with the general nature of arms control problems than with highly specific matters under discussion in the SALT talks.

The introductory chapter by Morton A. Kaplan discusses some of the reasons for engaging in arms control negotiations, problems of stability, and the general kinds of consequences for world order that negotiations of this type may have. Chapter 2 by Hedley Bull deals specifically with the interwar naval treaties. However, it was written less from the historian's point of view, which would examine reasons for highly particular choices at a particular time period, than from the political scientist's point of view, which asks what lessons can be learned from these particular negotiations that might possibly apply to arms control negotiations in the current time frame.

Since we often tend to mirror other nations, Johan Holst's chapter explores the character of Soviet arms choices, deployments, and strategic doctrines and how they may differ from the American strategies. Although, given the nature of the Soviet system, definitive knowledge in this area is not possible, the kinds of evidence provided by Mr. Holst should permit a more intelligent public understanding of this matter.

Richard Garwin and Richard Perle provide contrasting views of strategic stability and of the virtues of different kinds of arms control agreements that might be entered into by the United States and the Soviet Union. These chapters therefore deal with the central strategic issues in negotiations of the SALT type in the present time frame. Frederick Wyle's paper explores the possible consequences, or lack of consequences, of SALT for NATO. In this respect, he is concerned with both the nuclear and strategic balance. Although his point of view is controversial, it is also highly informative and well articulated.

The chapters by Leonard Beaton and Harry Gelber hypothesize reactions of proto-nuclear states to the bilateral SALT negotiations and to the assumptions made by the United States and the Soviet Union concerning such states. Leonard Beaton, who tragically died some months after his seminar, explores this problem primarily from the standpoint of European proto-nuclear states, while Harry Gelber does so from the standpoint of several of the major Asian proto-nuclear states. Both chapters provide important correctives to many facile assumptions currently being made in both the Soviet Union and the United States.

The distinguished physicist Freeman Dyson provides an important perspective for the relationship of the political and strategic factors from the standpoint of his long experience with and participation in arms control problems.

In choosing the authors of the various chapters, the director sought as wide a diversity of viewpoint as was consistent with technical expertise in the discussion of the issues. The authors were also chosen for their flexibility of mind and willingness to engage in genuine dialogue. Given this objective, consistency of viewpoint was necessarily impossible. However, the reader will note throughout, despite the diversity of perspectives, certain widely shared understandings that permit orderly dialogue and exploration of the major issues. Even if we end in disagreement, it is extremely important to understand why we disagree—whether the disagreements are based upon differences of basic assumptions, differences of assessment of matters of fact, differences of assessment concerning motivations, differences of projections concerning the future, differences concerning values, or differences concerning the kinds of risks, whether strategic or political, that ought to be run. Although the differences do not always emerge explicitly and systematically in the chapters, the discussions are sufficiently analytical and precise for the intelligent reader to grasp them without the necessity of didactic presentation. We do not provide the reader with a set of answers but with a set of questions. His thoughtful responses will provide a vantage point for his own perspectives.

1 • SALT and the International System

Morton A. Kaplan

Although agreements to limit the possession and use of armaments have seldom been achieved, and when achieved, seldom kept for long, the history of attempts to reach such agreements is several thousand years old. The reasons for the search may have changed over time, and even persistently sought objectives may be undesirable for reasons not understood by those who seek them, but it is at least a *prima facie* assumption that ends sought so long and so consistently must have some merit. The latest major attempt to agree on limitation of arms is currently being engaged in by the United States and the Soviet Union under the name SALT (Strategic Arms Limitation Talks). There are several considerations underlying the present set of negotiations.

Moral. Though necessary for morally defensible reasons, the proliferation of weapons designed to kill and maim is offensive to the civilized conscience. This is especially true in the age of nuclear weapons—an age in which a small number of weapons can accomplish so much in the way of incineration that the mind boggles at the thought.

In fact, no nation today fully accepts deterrence theory. If deterrence was the supreme objective, there would be two rather simple methods for achieving it. One method would be for the United States and the Soviet Union by agreement to plant nuclear mines under each other's cities; then, if a city in one country goes up, the other country can blow up a corresponding city in the first country. A second method is that of the doomsday machine, which, when a specified amount of destruction has occurred in a particular country, automatically explodes and destroys the entire world.

Whatever the possible technical deficiencies of either method, Herman Kahn used them very effectively as *reductios ad absurdum* by demonstrating to his audiences that these devices were psychologically unacceptable. In the same way, he did much to undermine the strategy of massive retaliation by referring to it as a "war-gasm." Although less attention has been called to it, at least until recently, the McNamara doctrine of assured mutual destruction has many of the same characteristics, albeit in somewhat less extreme form. Although assured mutual destruction may be defensible in the absence of an alternative, arms limitation conferences represent at least a hope, if not an expectation, that an alternative to such a doctrine may eventually be found. If many of the proposals for arms limitation are intellectually unsound and even dangerous, it still remains true that a world order that rests upon mutual terror is somewhat less than fully defensible morally.

Economic. Although the cost of the strategic arms race is greatly exaggerated in the public mind—for instance, the American strategic arms budget was $11 billion in 1961 and approximately $8 billion in 1971, despite a strong intervening inflation—and although many of the expectations concerning the savings that might occur as a consequence of arms control agreements are also exaggerated, there are undoubtedly strong economic motivations for the talks. Some of these involve nonmilitary uses of the savings but pressures for savings on the nuclear front come even from within the military, where nonstrategic forces have often been cut to the point of ineffectiveness.

Strategic. It is often argued that the mechanics of the mobilization systems were partly responsible for World War I. If Russia or Germany had been forced to mobilize and then to demobilize in the prewar period, for instance, either would have been virtually defenseless in an intervening period. Therefore, once mobilization was required, avoiding war was no longer believed possible. In the same way, in the post-World War II period when SAC constituted the deterrent force, the force would not have been utilizable for a period of forty-eight hours after a fail-safe operation. One motivation for arms limitation agreements would be to assure a system in which the mechanics of preparedness do not unnecessarily increase the probabilities of war.

On the other hand, the motivation to negotiate during some periods would have served to undermine strategic stability. For instance, when missile forces were powered by nonstorable liquid fuels, a freeze on qualitative improvements in weapons systems would have increased first strike incentives.

Political. The political motivations producing talks are both internal and external, intrinsic and extrinsic. American presidents, for instance, could no more be against arms control than they could be—or, at least before women's liberation, could have been—against motherhood. They must seek agreements, if only to establish their *bona fides.* Although our allies may distrust any particular set of negotiations, a general unwillingness to engage in negotiations on the arms control issue would interfere with our alliances and with our relations with uncommitted states. Moreover, arms control negotiations constitute a political forum. In this forum, governments seek to achieve objectives, whether they be establishing a more stable world order or achieving some particular advantage over other states. In this respect, arms control negotiations are as much a part of the normal international political process as are peace settlements, commodity agreements, alliances, and other bilateral or multilateral international activities.

Diplomatic. The diplomatic motivation is obviously closely related to the political. It rests upon the supposition that agreements are good in themselves, almost regardless of substance, because they create a climate of opinion in which other agreements become possible, or upon the supposition that talks are good in themselves, apart from any concrete outcomes, because they create a climate of shared expectations and understandings, thus increasing the probability of peaceful solutions with respect to non-conference-related activities.

SALT and International Order

There is a strong temptation to view SALT talks in isolation from the structure of the international system. Yet the agreements reached at SALT are likely to have important consequences for the behavior of other states not participating in these meetings and for the structure of the international system. Insofar as agreements emerging from SALT, if any, affect the weapons systems only of the United States and the Soviet Union, it might be argued that SALT sets no constraints on the rest of the international system. If anything, according to this view, SALT merely restricts the competition between the two nuclear superpowers and sets a limit to the superiority they achieve over the rest of the international system. This interpretation is dubious, however. Although an effort to relate the SALT talks to some conceptualization of the emerging international system might be counterproductive at this stage because it would force the United States and the Soviet Union to articulate their disagreement over that particular subject, an ultimate failure to resolve these issues will severely limit the value of SALT. Although, as Hedley Bull shows, it can be argued that the interwar naval agreements were quite effective during substantial periods of time, despite the fact that disagreements among minor powers removed particular classifications of ships from the ambit of the agreement, the nuclear age poses too many problems for satisfaction in the long run with results as modest as those that emerged from the naval agreements.

One solution to this problem, consonant with the Nuclear Non-Proliferation Treaty urged upon the world by both Russia and the United States, would be to use the SALT talks to establish a limited nuclear condominium between Russia and the United States. This world order would be based upon extant superior forces, for no rational political principle could be offered to support it. China is obviously opposed to this prospect and other potentially major states are likely to find it extremely disagreeable over the long run. Such a system would be highly vulnerable to political, economic, and technological surprises, and would depend upon limited but sustained joint interests between the United States and the Soviet Union over a long period of time, despite the many potential points of conflict that exist.

The Soviet Union and the United States might instead view the SALT talks as a halting but definite step in the direction of a nuclearly disarmed world, thus minimizing the invidious distinctions ensuing from the talks and providing a rationale for other states to refrain from major challenges to the regime established by SALT. This was indeed the basis on which a large number of states gave initial acceptance to the Nuclear Non-Proliferation Treaty. Unfortunately, however, there is no sign that either the United States or the Soviet Union has the intention or the capability to take any major steps in this direction. However, much such a world would respond to valid moral objection to the nuclear arms race, nothing in current nuclear doctrines (and strategic analysis provides no prospects) would seem to lower the risks to the point where genuine nuclear disarmament might become a feasible objective for either the Soviet Union or the United States, let alone both.

Alternatively, the SALT talks might be viewed as a first step toward a controlled nuclear situation in which several other nations or combinations of nations might become major participants. There are some signs that the United States may no longer be entirely hostile to this sort of development, but the Soviet Union remains adamantly opposed. Indeed, the Chinese continue to regard the talks, in part at least, as directed against them—a view they also had of the Nuclear Non-Proliferation Treaty. Moreover, political obstacles to the development of a nuclear force in Japan or in Western Germany or in the Common Market area (at least on a genuinely joint basis) are presently still so large that raising the issue in the near future would likely be counterproductive. Thus this idea appears to be one whose time has not come, even though its absence may limit the effectiveness of the SALT talks and increase the likelihood that resulting agreements will be disruptive politically in the intermediate future.

Whether a world with a large number of strategic nuclear systems seems likely to be more or less stable than the present one depends upon the kinds of assumptions one makes. If the additional nuclear forces were as unstable as the present French *force de frappe,* then these forces would be provocative, destabilizing for existing alliances, and inadequate for international security. If the doctrine for their use was that all other states must be deterred simultaneously, then the proliferation of weapons systems might indeed produce an uncontrolled arms race. If, on the other hand, the doctrine is to deter the first attacker—a genuinely achievable objective under some constraints—then this kind of proliferation might serve to dampen the arms race.

One of the incentives that maintains both the qualitative and the quantitative arms race on a bilateral basis is the fear that some mistake may provide the enemy with a decisive advantage which it might attempt to seize, despite various uncertainties, during some intense crisis that threatens its regime or bloc. Prudence demands forms of insurance that put premiums upon the speed and agility with which one makes qualitative improvements in one's weapons systems. If, however, the world consisted of a number of relatively equal and protected nuclear systems, with considerable second-strike capabilities, then a miscalculation by any one will likely not be fatal. A first strike by one of these powers against any other one, under most circumstances, would use up so much of its nuclear force that it would become extremely vulnerable to an attack by some other nuclear power. At the same time it would look extremely dangerous, as the attacking power would have demonstrated its willingness to make a massive use of its nuclear weapons to achieve victory.

By virtue of this, the first strike becomes a vanishing problem. Whatever plausible calculations the military planners might present to the leadership of a country contemplating attack that, despite uncertainties, the attack is a good risk because of the dangers threatening the regime or bloc, this argument could be made *vis-à-vis* only one particular state and not against the entire system. By turning what is only a marginally plausible calculation into an extremely implausible one, this would dampen the nuclear arms race by reducing the risks inherent in not continuing the qualitative arms race at a rapid pace. By dampening the arms race, it would lower the importance placed upon nuclear arsenals and, to that extent, diminish the relationship between international stability and mutual terror. Moreover, this development would place all major states or groups of states on an equal footing. Therefore, it would be more in accord with the equities of a normal international political process and would not rest upon a politically indefensible insistence by the United States and the Soviet Union on maintaining their nuclear hegemony over the rest of the system. If the quality of the systems of additional nuclear states were substantial but still not of "superpower" status, this argument would be weakened, but not irrelevant. Admittedly, an attempt to bring this consideration to the fore at the present time would be counterproductive with respect to the negotiations now going on at SALT. Neither the United States nor the Soviet Union is currently prepared to consider this kind of structure of world politics. Therefore, it is appropriate to turn toward the more specific constraints of the ongoing SALT talks.

SALT and Stability

The objectives of the parties in negotiations such as SALT bear some relationship to their respective economic strengths, political purposes, and existing strategic situations. If one nation is considerably superior to the other, it might seek negotiations to stabilize and regulate that superiority. For instance, if the United States had a first-strike capability against the Soviet Union and if the Soviet Union clearly lacked such capability against the United States, or vice versa, the superior state might seek to institutionalize this relationship through arms control negotiations. Alternatively, the weaker state might seek to evade such negotiations until it could bargain from a position of greater equality. If it perceived an opportunity to work upon the political will of the other state, it might seek negotiations to persuade the first state to give up its existing advantage. Or, if the advantage appeared to be increasing, it might seek to persuade it at least not to widen the discrepancy. Where neither state appears to be in a position to acquire a substantial advantage over the other either by means of the economic resources it is capable of diverting to military production or by virtue of political seduction, the states would seem to have a joint interest in what for want of a better term is often called strategic stability.

Strategic stability is not a simple term, for it has a number of different aspects. As Richard Perle points out, strategic stability may be viewed as the attempt to narrow the gap between first and second strikes, to minimize the advantage of striking first. However, stability may also be related to the susceptibility of the strategic systems to shocks, accidents, misinformation, and failures of command and control. It is not clear, in the absence of an investigation of particular solutions, whether the improvement of the mutual stability of a system in one respect improves it in others, causes no change, or worsens the situation. Moreover, solutions that improve the stability of the system in the short run conceivably could worsen it over the long run by diverting nuclear competition into uncontrolled channels that contain inherently greater instabilities than the existing ones. As any agreement can, and likely will, be evaded, if not violated, the effects of the agreement upon other aspects of the arms race —for example, a possible shift from submarine-launched ballistic missiles to retrofitted submarine-launched air-breathing missiles—should receive at least some consideration. Moreover, the effects of the agreement, although perhaps symmetrical with respect to deployed systems, may be asymmetrical to the point of instability with respect to dynamic factors. If, for instance, the climate of opinion in one of the two major nuclear powers, and not in the other, has a major effect upon research and development funding and recruitment of scientists, the situation might become dangerously unstable over time from the standpoint of that country.

Problems of stability are related to the specifics of the mutual deployment of nuclear systems. For instance, the layman might imagine that a situation of numerical parity is stable, whereas gross lack of parity is unstable. Yet this does not follow, at least in that abstract manner. Relatively small numbers of soft sites on both sides, although equal in number, might be susceptible to a successful first strike—and hence would make for instability—whereas even relatively large discrepancies in the number of attacking vehicles might make for a very stable situation if the sites were sufficiently hardened so that, given the megatonnage and the accuracy of the attacking vehicles, the attacked side could still do unacceptable damage, whatever that term might mean, to the other side. Indeed, from a purely mathematical point of view, equal numbers of small-sized systems tend to be more unstable than relatively unequal large-sized systems.

Of course, even this simple-minded approach to the subject overlooks the fact that the two countries may be asymmetrical in geography, population, industrial concentration, and strategic doctrine. These also can influence the stability of the system. Moreover, the context in which the calculation is made is also extremely important. Although nuclear interchanges are inherently far more calculable than other forms of military engagement, there are nonetheless potentially large uncertainties connected with them. Nations attempt to increase these uncertainties, thus buying an additional measure of protection against instability, by acquiring different kinds of strategic delivery and defense systems. This usually not only improves the marginal effectiveness of dollar allocations but also provides a basis of assurance against an unknown defect of a particular system that the enemy might exploit. Although, as Dr. Garwin points out, this mix may consist of systems of the same general type, as in the case of different kinds of submarine systems, rather than of systems of different types, land-based missiles and submarines, for instance, one runs a serious risk in the former case that an unanticipated defect may be common to the systems.

When one speaks of the context of the system in which the calculation occurs, one refers to the ways in which the preceding uncertainties are understood by the participants. Consider a scenario in which the world is at peace, there are as a consequence no major crises, and no overt political demands are being made. During this period, the military staff of one of the two countries tells the political leaders that careful calculation shows they can succeed in a first strike against the opposing forces. Although it is true that a few of the enemy's forces may survive, it seems virtually certain that the enemy will not use them against the attacker's homeland, because this would insure the destruction of the enemy's population and also because the withholding of these weapons would permit at least some bargaining over the political conditions that end the war.

I cannot imagine any political leadership that would fail to be appalled by this proposal regardless of the plausibility of the calculations and the strategic doctrine underlying it. To my mind, even the argument that if this opportunity is not achieved now, the other side might achieve a breakthrough that presents it with a similar opportunity would not be convincing. The political leadership would be appalled by the uncertainties inherent in the proposals and by the things that *might* go wrong, even if they were not likely to go wrong.

Although this conclusion assumes a high degree of conservatism in the leadership of the Soviet Union and the United States, at least *vis-à-vis* each other, if not *vis-à-vis* minor nuclear powers, the historical evidence supports it. This kind of view and scenario lies behind most theories of finite or minimum deterrence, which argue that the conservatism of political leadership with respect to nuclear weapons is so great that they will not conceivably be used and therefore that an emphasis on relative nuclear balance is ill-conceived and harmful.

Other scenarios, however, provide different contexts. Imagine a severe crisis, resulting from a largely uncontrollable situation, in which the Soviet regime or the maintenance of the bloc is at issue. In these circumstances, where the leadership faces ultimate political defeat, the same kinds of plausible calculations may not meet with quite the same horror and disbelief. In these circumstances, the risks may look different relative to the alternative losses. This might lead to acceptance of the suggestion for a first strike that might either work or that might plunge the world into catastrophe.

Consider this same situation from the viewpoint of the state that has allowed the other state to acquire the kind of superiority that makes this kind of calculation plausible. It will be aware that the other state can make that kind of calculation plausible. It will also be aware that it cannot make the same kind of calculation for a first strike by its own forces. Under these circumstances, it will be under tremendous pressure, not only in the crisis scenario just outlined but also in a crisis that has not gone quite that far, to make concessions that will prevent escalation. This will be particularly true if the other state has made demands and commitments based on an expectation that the first will back down. In short, the weaker state's diplomatic position will have eroded, although obviously the strategic balance is far from the only factor determining relative bargaining strength in a crisis.

Even if such crises or near crises are relatively low probability events, one would no more want to risk them, if they can be avoided at a relatively low price, than one would desire to play Russian roulette, even though the odds would strongly be with one. The facile assumption that the relative unlikelihood of a major crisis justifies the risk of potential instability is really based upon an unrecognized but false analogy between this kind of situation and repeated play games such as horse races or poker, where the bets are spread over a multitude of plays. Russian roulette is the better analogy if minimum or finite deterrence is accepted, because there will be only one history. Relatively low probability events will occur during it. And, in these cases, plausible risky calculations may play decisive roles unless great stability is built into the system. It is irresponsible to opt for a situation in which other states might be tempted to explore this kind of opportunity. No one in his right mind would desire to play this game if he recognizes it as such and if it can be avoided at a reasonable cost.

Thus, crisis stability is an essential element in strategic stability. It is quite true, as Freeman Dyson points out, that political factors are more important than strategic, and that a hundred years from now someone may view today's arguments over technical details as trifles that merely complicated the important job of reaching political agreements that desirably influence the course of world politics. Yet, the most one can say is that there are seven or eight chances in ten that this will be so. There might be two or three or even only one chance in ten that failure of attention to these technical "trifles" will result in grave, if not irreparable, damage to immensely important human and political values. One may wish to run this risk, but only if it can be shown that paying attention to these "trifles" involves a genuine and definite major cost with respect to other important values.

SALT and the Current Strategic Balance

The common assumption is that both the Soviet Union and the United States have strategic nuclear forces that provide the necessary type of stability. This is subject to serious question. The vulnerabilities of SAC are well known. Projected expansion of the Russian SS-9 would make Minuteman vulnerable by the mid-1970s, as would improvements in the accuracies of the SS-11 and other, relatively smaller, Russian strategic vehicles. Other techniques might result in the incapacitation of Minuteman with minimal warning. It is generally believed that the Polaris submarine missiles, and the succeeding Poseidon, are not vulnerable, but this is true only with respect to known technologies. Satellite tracking or undiscussed measures might change this situation. The system might become vulnerable because of either enemy ingenuity or design failures. For instance, the original design of SAC headquarters was vulnerable to unexpected "bullet-type" shoot-outs resulting from rock interface pressures or penetration devices not limited by surface-blast calculations. Thus the expectation that the headquarters would survive attack could have been "surprisingly" wrong.

Unfortunately, there is no point of permanent stability. New vulnerabilities are always being discovered, designed against, and exploited. No arms control agreement, short of one that establishes genuinely joint laboratories, will stop this, although certain kinds of dispersion of international power may lower the incentives with which these engineering solutions are pursued. Indeed, this very factor ought to, but likely will not, determine the design of an arms control agreement. An agreement that sacrifices considerations of stability, at least to some extent, to the need for symmetry or for acceptance of some existing force structure in setting limitations may increase rather than decrease the incentives for evasions or qualitative advances not outlawed by the treaty. The ease with which an important advantage may be secured is important among the factors that provide incentive to seek such superiority. Conversely the difficulty, and also the visibility, of the effort required to produce superiority will be important among those factors that dampen the incentive to seek it. Obviously, therefore, an effective arms control agreement may depend upon the search for the numbers and types of weapons systems consistent with the optimal amount of stability.

For this reason I find disappointing the apparent willingness of many in the United States to sacrifice ballistic missile defense to the search for an easy agreement in SALT. Ballistic missile defense improves stability in a number of ways. By increasing the mix of systems, it complicates the task of the attacker, thereby enormously increasing the difficulties of a first strike. By combining long- and short-range interceptors in the Safeguard system, ballistic missile defense enables the defensive side to ride out the first wave of an attack without initiating a nuclear World War III.

Since this first wave could be much smaller than many believe, and still be effective in the absence of ballistic missile defense, this is an important hedge against a mistaken war and an additionally strong deterrent to nuclear war. As it is marginally cheaper to expand missile defense than to expand offensive systems, contrary to the claim made by many opponents of defense, thin missile defense would be inconsistent with an offense-defense arms race, unless one of the states can devote enormously more in the way of resources to strategic weaponry than the other. Moreover, since a thin defense would have little effect on the second-strike capabilities of the Soviet strategic force, there is no reason for an offense-defense race unless the Soviet Union insists upon achieving a first-strike capability, which would in itself be a sign of dangerously hostile intentions. The elimination of ballistic missile defense would therefore reduce stability and drive the defending state back into a doctrine of striking upon warning, a doctrine advocated by Senator Fulbright and at one time by Dr. Garwin, who in the first draft of his paper for our conference was willing to take the decision out of the hands of the President and base it upon a stochastic device in order to enhance the deterrent value of the offensive forces. Moreover, given the Russian psychology on defense, there was a small, but not negligible, risk that the Soviet Union might have interpreted an agreement outlawing BMD as a green light to pre-empt the Chinese nuclear force.

In May of 1972, during the visit of President Nixon to Moscow, the Soviet Union and the United States reached a treaty on ABMs (BMDs) and an interim agreement on offensive missiles. In June, a statement of interpretations, divided into sections entitled Agreed Interpretations and Unilateral Statements, was issued. The ABM treaty is to last for five years and, according to American sources, is unlikely to have a longer life unless the interim agreement on offensive missiles is further refined and signed in treaty form. These first-stage agreements are not likely to reduce strategic military spending in either the Soviet Union or the United States. Secretary of Defense Laird has made it clear that he and the Joint Chiefs find the agreement acceptable only if an extensive R & D program is continued and only if we go forward with the Trident submarine and B-1 bomber programs. These agreements have little, if anything, to do with disarmament. Their importance lies in the manifestation of the intention of the two major strategic military powers to attempt to stabilize the strategic implications of their bilateral arms race.

The implications of the agreements will not become fully apparent for some time. There is much uncertainty about the implications of the ABM treaty. This treaty limits each side to 200 launchers in two sites. One site would be located around the national capital and a second in the vicinity of offensive missiles. These sites are to be at least 800 miles apart, which means that the second Soviet site would be behind the Urals. This distance between the sites is important because of strategic asymmetries between the Soviet Union and the United States. Due to the fact that the Soviet national capital is located in the heart of its industrial region, and because many of the Soviet offensive missiles are in Western Europe, two Soviet ABM sites in Western Europe might have given the Soviet Union a very significant advantage, even within the treaty terms, in establishing a light area defense and an important headstart in constructing a thick defense were they later to denounce the treaty. The provision on large phase-arrayed radars is important in limiting rapid expansion of the ABM systems, although the agreement on the size of the ABM site radar network apparently will permit significant expansion over existing facilities.

In the final analysis, the ABM treaty is probably favorable to the Soviet Union because of the concentration of industry and population in Western Europe. The extent of this advantage depends upon certain matters that are not yet clear. Are both the hen house and dog house type radars in the Soviet Union considered to be ABM radars? Both have ABM capabilities. Is the Tallinn system potentially part of an ABM network? Although it was not constructed for that purpose, and although there are important disputes concerning its slant range (160 to 1,200 miles, depending on who makes the estimate), the size of its warhead (one megaton) and its possible radar tie-ins indicate that this system may have such a capability. On the other hand, the slowness of the SS-5 missile, even given the fact that there are 1,000 of them, would seem to constitute a negative indication. Further disputes concern the meaningful quality of a light defense for the national capitals and of a single-site defense for an ICBM range. Most analysts in the United States do not believe that a single-site installation would significantly reduce the vulnerability of the American Minuteman force. Detailed analysis of this problem is required. On the other hand, the existence of two ABM sites would permit more rapid expansion if a decision were ever made to denounce the present treaty.

It is conceivable that the Soviet installations will make sense for the Kremlin not merely in terms of light defense against the United States but also in terms of defense against the Chinese strategic nuclear force. The two ABM sites might well constitute an effective interception system for any force the Chinese are likely to acquire before the 1980s. Moreover, if the Tallinn system has the 1,200-mile slant range that a minority among analysts suggest it may have, it could be useful in defending Moscow, as well as Leningrad, against a Chinese threat. Contrary to some expectations, there is apparently nothing in the ABM treaty that prevents research and development of advanced ABM systems, including laser types.

The executive agreement on offensive missiles is likely to produce somewhat more controversy than the ABM agreement, although some more astute analysts will deplore the sacrifice in potential stability that has been made as a result of the ABM treaty. The Soviet Union is permitted a 40 percent advantage in the number of ICBMs (1,408 to 1,000), 62 missile-launching submarines to 44 for the United States, 950 submarine-launched ballistic missiles to 710 for the United States, and a three-fold advantage in megatonnage of total missile payload. The agreement is believed to provide the United States with a two or three to one advantage in warheads. These estimates are based upon the common assumption that the United States has a two or three year lead in the development of MIRV systems. There are at least some substantial disagreements over the intelligence analyses of Soviet tests and of the extent to which American intelligence can monitor all aspects of Soviet testing. Moreover, the American ICBM system does not have a first-strike potential against the Soviet land-based force because of the small size of its MIRVed warheads and the smaller total megatonnage package its launchers are capable of handling, at least until the 1980s, and not even then unless funds are rebudgeted for accuracy improvements. The Soviet ICBM force, because of its larger payloads, may constitute such a first-strike threat against the American ICBMs even without MIRVing, if certain types of precursor attacks are launched. Moreover, the agreement is extremely ambiguous with respect to limitations by the Soviet Union on heavy SS-9-type launchers. Although as part of the agreed interpretation of the executive agreement the Soviet Union is limited to 313 launchers that are not more than 10 to 15 percent larger than the present SS-9 launchers, the failure to provide a common interpretation of what constitutes a heavy missile permits the Soviet Union to replace all other systems with considerably heavier launchers, with correspondingly greater capabilities. The unilateral declaration by the United States with respect to the difference between heavy and light missiles is clearly designed to provide a ground for

American renunciation of the executive agreement if the Soviet Union significantly increases the lift-capacity of launchers now smaller than the SS-9. However, whether the United States would respond would depend upon the political climate in the United States.

Presumably, the insistence by Secretary Laird on the need to go forward with the Trident submarine system and the B-1 bomber reflects concern about the vulnerability of the American land-based ICBMs—a vulnerability that the Soviet Union land-based ICBM force does not have. The decision to severely limit BMD and to accept the asymmetric vulnerability of the American ICBMs thus places the American second-strike potential primarily in two baskets: submarines and the new B-1. If the Soviet Union should desire to research a program capable of making vulnerable the entire American strategic force, this eases its task considerably. This is not to suggest that a first-strike would ever be a high-confidence strategy, for even an attack upon the highly-vulnerable ICBMs could hardly be pretested. Nonetheless the United States has taken a considerable risk, particularly with respect to its bargaining position during crises.

The foregoing discussion is not designed to suggest that the agreements reached by President Nixon are contrary to American interests, although I do believe that perhaps we might have bargained harder on some issues. The fact that Secretary Brezhnev signed for the Party, rather than Podgorny or Kosygin for the state, is a firm indication that there was considerable Party resistance to the agreement. Brezhnev's signature places the agreements beyond attack by the Party secretariat. This provides considerable evidence of the serious Soviet interest in détente. However, the numerical advantage provided to the Soviet Union may at some point be interpreted by them as acceptance not merely of an equal but of a somewhat greater than equal strategic role. This may be counterbalanced by the fact that the

Russians feel somewhat technologically backward, suspect their launchers are less accurate, and view the American external submarine basing system as providing the launchers with an advantage in terms of submarines in operation. On the other hand, the importance the Russians have always attached to strictly numerical factors and the concept of parity may lead them to have expectations that are somewhat destabilizing in an unpredicted crisis.

Some interpreters have suggested that the agreements return us to McNamara's city-busting strategies. This is not necessarily correct. This interpretation holds only if a Soviet first-strike could so reduce the American force that we would have no options except surrendering some important objectives or threatening the Soviet Union's major cities. The failure to provide a thin area defense does make this interpretation more reasonable. To the extent, however, that the Soviet Union lacks confidence in its first-strike capacity, or to the extent conversely that we have overestimated it, there are other war-fighting options open to the American force, particularly if American R & D continues to exploit these possibilities.

One final observation is in order with respect to the ABM agreement. Although the agreement may provide the Soviet Union with an ABM capability against either the Chinese or the French nuclear forces of the 1970s, if continued into the future the treaty would freeze the vulnerability of both the United States and the Soviet Union to secondary, but major, nuclear powers. Thus, despite the apparent intent of the drafters of the treaty to interfere with the proliferation of ballistic missile defense technology to other powers, in accordance with a general perspective that is opposed to the proliferation of nuclear systems, the agreement may in fact ease the process of transition to a multipolar nuclear world.

SALT and NATO

In addition to the bilateral consequences of SALT, it will have consequences for the United States in NATO. The

Russians' definition of strategic weapons—weapons that can hit either the Soviet Union or the United States—would transform the tactical nuclear aircraft in the NATO area into strategic weapons, while the IRBMs and the MRBMs in the Soviet Union that can hit Western Europe would not be considered strategic weapons. The Soviet IRBMs and MRBMs are obviously a major threat to Europe, a threat that the American strategic force could in any event not be used against, for the attempt to destroy them would, in part, disarm the United States and severely reduce its deterrence of the Soviet Union with respect to the American homeland. On the other hand, the tactical nuclear aircraft in Europe are only a marginal asset to the American strike power against the Soviet Union. Therefore, the Soviet insistence upon a definition that includes the tactical nuclear aircraft in NATO among the weapons to be controlled by a SALT agreement maximizes political friction between the United States and its NATO allies. Obviously, the United States cannot afford to negotiate this issue in a forum in which its allies are not present. At some point the European nations will become aware that they are held hostage by the MRBMs and IRBMs in the Soviet Union, whereas no comparable threat against the Soviet bloc exists. Moreover, as the vulnerability of the American force *vis-à-vis* the Russian increases, its value as a deterrent umbrella for our European allies is reduced.

This does not mean that the Russians would be likely to run the small but more than negligible risk that the Americans would indulge in an irrational counterattack if the Russians hydrogen-bombed Western Europe, but it does mean that the psychological pressure of the Soviet nuclear advantage may at some point become more apparent to Western Europeans than it now is, with important psychological and political consequences. This point is adumbrated in the paper by the late Leonard Beaton, who somewhat minimizes its effect because he misjudged the extent to which the American nuclear position has already eroded.

The poor quality of the American nuclear umbrella is somewhat compensated for by the fact that the conventional position *vis-à-vis* the Russians is not as bad as ordinarily supposed. On the other hand, the leading French strategist, General André Beaufre, emphatically disagrees with the position taken in Mr. Wyle's paper.[1] Since 1962, U.S. forces in Europe have decreased from 430,000 to 300,000, while the Russians have added five divisions. The Russians have a distinct advantage in aircraft and in tanks: there are nearly three times as many tanks in the Warsaw Pact as in NATO and an advantage of 2,500 tactical aircraft. Moreover, much of the logistics and support facilities of the NATO allies is extremely vulnerable to aerial attack, whether conventional or nuclear. It is not clear in the present situation that the degree of dispersal and hardening that would make the forces less vulnerable is politically or economically feasible. The NATO war-gaming in Germany, which is monitored by the Russians, hardly increases one's confidence in this respect. Moreover, as the Western nations, as democracies, cannot consider attack in secret and would find it difficult to control their population if an attack against them occurred, the disorganization occurring behind Western lines at the start of a war would not add to the defensibility of Europe. Although the French are now considerably more cooperative with NATO planning than they were under de Gaulle, the

---

[1] General André Beaufre, Director, Institut Francais d'Etudes Stratégiques, Paris, "Problems of Strategy and European Security," prepared for the Franco-American Symposium on Problems of Strategy and European Security, 15-18, September 1971, pp. 3–4: "The present state in the evolution of conventional arms is such that the extreme stability of conventional operations, which characterized the first half of this century, has been replaced by an extreme instability. This is due to the limits on the number of forces (because of their high cost), to the resulting discontinuity in defensive dispositions, and above all to the extreme mobility of offensive operations, both mechanized and airborne. . . . Actually, as at the beginning of the nineteenth century, *a battle can be won or lost in a day.*" General Beaufre believes it is the West that would lose this conventional war. Most European strategists agree with him.

lack of centralized planning and operations in NATO would be another distinct disadvantage for the West.

Mr. Wyle is quite right about the difficulties at the moment in the way of a European nuclear force, even one organized to use nuclear weapons under a strategy of limited retaliation under two, and only two, circumstances: a Russian nuclear first use or a massive Soviet incursion into Western Europe and refusal to withdraw upon notice. Nonetheless there appears no long-run solution to the problem of Europe that does not include Europe as a nuclear power. The failure of American will in Vietnam cannot fail to have its consequences for Europe. The unwillingness or inability of the United States to pursue a policy of extended deterrence against the Soviet Union that would increase the credibility of its nuclear defense of Europe must eventually be recognized. The pressures in the United States to reduce its forces in Europe cannot fail to have an enormous symbolic political importance for the Western Europeans. Although President Nixon has avoided these pressures for the moment, the handwriting upon the wall seems clear.

It is therefore important that nothing occur at SALT that would inhibit the unification of Europe or its eventual development of a joint nuclear force. This Europe would undoubtedly play an independent role that would create both political and economic difficulties for the United States. On the other hand, such a nuclear Europe would remove some of the tension from the arms race, would remove some of the burden of problems elsewhere in the world from American shoulders, would defuse the bipolarity of competition between the Soviet Union and the United States, would increase the deterrence of a Soviet decision to knock out China's nuclear force, and would help create a more stable as well as a more just pattern of international order. Moreover, such an independent and powerful Europe may be the only guarantor of Israeli survival and an important impediment to turning the Mediterranean into a Soviet lake.

Up to this point, Soviet diplomacy in the Middle East has been immeasurably successful. Although Senator Fulbright is correct when he points out that the Soviet Union in moving into the Mediterrannean is only doing what we have done, he overlooks the fact that this is to our distinct disadvantage and that the current position may have no prospect for long-term stability unless some alternative to the American role in the Mediterranean is found. Our navy is becoming increasingly obsolescent and, as our world role diminishes, our ability to maintain a firm position in the Mediterranean will probably weaken.

SALT and Asia

The SALT talks must also be considered in relationship to the Orient. Nothing we do at SALT should appear to provide the Soviet Union with a carte blanche to attack the Chinese. Such an impression would introduce a dangerous instability into world politics. This means that China eventually must be accepted as a full member of the nuclear club, even though the present Chinese strategic system is still quite weak. The Chinese in their turn are resisting the development of Japan as a nuclear power, a development not looked upon with great favor in Japan itself, although it so far has refused to ratify the Nuclear Non-Proliferation Treaty. Although Japanese nonnuclearization aids importantly the economic growth of Japan and although a nuclear force would introduce some grave strategic problems given the small area of the Japanese islands, the present Japanese position nonetheless rests upon the so-called American nuclear umbrella. The Japanese are also being very slow to recognize the porous quality of that umbrella and the extent to which the diplomatic bonds between the United States and Japan will weaken. However, as we give up our bases in Japan, as the situation changes in the south Pacific near Taiwan, as we continue our overtures to China, and as the

American political will weakens, the Japanese, particularly a younger generation, will come up against the problem of their own defense. Although nuclearization is a choice that should not be forced upon the Japanese by the United States, nothing that we do should appear to inhibit them in this choice or we may drive them into increasingly nationalistic directions. The nuclearization of Japan seems politically quite implausible within the next five years, unlikely within the next ten years, and almost natural within the next twenty years, as a second postwar generation comes into power and begins to question why it should be different from other major nations.

This development toward nuclear proliferation would likely be halted only if Russia knocks out the Chinese nuclear force and then increasingly develops a hostile and menacing attitude in order to prevent those proto-nuclear states which then see the Russians as aggressive and hostile from developing their own defensive nuclear weapons. This scenario would envisage so harsh a political climate that in my opinion no sensible or moral person would encourage it.

Indeed, what the SALT talks, if well directed, might do is to provide sufficient control over the future of the nuclear arms race to ease the problems for secondary nuclear powers in joining and becoming adequate members of the club. If we are farsighted and statesmanlike in this case, we will then provide know-how to the secondary powers in order to insure that they have the stablest nuclear systems possible, systems most compatible with arms control, with the avoidance of accidental war, and with the avoidance of firing upon warning. Whereas statesmen must avoid the issues of the next twenty years in order to reach the agreements of the day, it is quite correct for the scholars who consider this matter, whose judgments may inform the actions of the statesmen, to consider the agreements in the context of world order and international stability.

2 • Strategic Arms Limitation: The Precedent of the Washington and London Naval Treaties

Hedley Bull

Though in some respects unique, the problems of Soviet-American strategic arms limitation have in other respects been encountered before. The most important precedent would appear to be that of the system of naval arms control established by the Washington Naval Treaty of 1922 and the London Naval Treaties of 1930 and 1936. These attempts to limit naval armaments in the interwar years may be compared with present-day attempts to limit strategic armaments as follows:

First, the naval treaties were the result of realistic and businesslike negotiations designed to establish formal limitations on a particular category of armaments of major strategic importance. At the present time the Strategic Arms Limitation Talks (SALT) are distinguished from the discussions of comprehensive disarmament conducted between 1946 and 1960 by their apparently realistic and businesslike nature, and from the negotiations leading up to the Partial Test Ban Treaty, the Outer Space Treaty, and the Non-Proliferation Treaty by the greater strategic significance (at least for the superpowers) of the limitations contemplated. Similarly, in embodying the approach of "partial" arms limitation, the naval treaties in the interwar period stood in contrast to the discussions of comprehensive disarmament that began with the Temporary Mixed Commission and the League Preparatory Commission in the 1920s and culminated in the abortive World Disarmament Conference of 1932. Among the various formal arms control agreements that were concluded (the others, apart from the disarmament provisions of the peace treaties, were the Geneva Protocol of 1925 on chemical and bacteriological warfare and various other attempts to restate or adapt traditional "rules of war"), they were clearly the most important.

Second, the naval treaties were concerned with quantitative limitations. Unlike the negotiations that led up to the Partial Test Ban Treaty, the Outer Space Treaty, and the Non-Proliferation Treaty, SALT is concerned not just with prohibition of a whole class of arms or arms activity but also with numerical limitations in categories of arms that are to be retained.[1] In other words, SALT is faced with the classic "problem of the ratio": what will be the relationship between the numerical limitation to be imposed upon one party's arms and that imposed upon another's? The naval arms discussions revolved around this "problem of the ratio" among British, American, Japanese, Italian, and French warship levels (even though purely qualitative prohibitions were also contemplated: the British, for example, initially sought to abolish the submarine, and thought was later given to abolishing the battleship).

Third, in attempting to deal with "the problem of the ratio" the naval arms negotiators accorded a central place to the idea of "parity." The Washington Naval Treaty established parity between the British Empire and the United

---

[1] A quantitative limitation always presupposes some element of qualitative limitation, to the extent that the limitation must spell out the nature of what is being quantitatively restricted. Prohibition of a category of arms or arms activity, however, is purely qualitative.

States in total tonnage of capital ships and aircraft carriers, and in the London Naval Treaty of 1930 this parity was extended to cruisers. The Washington Naval Treaty also established parity between France and Italy in capital ships and aircraft carriers, but because France was unwilling to accord parity to Italy in cruiser strength, the two countries refused to sign the provisions relating to cruisers in the London Treaty of 1930. Japan was denied parity with the British Empire and the United States in the treaties of 1922 and 1930; because the two dominant naval powers were unwilling to accord it to her, Japan announced her withdrawal from the treaty system in 1934. In SALT, likewise, the idea of "parity" clearly has a central place, together with the problem of how to express it, and to assess its strategic meaning, if any.

Fourth, the naval treaties were an attempt to determine an agreed ratio of naval strength among the dominant naval powers, especially the British Empire and the United States. Yet the naval arms levels of the dominant powers were throughout affected by the arms levels of lesser powers left outside the system of limitation. The Washington Naval Treaty (and this, of course, is a point of contrast with SALT) limited all five of the principal naval powers, but even here the signatory powers were concerned about the ratio of their naval strength to that of outside powers such as Russia and disarmed Germany. However, by the time of the 1930 treaty France and Italy had to be counted out of the system of cruiser limitation, and by 1936 Japan was outside the system altogether, and Germany had acquired significant naval strength. When the London Naval Treaty of 1936 expired in 1942, the naval strength of the "outside" powers (especially Japan, now dominating the Pacific) had grown so dramatically that the ratio of naval strength between the British Empire and the United States, the principal element in the system of naval arms control, now seemed of little consequence to either party.

It is obvious that SALT, ostensibly concerned only with the strategic relationship between the superpowers, must also reflect the views of each (if not joint views) as to what ratios of strategic arms are desirable as between them and outside powers. In SALT as in the naval disarmament discussions the two dominant powers are bound to consider such questions as whether limitations should be sought on the arms levels of "outside" powers. If so, should they be incorporated within the system, or should supplementary limitations be devised; if not, how should the limitations on their own strength take account of these other relationships?

Fifth, like SALT the attempt to limit naval arms was part of a wider long-term disarmament effort. The United States and the Soviet Union are negotiating about strategic arms partly to fulfill the expectations of a wider community of nations that they will do so, and in particular the expectations of nonnuclear signatories of the Non-Proliferation Treaty that the superpowers should seek to halt "vertical proliferation" as an "equivalent sacrifice" for the renunciation by the former of "horizontal proliferation." In the same way the Washington Naval Treaty was viewed as "making a start" toward the goal of a general and comprehensive reduction and limitation of arms, upheld in the League Covenant. In some respects the position now occupied by the principal potential nuclear powers in relation to SALT was then occupied in relation to the principal naval powers by Germany, who had accepted her disarmament under the terms of the Versailles Treaty on the understanding that this would be followed in due course by the agreement of the victorious powers to a general system of disarmament which would remove the element of discrimination against her. The main theme of the interwar disarmament discussions was the attempt to reconcile the German desire for "equality" (which could in principle be achieved either by disarmament of the victors or rearmament of the vanquished) with the French desire for "security" (which in the absence of firm Anglo-

American guarantees could in the French view be met only by superiority over Germany). It was against this background that the limitation of naval arms was pursued.

Sixth, in the naval arms conferences as in SALT, the discussions assumed that verification of any agreement would not require formal inspection procedures, "reciprocal" or international, but would be carried out by unilateral intelligence. Although in SALT consideration may well be given to proposed requirements for formal inspection (the United States is reported to have proposed "on site" inspection in connection with a ban on MIRV deployment), it appears both sides realize that intrusive formal inspection is unacceptable to the Soviet Union and that, realistically, the negotiations should be confined to agreements that can be verified unilaterally. The Washington and London naval treaties contained provisions for exchange of information; the United States proposal of July 1970 reportedly requires the parties to cooperate on unilateral verification.

I now propose first to expound the naval arms treaties; second, to discuss how they were achieved and what their results were; and third, in the light of this and other historical experience of arms control understandings, to advance a number of propositions relevant to SALT. The present draft is based only upon a knowledge of the secondary literature concerning naval arms limitation.[2] The documentary material does not appear to have been much studied in relation to the questions here considered.

The naval discussions at the Washington Conference

---

[2]See especially H. and M. Sprout, *Toward a New Order of Sea Power, American Naval Policy and the World Scene, 1918–1922,* Princeton University Press, 1940; Stephen Roskill, *Naval Policy between the Wars,* Vol. I, *The Period of Anglo-American Antagonism 1919–1929,* Collins, London, 1968; R. G. O'Connor, *Perilous Equilibrium, the United States and the London Naval Conference of 1930,* University of Kansas Press, 1962; Thomas H. Buckley, *The United States and the Washington Conference 1921–1922,* University of Tennessee, 1970; R. L. Buell, *The Washington Conference,* Appleton, 1922.

(21 November 1921–1 February 1922) related to three separated naval balances: the global balance of Britain and the United States, the Pacific balance of these two powers and Japan, and the European balance of Britain, France, and Italy. The British Empire (it is important to note that Canada, Australia, New Zealand, South Africa, and India were represented in this and subsequent naval negotiations as part of the Imperial delegation) was the only power involved in all three.

At the end of World War I, the determination of the United States Navy to build "a navy second to none," if not actually to achieve superiority, together with British reluctance to abandon historic naval primacy, implied an Anglo-American naval arms race. Britain in 1921 still had a clear lead over the United States in most indices of naval strength, but the United States Navy was expanding at a much faster rate; it was clear that the United States had the resources to achieve primacy, if it decided to devote sufficient resources to this end. Agreement on "parity" between the two Anglo-Saxon powers required the triumph of "enlightened" views of the national interest in the two countries: in Britain, that the national interest lay in an agreement that would at least hold the United States to equality and avert what to Britain might be a ruinous competition, even if it implied a formal acceptance of decline; in the United States, that the national interest was best served by an agreement which secured only equality, but saved money, promoted the cause of disarmament, and cemented Anglo-American understanding.

The Anglo-American naval balance, however, could not be separated from the triangular balance in the Pacific. The United States would not accept equality with Britain if there was a possibility that in the Pacific Britain and Japan might be combined against her: accordingly, the American concession of equality was matched on the British side by agreement to terminate the Anglo-Japanese alliance of 1902. Thus abandoned by their ally, the Japanese would not accept a

60 percent ratio in relation to the two major powers unless their local superiority was preserved by an agreement to freeze the construction of naval bases and fortifications in the Pacific; this accordingly was included in the Treaty.

The principal elements in the European naval balance were the determination of Britain to maintain her historic "two-power standard" at least in relation to European rivals; the desire of Italy for nominal equality with France; and the determination of France not to disarm without Anglo-American guarantees of her security.

The main elements in the Treaty for the Limitation of Armaments signed on 6 February 1922 were:[3]

1. Capital ships (battleships and battle cruisers) were to be limited by total tonnage displacement: 525,000 tons each for the United States and the British Empire; 315,000 for Japan; 175,000 each for France and Italy. Some points to note about this famous ratio are that:
   a. These figures represented goals to be reached after replacement of old ships. The actual totals to be retained (the Treaty named each individual ship) were 500,650 tons for the United States; 580,450 for the British Empire; 301,320 for Japan; 221,170 for France; 182,000 for Italy.
   b. Replacements of capital ships were not to take place until twenty years after the date of their completion.
   c. There was to be no new capital ship construction for ten years from November 1921.
   d. Capital ships were not to exceed 35,000 tons displacement and not to carry guns larger than 16″ caliber. No reconstruction of retained capital ships could take place except as a defense against air and submarine attack, and subject to certain rules.

---

[3]The text of the Washington Naval Treaty is given in H. and M. Sprout, *op. cit.*

e. The major naval powers were to "scrap" large quantities of shipping: the United States, 15 pre-Jutland ships and 11 unfinished ones; the British Empire, 20 pre-Jutland ships and 4 unfinished ones (the prized "Super-Hoods"); and Japan, 10 pre-Jutland ships and 6 unfinished ones. No vessels were to be scrapped by France or Italy. The ships to be "scrapped" were listed in the Treaty and precise instructions were given as to how and when to "scrap."

2. Aircraft carriers were to be limited by total tonnage displacement: 135,000 tons each for the United States and the British Empire; 81,000 for Japan; 60,000 each for France and Italy:
   a. These figures far exceeded the tonnage of aircraft carriers then possessed or under development; indeed, neither France nor Italy later constructed any carrier in the interwar period.
   b. Carriers, like capital ships, could not be replaced for twenty years, but carrier tonnage in existence or building at the time of negotiation of the Treaty could be replaced without regard to its age, and the ten-year moratorium on capital ship construction was not extended to carriers.
   c. Carriers were not to exceed 27,000 tons displacement and not to carry guns of more than 8″, except that (to allow the United States to complete *Lexington* and *Saratoga*) parties could build two of 33,000 tons.
   d. Needless to say, no carriers were to be "scrapped."
3. There were no limitations on "auxiliary vessels" (cruisers, destroyers, and submarines), except that (because this was essential to the definition of "capital ship") the maximum size of a cruiser was fixed at 10,000 tons and 8″ guns. The smaller naval powers insisted upon retaining the submarine, which the British would have liked to abolish: a

separate treaty restricted the use of submarines in warfare.

4. The United States, the British Empire, and Japan agreed upon where in the Pacific they would maintain the status quo with regard to naval bases and fortifications. The area included the Philippines, Guam, and Wake among American possessions (but not the West Coast and Hawaii), Hong Kong and British island possessions in the Pacific (but not Singapore, Canada, Australia, New Guinea, or New Zealand), and such Japanese possessions as the Kuriles, Bonins, Formosa, and the Pescadores.
5. Clauses in the Treaty restricted conversion of merchantmen, prohibited dissemination of capital ships and carriers to nonsignatories, and provided "escape clauses" and a revision procedure.

The Washington Naval Treaty had failed to restrict cruisers, destroyers, or submarines; naval competition thus concentrated in these areas. The attempt to extend the Washington ratios to these classes of vessel—in discussions in the League Preparatory Commission, in the abortive Geneva Naval Conference of 1927 ("the Coolidge Conference"), and in numerous bilateral discussions culminating in Ramsay MacDonald's visit to Washington in 1929—was long and arduous; in the end it was only partly successful.

The bargaining centered chiefly upon the cruiser. The British, with far the largest cruiser force, were determined to retain a high level (which they justified by a doctrine of the "absolute requirements" of protection of Imperial communications, unrelated to the force levels of other powers). At the 1927 Geneva Conference they insisted on 70 ships. Their chief requirement, however, was for light cruisers and they did not want a limitation that would leave other powers free to build all their cruisers up to the maximum limit of 10,000 tons and 8″ guns.

The Americans were pulled in a number of directions. The United States Navy, seeking formal parity with Britain in cruiser strength, opposed an agreement that would perpetuate British superiority. On the other hand, they did not need 70 cruisers and recognized that no matter what the treaty permitted, Congress would not provide funds for as many as that. They therefore sought parity at a lower level than that of actual British cruiser strength. In addition, the vast distances of the Pacific and America's comparative lack of bases justified a high proportion of heavy cruisers, built up to the maximum level: the American Navy, for example, hoped to get 25 to 30 such cruisers from the Geneva Conference; the British wanted 15.

The Japanese, restive under the Washington ratio, wanted to improve their position to 70 percent of the Anglo-American level in cruisers and destroyers, and parity in submarines. If, however, the United States were to be allowed the 25 or more heavy cruisers it wanted, then 70 percent of this level for Japan was unacceptable to the British, whose cruiser force (partly because of pressure from the increasingly vocal Dominions) was spread over the seven seas.

At the 1930 London Naval Conference a number of compromises were effected. Cruisers were divided into two classes, the Americans being assigned superiority in heavy cruisers and the British in light. Japan was given equality in submarines and a 70 percent ratio in light cruisers and destroyers, but only a 60 percent ratio in heavy cruisers. France and Italy, unable to resolve their disagreement over parity, did not sign the crucial provisions of the Treaty.

The London Naval Treaty thus extended the Washington ratios to cruisers, destroyers, and submarines, with an alteration in Japan's favor, and established Anglo-American "parity" more clearly than the Washington Treaty had done. The limitations agreed, however, were at levels higher than the actual tonnage of the powers; by contrast, the 1922 Treaty had brought substantial reductions. Moreover, its essential provisions bound only three powers, not five, causing the three to include an "escalator clause."

The main elements in the London Naval Treaty signed on 22 April 1930 were as follows:[4]

1. The United States, the British Commonwealth (as it was now called), and Japan accepted limitations on their cruisers, destroyers, and submarines:
   a. in heavy cruisers (those with guns more than 6.1″) the United States was allowed 180,000 tons and 18 ships; the British Commonwealth 146,800 tons and 15 ships; and Japan 108,400 tons and 12 ships.
   b. in light cruisers (those with guns of 6.1″ or less) the United States was allowed 143,500 tons; the British Commonwealth 192,200 tons; and Japan 100,450 tons (there were no limits on the number of ships).
   c. in destroyers the United States and the British Commonwealth were each allowed 150,000 tons and Japan 105,500. No more than 16 per cent of the allowed tonnages was to be employed in vessels of over 1,500 tons.
   d. in submarines the United States, the British Commonwealth, and Japan were each allowed 52,700 tons.
   e. the "escalator clause" provided that if the national security of any of the parties was materially affected by new naval construction of a nonsignatory, it should inform the other parties about the increases it proposed to make, and they should be entitled to make "a proportionate increase."
2. The other provisions in the Treaty were accepted by all five of the naval powers:
   a. the moratorium on new capital ship construction was extended to 1936. The United States was to scrap 3 more capital ships, Britain 5, and Japan 1.
   b. submarines were not to exceed 2,000 tons or 5.1″ guns,

---

[4]For the text of this treaty, see O'Connor, *op. cit.*

apart from a quota for each power of three up to 2,800 tons and 6.1″.

c. certain classes of naval vessel were exempted from all restrictions: all naval surface combat vessels of 600 tons up to 2,000 not having certain characteristics of armament and speed; and naval surface vessels not having combatant purposes. This served to establish limits in relation to the restrictions laid down in other parts of the Treaty.

The treaties of 1922 and 1930 were to expire at the end of 1936. In December 1935 the Second London Naval Conference assembled to discuss prolonging the limitations. By this time, however, the world political situation had been transformed. In November 1931 Japan invaded Manchuria, in January 1933 she withdrew from the League of Nations, and in 1934 gave the required two years' notice of her intention to terminate her obligations under the naval treaties. At the same time Japan made it clear that she would contemplate further limitations only on the basis of "a common upper limit," i.e., parity with the United States and Britain in all categories.

British policy at this time was directed toward appeasement, one expression of which was the 1935 Anglo-German Naval Agreement, which accorded Germany the right to 35 per cent of British naval tonnage and parity in submarines. By concluding this agreement Britain assented to Germany's violation of the naval disarmament provisions of the Versailles Treaty. Appeasement of Japan was also being urged in London, especially since Britain could not contend with both Japan and Germany, and (in the words of a report considered by the Committee of Imperial Defence in February 1934) while Japan presented the more immediate threat, Germany was "the ultimate potential danger." The "pro-Japanese" school in London in 1934 was contemplating a separate

Anglo-Japanese naval understanding that would have placated Japan at the price of alienating the United States.[5]

While the United States was opposed to Japanese claims to naval parity, it was at the same time against any upward revision of British levels: President Roosevelt's emissaries at the preliminary conversations in London in the summer of 1934 not only rejected the Admiralty's proposal to restore British cruiser strength to 70 ships, but even at this late hour advanced the idea of a one-third reduction in the general level of naval armaments.[6]

At the London Naval Conference of 1935, however, the United States and Britain worked together to reject Japan's demands for parity and to agree on upward revision of naval tonnages, including the restoration of the 70 British cruisers. But the London Naval Treaty signed on 25 March 1936 by Britain, the United States, and France alone, preserved only the shadow of a system of formal arms control. It had so many "escape clauses" and "escalator clauses" as to be virtually meaningless. When in June 1938 these three powers met, in the last act of the drama, to raise the permitted tonnage for capital ships from 35,000 to 45,000 tons the Japanese had already secretly laid the keels of *Musashi* and *Yamato,* each of 63,700 tons.[7]

The system of formal naval arms limitation had in effect collapsed by the end of 1936, but it had lasted for fifteen years. Leaving aside for now the question of the effects of the treaties, beneficial or otherwise, how do we account for the fact that they were established and maintained?

---

[5] For an account of the conflict between "pro-Japanese" and "pro-American" views of the Far Eastern and naval problem, see D. C. Watt, *Personalities and Policies, Studies in the Formulation of British Foreign Policy in the Twentieth Century,* Longmans, London, 1965, pp. 83–99.

[6] *Ibid.,* pp. 91–92.

[7] Samuel Eliot Morison, *History of the United States Naval Operations in World War II,* Vol. III, *The Rising Sun in the Pacific 1931–April, 1942,* Little, Brown, 1947–62, pp. 30–31.

One answer is that the naval treaties were part of a basic political understanding among the original five parties. The Washington Naval Treaty itself was part of a wider structure of agreements about political and territorial position in the Pacific. Along with the naval treaty and a treaty restricting the use of submarines and noxious gas in warfare, the Washington Conference produced a Four Power Pact in which the signatories recognized their rights to Pacific dependencies, a Nine Power Treaty reaffirming the integrity of China and the Open Door, and several ancillary agreements, making a total of nine. These understandings stabilized, as between the powers that most profited from it, the new situation that had been brought about in the Pacific as the result of World War I. They also induced a relatively relaxed attitude about the possibility of naval conflict in the area. At the same time the fact that the naval agreements were part of this larger package provided a deterrent to their violation, which might jeopardize all aspects of the settlement. In 1931 and thereafter, Japan was challenging the whole complex of agreements.

The political relations of the five powers, however, transcended the Pacific area, and the political accord that underlay the naval treaties had deeper roots than the Pacific settlement. The comity of the great powers was to be the basis of the repose and tranquillity which the postwar world seemed to need; arms limitation symbolized that comity.

Japan and the United States (and to a lesser extent Japan and Britain) were divided over the Pacific; France and Italy over the Mediterranean; and the United States and Britain over commercial competition, war debts, and naval rivalry itself. Moreover, in their approach to arms control the powers were often willing to insist upon "political linkage" (although this can facilitate an arms agreement as well as obstruct it), as when the United States, at the Paris Peace Conference, used the threat of naval expansion to induce Britain to accept the League Covenant, with a reference to the Monroe Doctrine, and later at the Washington Conference, used the same threat to bring about the dissolution of the Anglo-Japanese Alliance.

But in all five countries, only by overruling the advice of naval authorities intent upon achieving a favorable military balance could the political leaderships concerned secure the naval agreements that would help to cement "the system."

This was especially important in the relations between Britain and the United States. The Americans were outside the League of Nations but this made their participation in the disarmament system all the more important, as the chief symbol (along with the agreements about reparations) of their involvement in world affairs. The political leaderships in London and Washington were willing to overrule their naval advisers because they were reluctant to allow disagreements that might undermine Anglo-American concord.

A second answer to our question is that the naval treaties were expedited by the obsolescence of the capital ship, especially in relation to the submarine and naval air power. It is true that in 1921 the naval staffs of all the major powers believed faithfully that the principal element in command of the sea was the main battle fleet, that this remained the predominant official view right up to the outbreak of World War II, and that it would thus be quite wrong to conclude that the treaties merely sanctified a junking of useless vessels that would in any case have been carried out unilaterally.

On the other hand, the orthodox belief in the supremacy of the battleship had been badly shaken by the German U-boat campaign of 1917–1918, and in the summer of 1921 it had been jolted by the sinking by test aerial bombing of the old German battleship *Ostfriesland.* At the time of the naval treaties, adherents of the battleship were on the defensive, and the submarine and naval air power (both land- and sea-based) were clearly on the rise. This was reflected in the failure of the naval treaties to impose restrictions on the latter comparable to those provided for the former.

At Washington the British, who had most to lose from the submarine, proposed abolishing it; failing to get support, they asked for quantitative limitations. The only limitations to result, however, were a restriction in 1922 on use in warfare and a limit in the 1930 treaty on size of individual submarines.

The Washington Conference discussed limitation of air power, but concluded that because aircraft were so easily converted from civil to military use, there could be no such thing as air disarmament short of the abolition of aviation itself. Although the conference did impose restrictions on aircraft carriers, then in an experimental stage, these were markedly more permissive than those applied to battleships and battle cruisers.

A third element facilitating an agreement in which the central element was the principle of parity between Britain and the United States was that there was a crude parity in the actual naval balance between them. If either power had been clearly superior in quantity and quality of naval arms, then, given the state of public feeling in the two countries at the time, an agreement of this nature could hardly have been reached.

Britain in 1921 was superior to the United States in total naval tonnage, and in total tonnage of each category of vessel.[8] On the other hand, the United States was spending more on its navy, had more post-Jutland ships in commission or under construction, and had greatly superior economic resources. The notion of overall relative naval power (and hence "parity" and "superiority"), which seeks to reduce the manifold dimensions of naval strength to a common denomi-

---

[8]According to U.S. Naval Estimates Britain in 1921 had a total tonnage of 1,753,539 to 1,302,441 for the U.S.A. The three-power ratio in total tonnage was Britain 13.5, U.S.A. 10, Japan 4.9; and in capital ships it was 13.9–10–6.8. If, however, ships under construction were counted, the capital ship ratio was 10.6–10–8.7. Buckley, *op. cit.*, pp. 23–24.

nator, may not have any meaning. But people think in terms of these notions, which therefore acquire an importance of their own. The notion of a rough, though possibly fleeting, equality was deeply imbedded in naval minds on both sides of the Atlantic; it led naturally to Secretary Hughes' proposal at the opening session of the Washington Conference that the limitations should be determined on the basis of "existing strength."[9]

It seems doubtful whether "parity," expressed as equal numbers or tonnages of ships, bore any relationship to the actual strategic needs of either Britain or the United States. A country needs the amount and the kind of forces that are adequate to fulfill its strategic requirements. The goal of "parity" implied that Britain and the United States both needed the same *kinds* of naval forces, as well as the same amounts of each kind. This was very doubtful, as was contended in Britain by the advocates of a large light cruiser force determined not by the size of the American cruiser force but by the needs of a worldwide maritime empire.

"Parity" also implied that Britain and the United States might possibly go to war with one another. The United States Navy's General Board in the 1920s took the view that they might, whereas the Admiralty thought (or at least said) that such a war was "unthinkable."[10] If they had gone to war, "parity" from the British point of view would have been quite insufficient. The British Navy by itself could not adequately protect the British Empire in World War II even against the naval forces of Germany, Italy, and Japan. Alone, Britain could provide for the security of her scattered Empire only if, as the traditional doctrine proclaimed, she had naval dominance. Given that she had lost it, her interest lay not in matching the United States Navy but in securing its cooperation.

Because in the naval arms negotiations all the parties

---

[9]H. and M. Sprout, *op. cit.*, p. 149.
[10]Roskill, *op. cit.*, p. 25.

wanted arms of the same sort and the issue essentially concerned how many of each they should retain (by contrast with negotiations between a land power and a sea power, or a "submarine power" and a "surface fleet power"), they raised "the problem of the ratio." There are perhaps three aspects of this problem that deserve mention.

First, there is the question of the standard or principle on which the ratio should be based. Secretary Hughes in 1921, as we have seen, said it should be based on "existing strength." Proposals which take this as their basis (other examples are the Hoover proposal to the World Disarmament Conference in January 1933 for an all round one-third cut, and similar proportional cuts suggested in the comprehensive staged disarmament plans of the 1950s and early 1960s) are open to the objection that they are "unjust" to parties which are dissatisfied with the existing balance, or believe that it is changing in their favor.

The alternative standard to the "existing ratio" is presumably the "just ratio." The British Admiralty, for example, conducted a study in which the criterion used was that of Point 4 of the Fourteen Points, that each country's arms should be "the minimum consistent with national safety." They then argued that Britain needed a large navy whereas America did not, and demonstrated this by comparing lengths of coastline, volume of trade, and size of mercantile marine to be protected.

Once a standard or principle has been laid down, a second question arises: how shall it be expressed in terms of numbers and kinds of arms? Naval authorities considered such alternatives as naval expenditure, personnel, total tonnage, and total numbers of ships. Others added such factors as a ship's armament, speed, and armored protection. One American study, taking into account naval bases and merchant marine, contended that because of Britain's superiority in these, "parity" could be achieved only by a vast American superiority in warships.

Choice of the means of expressing the principle can of

course provide the opportunity to subvert the principle itself. Hughes, for example, having appealed to the "existing ratio," went on to say that the best way of gauging it was by "total capital ship tonnage, in being and under construction," a formula that led to equal numbers for Britain and the United States.[11] He then argued on the basis of this formula that Britain should reduce her total naval tonnage to the American level; his purpose, in other words, was to change the existing ratio in America's favor.

The third problem, once the standard has been chosen and given quantitative expression, is how to negotiate an agreement about it. A basic question is whether the negotiation has to include discussion of the standard and how it is to be expressed, or whether it can proceed directly to bargaining about forces each party will retain.

An example of this problem was the controversy within the American government in 1929–30 about how to negotiate cruiser ratios. Naval authorities had devised what was called a "yardstick," a formula for computing the equivalent value of ships in terms of combat effectiveness rather than just tonnage and gun caliber, and had proposed to present this in the negotiations. General Dawes, the chief American negotiator, commented that this would lead to a "yardstick drawn up to fit the settlement . . . instead of the settlement fitted to the yardstick."[12]

What effects did the treaties have? So far as I have been able to discover, the treaties were respected. The Japanese terminated their obligations as they were entitled to do, but they were at no stage charged with violating the system. It does not follow that no violations were detected (we know that Britain deliberately refrained from making an issue of German violations of the Versailles disarmament provisions of which she was aware), still less that they did not take

[11] See above, n. 8.

[12] O'Connor, *op. cit.*, p. 42.

place. This is a matter on which documentary research is needed.

Did the naval treaties restrain naval competition? Their effects were ambiguous. The fifteen-year moratorium on capital ship construction undoubtedly slowed qualitative improvements and drastically reduced expenditures in this area. Moreover, *overall* naval expenditure in both Britain and the United States fell in 1922 and did not reach pre-Treaty levels again until 1938–39. But economic retrenchment and anti-navalism in Congress and Parliament might have produced this result in any case. Furthermore, the 1922 Treaty channeled competition into the field of cruisers, destroyers, and submarines. Within two years of its conclusion all signatories were laying down cruisers up to the maximum treaty limits, and in 1927–29 the Anglo-American cruiser race became a source of serious friction.

The course of naval arms competition was determined by many factors, among which the treaties were only one. In some cases governments built up to the treaty limits, in other cases (e.g., the 1929 Labour Government) they allowed force levels to fall well below them. Economic policies in the pre-Keynesian era worked in favor of disarmament, but under Roosevelt in favor of rearmament. After the rise of Hitler, British expenditure rose. This particular formal arms treaty did not determine the course of the arms competition, but simply settled one parameter.

It is often argued that the naval disarmament system weakened the democracies in confronting Japan in the 1930s and contributed to their reverses in 1942.[13] It is pointed out that the nonfortification clauses of the Washington Treaty left the Philippines, Guam, and Wake exposed to Japan and inhibited the United States and Britain from bringing pressure to bear on that country after 1931. It is also said that

---

[13]See, e.g., Morison, *op. cit.,* Chapter 2.

the formal denial of "parity" to Japan contributed to the emergence of the "militarist" ascendancy in Japan, rather as overselling of the Non-Proliferation Treaty by the United States and the Soviet Union a few years ago was said to have stimulated interest in nuclear weapons in potential nuclear countries.

These views perhaps attribute to the treaties a greater importance in determining events than they actually had. The reluctance of the United States and Britain to threaten Japan after 1931 also had many other causes. The weakness of the Allies in the Pacific in 1942, relative to Japan, was not the consequence of the treaty system, which also limited Japan, so much as of the failure of the Allies to build up to their treaty limits.

The political and strategic context of SALT is so radically different from that of the interwar naval limitations that it would be foolish to derive "lessons" from the latter directly applicable to the former. However, there are a number of questions that arise about SALT which the above may clarify.

The question is often asked whether Soviet-American strategic arms limitation is best pursued by means of formal or "informal" restraints. The latter concept includes a number of quite different things, and we are handicapped by the fact that none of them has been adequately studied. In addition to formal arms control treaties there are:

1. agreements which, although not treaties, are written (e.g., the Kennedy-Kruschchev agreement over the Cuban missile crisis);
2. agreements which are verbal, having been put into words and assented to by both parties (e.g., the House-Cecil understanding at the Paris Peace Conference, in which the Americans agreed to halt their naval construction program in return for British diplomatic support);
3. agreements which are not verbal but are reached by a process of "negotiation by maneuver" or "exchange of

signals," verbal and not verbal (i.e., "tacit agreements" like limitations observed in the Korean War);
4. strictly unilateral acts of arms control which are not conditional upon reciprocal action by the other party, nor necessarily aimed at it (e.g., nuclear command and control procedures).

It is obvious that past formal agreements have made a contribution to arms control. In relation to the varieties of informal understanding, they are more precise, more explicit, more inflexible or rigid, and better able to confirm mutual expectations about future behavior. They have the advantage of settling (within limits and for the time being) friction over the existence or the utility of an agreement, of taking it off the agenda of international conflict. It is difficult to see how the capital shipbuilding holiday from 1922 to 1936 could have been effected except by a formal treaty, or more recently the cessation of atmospheric nuclear tests or the abstention of the powers from placing weapons of mass destruction in outer space.

On the other hand, there are situations in which an informal agreement is more feasible or more likely to advance the purposes of arms control. Where (like the naval treaties in relation to Japan and the Non-Proliferation Treaty in relation to certain potential nuclear powers) an agreement that makes explicit the basis of the understanding is likely to provoke friction, there is a case for an agreement that leaves it vague. Where (as in the case of the developing of air power between the wars) there is a rapidly changing military technology, an agreement that preserves flexibility may be preferable. Where (as with submarines) the parties are not able to conclude a formal agreement, an informal one may be better than none at all. Sometimes mutual expectations are *better* confirmed by actions than by formal obligations: reciprocal restraints, e.g., have been more effective than "rules of war" in limiting war in this century.

Moreover, where a formal treaty does exist and is being

observed, there may still be a need to supplement it with informal understandings of various kinds. The naval treaties, while they stabilized certain aspects of the naval arms contest, left others untouched: they did not determine whether or not the parties armed themselves to the maximum limits laid down in the treaties; whether they merely redirected their competition to areas of the contest that were not limited, or achieved an "overall" slowing down; or how effectively, within the limits of the treaty, they provided for their national security or cooperated to preserve the peace.

In the case of SALT the question is not whether formal or informal agreements are to be preferred as a general formula, but which aspects of the Soviet-American competition are most amenable to formal restraints and which to one or another variety of informal restraint. United States and Soviet strategic arms are already subject to both sorts of limitation (on the one hand, the Partial Test Ban Treaty and the Outer Space Treaty; on the other hand, certain understandings about deployment and use). It will be important to ensure that if formal agreements are concluded, perhaps on the lines of the United States proposal of July 1970, these would not become a substitute for informal understandings and unilateral restraints where these are more appropriate.

In the wider field of arms control studies, advocates of general and comprehensive disarmament or arms control have argued that "the arms race" can be controlled only if arms control is "general," restricting all powers, and "comprehensive," restricting all categories of armaments. According to this thesis, "partial" arms control, such as the attempt to limit naval armaments only, merely has the effect of redirecting the arms race. The difficulty with this view is that (apart from the problems of negotiation) it is difficult to conceive of an agreement which would be genuinely comprehensive, inasmuch as however widely "armaments" are defined, some categories of military activity always escape the net.

The same problem arises with control of a particular

field of arms activity. Thus the advocate of comprehensive naval arms restraint argues that limiting capital ships and carriers only will merely lead to increased competition in "auxiliary vessels," and that including these later was bound to turn attention to naval aircraft, speed, gun elevation, and other factors not regulated by the system. In relation to SALT the argument is that missiles must be limited by payload as well as number, that numbers of warheads cannot be left out, that improvements in accuracy will undermine the system if missile testing is allowed to continue, that tactical aircraft and missiles must be taken into account, that ASW degree of silo hardening, etc., must be considered.

It is clear that the notion of a genuinely comprehensive strategic arms agreement does not make any more sense than that of a genuinely comprehensive disarmament agreement. To a greater or lesser degree all possible strategic arms agreements will contain loopholes. It is for this reason that it is best to think of the task of SALT as to produce over time not a single system but a series of agreements. The necessarily "partial" nature of any particular agreement, moreover, reinforces the argument that formal agreements by themselves must be insufficient.

The question to be asked in assessing proposed agreements is not how comprehensive they are, how wide an area of the strategic competition they cover, but how closing off the particular area of competition will affect the competition as a whole: whether, e.g., it will lead to greater or lesser expenditures, channel the contest into more or less "stabilizing" directions, make the Soviet-American relationship more or less proof against the danger of war, fulfill or not fulfill the political objections of the negotiations.

A nation's choice of the kinds and levels of its armed forces is, or should be, the result of an intellectual process of defining goals and assessing the cost and effectiveness of the military instruments required to fulfill them. When two or more nations meet together so as jointly to determine the kinds and levels of force they require, can this and should this also include such an intellectual process, or do they have to proceed by straight bargaining?

Arms control negotiations clearly presuppose at least some elements of common strategic understanding, at least about the characteristics of weapons, and their effects and uses in war. But it may be argued that arms control agreements have been arrived at in the past essentially by a process of bargaining, in which the rationale of the positions adopted, if not actually an obstruction, has been irrelevant to the outcome. The arguments in the naval disarmament negotiations about what principles shall determine "the ratio," what "yardsticks" measured it most successfully, what size navy the United States "needed," were in fact the process of bargaining in disguise. The real question was: how many ships of what sort would the powers agree to allow each other to retain?

In SALT, should questions of strategic and arms control doctrine (e.g., defense vs. mutual deterrence as a goal) and questions of the computation of appropriate force levels enter into the substance of the negotiations? It is important that SALT should be an exchange of strategic ideas and a process of mutual education about the bases of strategic thinking in the two countries. But it would be a mistake to proceed as if each country could do the other's strategic planning for it, and the issue were to define a common goal and find a route to it, rather than to explore by negotiation whether there is common ground between two positions arrived at by necessarily separate processes of decision.

In SALT, as in the Anglo-American naval talks, the fact of "parity" provides the background of the negotiations and the idea of ratifying it an implicit objective toward which they are directed. It is clear, however, that "parity" has no more strategic meaning now than between 1922 and 1936.

"Parity" in offensive vehicles (or in these plus ABMs, plus MIRVs) could be *compatible* with strategic stability (in the sense of an in-built tendency of mutual deterrence to persist) but it bears no necessary relationship to it; for this purpose each power requires the levels and kinds of forces (quite possibly different levels and kinds) necessary to deter the other. Nor does a matching in particular categories of weapon subserve any strategic purpose: the United States ABM level is related strategically to the Soviet offensive force rather than to the Soviet ABM level, the United States offensive force to the character of Soviet defensive weapons, and so on.

But in SALT, as in the Anglo-American case, "parity," and its desirability as the basis of a settlement, have great political importance. These notions must be taken into account without allowing them to obscure SALT's primary strategic goals.

The position of the United States and the Soviet Union in strategic arms today is much more clearly preeminent than was that of Britain and the United States in naval arms in the interwar period (Japan, after all, possessed comparable naval technology and had a chief quantitative inferiority). But they face the same problem that the "central balance" about which they are negotiating is only part of the global balance in this category of arms.

Whether or not it is made explicit, there must enter into any structure of Soviet-American agreement some equivalent of the "escalator clauses" to which the naval powers resorted to take account of those who had not joined the system or had left it. This is not to say (indeed, the "escalator clauses" did not state this) that rises in the nuclear strength of China or of other nuclear powers should be met by proportionate increases in Soviet and American force levels, nor necessarily by increases or improvements at all. It is rather that the rise of new strategic nuclear powers will create new situations, which will require adjustment of the system as a whole.

In the event that the United States and the Soviet Union

elect to incorporate China within their system of strategic arms limitation, however, they may find that if "parity" has been made the basis of the ratio agreed between themselves, they have either to extend that parity to China, or face the same consequences of denying it to her that Britain and the United States faced when they denied it to Japan.

3 • Comparative U.S. and Soviet Deployments, Doctrines, and Arms Limitation

Johan Jorgen Holst

It is commonplace to observe that the evolving strategic relationship between the two superpowers is critical to the future structure and process of the international order. This relationship may, however, become less central than it was during the 1950s and 1960s. Perceptions of the political utility of strategic forces and concepts of international order will to a significant extent determine the role of the "central balance" in the system of international politics. Predictions about such perceptions and concepts are extremely tenuous. In the United States attention and resources are shifting to other areas of social concern.

Strategic weapons may be viewed as largely irrelevant to the solution or management of important political issues in the international arena,[1] and largely nonconvertible into politically usefully currency. The Strategic Arms Limitation Talks (SALT) may be an attempt to avoid the fate of the dinosaur. Part of the difficulty confronting an analyst in this context is mapping the distribution of this particular

---

[1]See, e.g., McGeorge Bundy, "To Cap the Volcano," *Foreign Affairs,* 48, No. 1 (1969): 1–20.

attitude both *between* the two superpowers and *within* the decision-making systems of each. How will the interaction of Soviet and American attitudes affect the distribution? And how will expectations about possible distribution affect the interaction?

The attention and resources allocated to strategic forces will be determined also by the *intrinsic* stability of the strategic balance. Improved accuracies of long-range missile systems, development of multiple reentry vehicles, availability of active defense systems against missiles are all factors which individually and in combination strain the intrinsic stability of the central balance. Trends in expenditure levels and budget profiles and quantitative expansion of the strategic forces also tend to force decision-makers to continue to concentrate on strategic force issues. Maintaining a credible and reliable deterrent posture is a continuous process.

The central balance is subject, furthermore, to strains *extrinsic* to the balance proper. The actual and potential emergence of other nuclear powers will influence both the quantitative level of strategic arms maintained by the superpowers and the composition or profile of their postures. The two superpowers may have many interests that coincide, but the extrinsic strains on the central balance also provide opportunities for competitive strategies aimed at emasculating the extended deterrence potential of the adversary. The politics of providing and denying protection has very strong competitive elements providing links between the calibration of the central balance and the quest for influence and the construction of a compatible milieu. In the dimension of strategic nuclear power the two superpowers are likely to remain preponderant. They may decide to ensure that preponderance by the adoption of a high posture vis-à-vis emerging great powers. Such policies, serving rather narrow national power interests, are also compatible with reasonable concepts of world order. Thus, from the point of view of many smaller and middle powers, the interests of international society are better served in nuclear matters by a limited condominium of superpowers than by a more widely diffused capability to challenge and manipulate the basic structure of the international order. The Non-Proliferation Treaty (NPT) could serve as a symbolic monument to that particular conception.

Some of the current problems in international relations stem from the coexistence of a bipolar central balance of deterrence and an increasingly multipolar political order. Nuclear power is to a large extent unusable power in a world of more than one nuclear weapon state. Superpower is for many purposes paralyzed power. However, as ambitions and role perceptions change the multipolarization of the political order may contain the seeds of challenge to the strategic preponderance of the superpowers. The statesmen of the world are thus inevitably confronted with the perennial enigma of engineering peaceful change. The NPT reflects a holding action. It does not deal with the issues of reconstruction. These issues, all in some way extrinsic to the inherent stability of the strategic balance, will somehow have to be incorporated into the negotiations.

SALT is concerned with two kinds of stability: (1) *crisis stability,* or the relative absence of preemptive pressures deriving from the qualitative characteristics of particular weapons systems or the quantitative distribution of such systems, and (2) *dynamic stability,* or the relative propensity of the strategic postures of the two superpowers to remain basically unchanged over time. To some extent it could be said that SALT reflects or ought to reflect a recognition of the fact that unilateral rationalities (e.g., deterrence calculations) may produce an objectively irrational outcome (e.g., an arms race). Hence it is possible to view the problem as one of reducing the final irrationality, possibly by way of promoting a more unified attitude to deterrence.

SALT encompasses several levels of negotiation, only

one of which is found in Vienna and Helsinki. Perhaps the most important set of negotiations will take place inside the decision-making systems in Moscow and Washington. One of the more interesting ways to analyze SALT may be to focus on the ways in which the formal negotiations in Austria and Finland affect the decision-making processes, and the outcomes of these, in the capitals of the superpowers. It may be that the very fact of SALT will affect the *level* at which substantive decisions are made, the distribution of *bargaining power* inside the decision-making structures, and the *access* of various interests to the centers of decision in Moscow and Washington.

SALT can be viewed also as an educational exercise. By a process of mutual education the two superpowers could possibly acquire somewhat greater empathy for the doctrinal framework for decisions on strategic forces on both sides. An appreciation of the differences in doctrinal outlook may reduce latent propensities to view weapons procurements and configurations of the other through one's own doctrinal framework. A greater convergence of doctrines through education in turn might reduce misunderstanding. The impact of such doctrinal convergence on the stability of the strategic balance would depend critically on the substance of the doctrine. Some American analysts and decision-makers see the Soviet-American strategic arms dialogue as an attempt to "educate the Russians." This perspective begs both operational and normative questions: is it feasible or even desirable, to influence the Russians to adopt, e.g., American doctrines of assured destruction? There is logically, of course, nothing objectively finite about the relationship between deterrence on the one hand and such concepts as "assured destruction" and "damage limitation" on the other.

Mutually "negotiated" doctrinal convergence may amount to a "doctrinal freeze." It could thus come to be a straitjacket preventing desirable and feasible adjustments to novel opportunities. Personal and social ethics, largely by the intrinsic content of the doctrine, would also affect desirability, as would the relative congruence of the value judgments implicit in or to be derived from the doctrine on the one hand, and the value consensus prevailing in American (and Soviet) society on the other. What value content is likely to *reduce* rather than *induce* social alienation? Doctrinal flexibility may be forfeited also by the negotiation of certain quantitative or qualitative restrictions on strategic forces. Certain kinds of flexibility may be useful, others not.

Before we examine Soviet doctrinal perspectives, we need to delineate the present strategic capabilities of the Soviet Union and the trends and peculiarities of the Soviet strategic posture.

For the first time in its history the Soviet Union has emerged as a serious *global* power with the military means to support extensive aspirations for influence. The exclusive emphasis on power to dominate the rimlands of the Soviet landmass has given way to intercontinental capabilities in some respects equal to or larger than those of the United States. The most dramatic evidence of Soviet global prowess is the growth of the intercontinental missile force. The current deployment buildup of the Soviet ICBM force started some time in the mid-sixties. It has often been suggested that the buildup reflected a series of decisions made in the wake of the Cuban missile crisis and the subsequent leadership struggle which produced the ouster of Nikita S. Khrushchev. Actually, the Brezhnev-Kosygin leadership probably reconfirmed and possibly accelerated the program which had been initiated under Khrushchev.

The Soviet Union fired its first ICBM, SS-6 "SAPWOOD," in August 1957. This large missile, based on nonstorable liquid fuel, was mounted only in very small numbers. In fact, the Russians had only a handful by 1961[2]

---

[2] *The New York Times,* April 5, 1965.

and thus the fears of a missile gap evaporated in the United States. For some years, however, the Russians had done much to nurture an inflated Western perception of Soviet capabilities.[3]

It now seems likely that Moscow laid the basis for the missile program of the sixties by substantially expanding military research and development expenditures in 1954–58 when actual procurement remained constant or even declined. The Seven Year Plan (1959–65) provided for substantial increases in military expenditures. This gave room for the missile buildup which was concentrated first on the medium- and intermediate-range missiles oriented against Europe.

Simultaneously with the M/IRBM deployment Moscow was making leisurely progress on the second generation ICBMs, SS-7 SADDLER (1962) and SS-8 SASIN (1963). They were deployed at an approximate annual rate of 50 missiles, producing a force of 200+ missiles by 1965. From about 1964 the Russians have been deploying the large SS-9 SCARP missile, which it was estimated could carry a warhead of some 25 MT, and the liquid-fuel 1MT ICBM, SS-11. A solid-fuel ICBM, SS-13 SAVAGE, which was first shown in the May Day parade in 1965, has been deployed in relatively small numbers since 1968. It exists also in a mobile configuration.

The Soviet intercontinental missile force comprised 250 launchers by mid-1966, 570 by September 1967, 900 by September 1968, and 1,060 by September 1969. By the end of 1970 the operational force included some 1,400 missiles with about 100 under construction. There are signs that the Soviet ICBM buildup is leveling off. The Soviet force includes 900+ SS-11s operational or under construction. According to some reports the Russians have

---

[3] Arnold L. Horelick and Myron Rush, *Strategic Power and Soviet Foreign Policy,* University of Chicago Press, 1966.

not started any new SS-11 silo constructions for more than a year;[4] since average construction time seems to be about eighteen months, the force would level off at current strength unless new constructions begin. According to official U.S. estimates the Soviet force includes some 300 SS-9s operational or under construction with 250+ presently operational. It has been acknowledged officially that SS-9 deployment has slowed, and according to other reports no new SS-9 silo constructions have been initiated for six months.[5] The SS-9 deployment program has been erratic. Since 1964 deployment starts have averaged 47 per year, but they have varied from 66 (1968) to 30 (1967).[6] The SS-9 missiles are deployed in groups of six.[7] There are also some 100 SS-13s and the 200+ SS-7s and SS-8s. The Soviet buildup since 1968 has resulted in a fourfold increase in the megatonnage of the Soviet strategic force. (The U.S. blast power diminished by 40 per cent over the same period.[8]) The Soviet ICBMs are deployed in a broad zone along the Trans-Siberian Railroad from Moscow to Transbaykal Military District. Some of the base complexes are located fairly close to Soviet cities. The SS-11 missiles are deployed in dispersed and hardened silos, while some of the SS-7s and SS-8s are mounted in soft firing complexes. The SS-9 silos are apparently not hardened to the same degree as the silos

---

[4] *International Herald Tribune,* December 17, 1970.

[5] *Ibid.;* see also letter to *The New York Times,* December 17, 1970, by Robert R. Neild, Director, Stockholm International Peace Research Institute.

[6] The figures were (cumulative total in parentheses): 42 in 1964 (42); 66 in 1965 (108); 54 in 1966 (162); 30 in 1967 (192); 36 in 1968 (228); 54 in 1969 (282); thus there have been fewer than twenty new constructions in 1970. (Source for figures: *International Herald Tribune,* July 10, 1970.)

[7] Computed on the basis of information given by Secretary of Defense Melvin Laird in *Authorization for Military Procurement, Research and Development, Fiscal Year 1971, and Research Strength,* Hearing before the Committee on Armed Services, U.S. Senate, 91st Congress, Second Session, Part 3, p. 2196 (Hereafter: *1971 Authorization Hearings*).

[8] *International Herald Tribune,* April 21, 1970.

of the SS-11. There are reports that the Russians have recently deployed some 100 SS-11s in the firing complexes in southwestern Russia which previously housed only M/IRBMs.[9]

The Soviet M/IRBM force has remained quantitatively stable since about 1964. The early emphasis on medium- and intermediate-range missiles was probably to some extent a function of a traditional proximity concern in the Soviet strategic outlook. Europe has been a primary arena for Soviet diplomacy, and the deployment of the force coincided with the re-equipment and reorientation of the ground forces for tactical nuclear war. The M/IRBM forces were evidently conceived as war-fighting forces assigned to destroy military forces and installations in Western Europe to pave the way for the Red Army in a war situation. Such an outlook was consistent also with the strong artillery tradition in the Soviet Armed Forces. Artillery officers dominated in the Soviet missile program which produced the first improvements of the German V-2, SS-1 SCUNNER (1947) and SS-2 SIBLING (1951). It now seems likely that the first generation MRBM was in small-scale production by 1955–56 (SS-3 SHYSTER). By 1958 deployment of SS-4 SANDAL had begun. The 2,000-mile range IRBM SS-5 SKEAN was first deployed in 1961. Moscow deployed more than 500 M/IRBMs in the period 1961–63, stabilizing the total force at about 700 launchers. The present force comprises some 600 SS-4s and 100 SS-5s. About 50 per cent of the sites for these weapons are hardened. The soft sites have a reloading capability. The total number of launch installations is apparently about 250. Most of the missiles are deployed in Western Russia. Some 70 missiles have been deployed in the Turkestan and Far Eastern Military Districts, but there are reports of some of these being disman-

[9] *New York Times,* February 11, 1970 and December 17, 1970.

tled lately.[10] The Russians have also been introducing the SS-12 SCALEBOARD, a counterpart to the American short-range missile (SRM) Pershing.

Until recently the Soviet Union did not have an operational system comparable to the American Polaris SLBM. A 300-mile missile, SS-N-4 SARK, became operational in 1959. It was emplaced in diesel-powered submarines (G and Z class) capable of surface-launching the missile, and later also in the first nuclear-powered submarines (H class). In 1964 the 700-mile SS-N-5 SERB entered the operational inventory. The present force comprises 75 SARK and 50 SERB missiles on 15 nuclear-powered and 25 conventional submarines. Since 1968 the Russians have been deploying the 1,500-mile SS-N-6 in the new Y-class submarines carrying 16 missiles each. The Y-class submarines are constructed at Severodvinsk, which has a total capacity for ten complete hulls at a time. Estimated total rate of production is six to eight vessels per year, with production time per hull about eighteen months. Ten to fifteen Y-class submarines were apparently operational, or close to operational, at the end of 1970. By 1974–75, the Soviet Union could have 35–50 Y-class submarines with 560–800 SLBM launchers.[11]

The Soviet Long Range Air Force, like the missile forces until the mid-sixties, emphasizes medium-range targets. The Russian copy of the B-29, the TU-4 "Bull," ready in 1947, was mass-produced into an operational force of 1,000 aircraft by 1953. The planes could have mounted one-way attacks on the United States, but it is unclear whether such tactics were included in the Soviet war plan. The follow-on jet bomber, TU-16 BADGER, was first shown in 1954, and by 1959 there was an operational force of 1,000

---

[10] *New York Times,* December 17, 1970.

[11] Address by Secretary of Defense Melvin Laird at the Annual Luncheon of the Associated Press, New York City, April 20, 1970, *DOD News Release* No. 316-70, p. 11.

aircraft. The third generation, TU-22 BLINDER, appeared in 1961 and is currently replacing the TU-16 at the rate of one TU-22 for every three TU-16s. The present force of medium-range bombers includes 600 TU-16s and 150 TU-22s. The Russians have been flight-testing two prototypes of a new Tupolev swing-wing bomber believed capable of supersonic penetration at high and low altitudes.

There are no indications that the Russians are developing a new heavy bomber. The present fleet of long-range heavy bombers includes some 110 M-4 BISON (1954) and 90 TU-20 BEAR (1955), of which 50 are configured as tankers. In addition, the Naval long-range air force includes 300 TU-16s and 50 TU-20s configured for reconnaissance. An improved M-4, the M-201 BOUNDER, was shown in 1967 but is not part of the operational inventory.

The Russian emphasis on active and passive defense has made their military posture structurally quite different from the U.S. offensive emphasis posture. Thus the Soviet Union has spent some $125 billion on active defenses since 1945, while the U.S. was spending $50 billion.

A very large portion of the Soviet defense budget went for construction of a modern air defense system in the immediate postwar years, with procurement of early warning radar and jet fighter interceptors (YAK-17, MiG-9, MiG-15). By 1955 the Soviet Air Defence Forces comprised some 4,000 jet interceptors, primarily equipped for clear weather/daylight interception. The current Soviet strategic interceptor force consists of some 3,000 aircraft, with a small numerical decline in recent years. A large part of the force is subsonic or low supersonic models, mostly day fighters, from the mid-fifties (MiG-17, MiG-19, YAK-25). A smaller portion is supersonic all-weather interceptors from 1959–64 (MiG-21, YAK-28, SU-9). Over the last years there has been a 5 per cent increase in new interceptors (YAK-28, TU-28, SU-11, MiG-23). The first Russian deployment of surface-to-air missiles (SAM) around Moscow took place in the early fifties; it is interesting that the deployment of the SA-1 GUILD apparently was limited to the national capital area. More than 3,000 missiles were reportedly deployed around Moscow.[12] However, by 1958 the SA-2 GUIDELINE deployment was initiated. This missile, which has undergone substantial improvements, has been widely deployed in the Soviet Union. A short-range interceptor missile against low altitude attacks, SA-3 GOA, was first shown in 1964. There are also two mobile systems, SA-4 GANEF and SA-6 GAINFUL. A new anti-aircraft missile, SA-5 GRIFFON, is currently being deployed in northwestern Russia in the so-called Tallinn line. While the systems are generally thought to have been designed as anti-aircraft systems, there is some concern in the United States about the possibility of upgrading the 1,000+ SA-5s and 8,000 SA-2s[13] to act as ABMs, particularly if they can be commanded by the big hen house and dog house ABM-radars.

In November 1966 U.S. Secretary of Defense Robert S. McNamara announced that the Soviet Union had begun to deploy a ballistic missile defense (BMD) around Moscow based on the SA-7 GALOSH missile. Some 64 launchers were under construction or operational in 1969 there. The four complexes of 16 relocatable launchers each have reached their initial operational capability.[14] The long-range capability of the GALOSH missile enables the system to provide a thin area coverage for substantial portions of western Russia. There are no reports of new ABM site constructions. In their original configuration the GALOSH radars were deployed against American strategic attacks only, but they have since been directed also against China.

---

[12]Herbert Scoville and Robert Osborn, *Missile Madness,* Houghton, Mifflin, 1969, p. 14.

[13]*New York Times,* January 11, 1970.

[14]*ABM, MIRV, SALT and the Nuclear Arms Race,* Hearing before the Subcommittee on Arms Control, Internation Law and Organization of the Committee on Foreign Relations, U.S. Senate, 91st Congress, Second Session, 1970, p. 609.

Since the late fifties the deployment of the HEN HOUSE radar has built up a substantial missile tracking capability along the periphery of the Soviet Union. Such long leadtime tracking capability provides Moscow with a certain ABM mobilization base. The radar, which operates on approximately one-third the frequency of the Safeguard perimeter acquisition radar, may, however, prove quite vulnerable to the ionization effects of high altitude nuclear explosions; they must be backed up by DOG HOUSE type radar in closer proximity to the ABM launchers. The Russians may have cut back their ABM deployment. But the available evidence does not permit a judgment about whether the Russians started off with a more ambitious deployment schedule for their first generation ABM system. Soviet deployment of other weapon systems indicates that the Russians may view initial deployment of new systems as an extension of the research and development phase. The evidence does not yet permit a judgment on whether the limited deployment reflects a *general* disillusionment with BMD or a *specific* desire to improve the technology before substantial resources are committed to extensive deployment.

The Soviet Union has caught up with the United States quantitatively in long-range strategic systems. With rough quantitative parity Soviet decision-makers must now ask, "Where do we go from here?" The competing conceptions and interests that then open up could once be reconciled under the common denominator of catching up with the United States. From such a perspective SALT seems to be ideally timed for influencing Soviet priorities and choices. The Soviet options are, however, circumscribed by technological, economic, doctrinal, bureaucratic, and ideological constraints.

In the technological sector the Soviet Union seems to have an extensive test program of new and improved ABM systems at Sari Shagan in Southern Siberia, close to the

Mongolian border. The improved interceptor reportedly has a loiter capability, permitting it to coast for a brief period after it has been fired until it has selected a target, at which time it will be restarted and maneuvered to the target.[15] The Russians have also been testing an asphalt cloud technique designed to destroy or blunt the effectiveness of ICBM warheads.[16] The development program apparently includes second generation acquisition and terminal guidance radars.

The Russians have since August 1968 been testing a triplet multiple reentry vehicle (MRV) system with the SS-9 booster. The triplet reportedly has a fairly small footprint. Such a closely spaced reentry system with three 5 MT warheads seems ill-suited for counter city missions; a single 25 MT warhead would have a greater area of destruction (assuming that an overpressure of 10 psi will destroy an urban target). In July 1970 the SS-11 was tested with a triplet multiple reentry system. The Russians do not seem to have a real MIRV capability yet, but most analysts would agree that if the Russians should decide to develop MIRVs they could do so.

Retrofitted SS-9 missiles have been flight-tested in depressed trajectory and FOBS (Fractional Orbital Bombardment System) configurations. It is unclear whether such capabilities are in the operational inventory. Such configurations would presumably be designed to underfly radar (reducing the warning time) and could constitute a threat to airfields, command centers, etc. The SS-13 has till now not been flight-tested with multiple warheads, but it may become the missile in a mobile land-based ICBM system. There are no reports of Russian multiple warhead or de-

---

[15] *Safeguard Antiballistic Missile System,* Hearings before the Subcommittee of the Committee on Appropriations, House of Representatives, 91st Congress, 1st Session, 1969, p. 10–11.

[16] *Aviation Week and Space Technology,* June 13, 1970, p. 19.

pressed trajectory SLBM tests. However, in the November Day parade in 1967 the Russians showed a new SLBM, SS-N-XZ SAWFLY. This long-range (3,000 miles) missile has been flight-tested.

The M/IRBM force is probably approaching obsolescence; SALT may influence Soviet decisions about follow-on systems. Such decisions are, however, intimately connected with Soviet objectives and strategy in Europe. In 1965 the Russian showed a mobile IRBM system, the SS-XZ SCROOGE, and in 1967 a two-stage MRBM version of the SS-13, the SS-14 SCAPEGOAT missile (part of the mobile SCAMP system). These systems presumably constitute potential follow-on systems to the SS-4 and SS-5 missiles.

It is extremely hard to extrapolate Soviet strategic plans and doctrine from the operational force of the Soviet Union. There is no official Soviet presentation of procurement decisions or any document discussing posture and strategy similar to the annual "Posture Statement" of the American Secretary of Defense. In fact, the content and timing of major decisions have to be inferred *ex post facto* as the weapons emerge and are deployed. It is also not feasible to extrapolate the probable direction of Soviet procurement decisions on the basis of an analysis of Soviet discussions of doctrine and strategy.

Certainly, there has been an important output of Soviet literature dealing with questions of doctrine and strategy in recent years, particularly compared to the situation in the 1950s.[17] But such analyses are not necessarily relevant

---

[17]For an analysis of Soviet strategic doctrine in the 1950s see Raymond L. Garthoff, *Soviet Military Doctrine,* Free Press, 1953; *Soviet Strategy in the Nuclear Age,* Praeger, 1958; *The Soviet Image of Future War,* Public Affairs Press, 1959. The debates of the 1960s are analyzed in Thomas W. Wolfe, *Soviet Strategy at the Crossroad,* Harvard University Press, 1964 and *Soviet Power and Europe 1945–1970,* The Johns Hopkins Press, 1970. A representative sample of Soviet writings is contained in William R. Kintner and Harriet Fast Scott (eds.), *The Nuclear Revolution in Soviet Military Affairs,* University of Oklahoma Press, 1968. The most important recent Soviet works are first of all the three editions of Sokolvskij's *Voennaya Strategiva (Military Strategy)* (last edition: 1968). The

to procurement decisions; they constitute explorations of options inherent in a given set of technology. To a large extent it is likely that Soviet doctrine has followed, rather than structured, procurement decisions. The absence of a serious Soviet discussion about flexible and controlled response strategies until quite recently is possibly connected with the state of Soviet technology for guidance, command, and control. The considerable transmission of concepts, ideas, and perspectives from the American strategic analysts may have facilitated mutual comprehension and stimulated discussion and analysis—although it has failed to produce a convergence of views.

There is no intellectual defense establishment outside the professional officer corps in the Soviet Union. Some such may be emerging among physical scientists who develop interests in doctrinal issues through association with hardware development and contacts with colleagues in the West. As strategists, however, they seem likely to get into conflict

---

five editions of *Marksizm-Leninizm o Voyne i Armii (Marxism-Leninism on War and the Army)* (last edition: 1968) present the ideological perspective on military affairs. The two editions of *Metodologicheskie Problemy Voennoy Teorii Praktiki* (last edition: 1969) are by the young colonels from the Lenin Military Political Academy. There are also a number of monographs and collective works: P. A. Kurochkin (ed.), *Osnovy motodiki Voenno-Nauchnogo Issledovaniya (Fundamentals of Military-Scientific Investigation)*, 1969; S. N. Kozlov, et al. (eds.), *O Sovetskoy Voennoy Nauke (On Soviet Military Science)*, 1964; N. A. Lomov, *Sovetskaya Voennaya Doktrina (Soviet Military Doctrine)*, 1963; M. V. Popov, *Sushehnost Zakonov Vooruzhennoy Bor'by (The Essence of the Laws of Armed Struggle)*, 1964; N. P. Prokop'ev, *O Voyne i Armii (On War and the Army)*, 1965; N. V. Pukhovskij, *O Mire i Voyne (On Peace and War)*, 1965; E. I. Rybkin, *Voyna i Politika (War and Politics)*, 1959; I. A. Seleznev, *Voyna i Ideologicheskaya Bor'ba (War and the Ideological Struggle)*, 1964; A. A. Sidorenko, *Nastuplenie (The Offensive)*, 1970; P. V. Sokolov, *Voenno-Ekonomicheskiye Voprosy v Kurse Politekonomii (Military-Economic Problems in a Political Economy Course)*, 1968; P. I. Trifonenkov, *Ob osnovnykh zakonakh khoda i iskhoda sovremennoy voyny (On the Fundamental Laws about the Course and Outcome of Contemporary War)*, 1962; S. A. Tyushkevich, *Neobkhodimost' i sluchaynost v voyne (Necessity and Chance in War)*, 1962; M. S. Shifman, *Voyna i Ekonomika (War and Economics)*, 1964; V. S. Yarovikov (ed.), *Problemy Revolyutsii v voennom dele (The Problems of the Revolution in Military Affairs)*, 1965.

with important military prerogatives. Many Soviet procurement decisions become comprehensible only in the context of the traditions, vested interests, distribution of bargaining power, system of decision-making, etc., in the Soviet military establishment.

It is hard to demonstrate a consistent pattern of action-reaction in the interactions between the Soviet and American strategic postures. We just do not have an adequate explanatory model for the Soviet-American arms race. There is a sense in which the very development of defense technology acts as a built-in escalator. There appears to be a large element of unilateral parallel racing with offense competing against defense in the laboratories and in the minds of men. The quantitative targets for a particular weapon system may set the scale for the imitative effort of the adversary, as indeed the American missile buildup in the early sixties may have done for the Soviet effort in the late sixties. The Soviet timing of the programs, however, seems to be determined largely by indigenous factors, and the configuration of the force reflects particular Soviet traditions (massive fire power, counterforce). The Soviet Union does not seem to offset American defenses by augmenting its own offensive capabilities. However, such a pattern might emerge in a parity situation should the United States deploy, for example, a comprehensive BMD system. The question is open.

The Russians acknowledge that offensive systems tend to generate defensive countermeasures, which in turn encourage development of new offensive systems. They refuse, however, to consider the Soviet-American arms race as a process of reciprocal stimulation:

> If we turn to the question about the causes for the contemporary arms race, we consider that its driving force is not the "action-reaction phenomenon" per se, as R. McNamara claimed, but rather the political objectives of imperialism, particularly American imperialism. In their evaluation of the future of the arms race many American ideologists and

theoreticians proceed on the assumption that military force constitutes the only determining factor.[18]

It is not clear that the Russians relate their force levels to quantitative assumptions about the relationship between deterrence and second strike population hostages. Though such assumptions may structure the procurement decisions, they have not crystallized into official doctrine around such concepts as assured destruction. The Soviet view appears to be an extension of classical war strategy, focusing on relative war outcomes and the need to come out best rather than on absolute levels of destruction. Such an outlook is in principle more compatible with mutual force reductions than that of "assured destruction." The following is a rather cogent summary of a representative Soviet viewpoint:

> In war it is the stronger who is victorious. At first glance this may sound trivial. However, it expresses a profound, substantial, necessary, firm and recurrent link, both between the various aspects of war and between the various sides within these aspects. In this sense one can speak of the correlation of forces between states or coalitions of states during the period of preparation for a potential war, during the period of the beginning of armed struggle and during the various concrete combat actions and operations.

Superiority over the enemy is not only achieved by destroying his forces, but also by saving one's own forces.[19]

It is hard to identify the Soviet position on the "superiority versus parity" issue. Military commentators tend to emphasize the need to maintain a superior position, but they also seem to imply that the Soviet Union occupies such a position, largely by reference to the presumed superiority

---

[18] V. Kulish and S. Fedoreko, "Po povodu diskussil v SShA o strategicheskikh Vooruzheniyakh," *Mezhdunarodaya Ekonomika i Mezhdunarodyne Otnosheniya,* 3 (1970): 48.

[19] Rear Admiral V. Andreyev, "Dialektika sootnosheniya sil," *Krasnaya Zvezda,* December 13, 1967.

of the Soviet social system. Here, the "hawks" among Soviet military analysts seem to come predominantly from the Lenin Military Political Academy, under the Main Political Administration of the Soviet Army and Navy.[20]

Political commentators, in relation to SALT, however, have emphasized that the two superpowers are talking from positions of equality. Probably there is no firm Soviet view on this issue. Till recently it has not presented any concrete procurement decisions; the Soviets have been catching up. Statements on the issue have to be interpreted in the context of the prevailing position of the Soviet Union, and the audience: Soviet statements downgrading superiority when the Soviet Union was clearly inferior to the United States are a poor base for projecting Soviet views in a different situation. A strong statement about the need to maintain superiority may likewise be best understood in the context of indigenous bargaining over the allocation of resources to defense and the legitimation of a certain allocation.

Several dynamic elements complicate the prediction about Soviet doctrine and deployment. The Senior Command Group of the Soviet Union over the last decade has been characterized by old age. The group was the youngest in the world in 1945, with an average age of 45; by 1965 it was the oldest, with the average age over 60. Since 1965 there appears to have been a drive to rejuvenate the top commands. The 1967 "Law on Universal Obligation for Military Service" made senior generals liable to transfer to the lowest category of reserve forces (Group 3) and set the retirement for one- and two-star generals at 55 and colonels at 45. Rejuvenation is most marked in the Air Defense Command and in the Military District commands. Increasingly, the senior command group will be made up of officers who were

---

[20] The Lenin Military Academy publishes the journal *Kommunist Yooruzhennykh sil* while *Voennyj Vestnik* is published by the Frunze Academy and the classified journal *Voennaya Mysl'* by the Military Science Administration under the General Staff.

not senior commanders in World War II, and whose professional careers are associated primarily with the postwar military establishment. Such a change may pave the way for new outlooks, priorities, and emphases.

Modern analytical techniques from operational research and systems analysis may contribute also to a greater convergence of Soviet and American decisions on weapons procurement.[21] The configuration of the Soviet strategic posture seems to have been decided largely by the military professionals, within certain broad economic parameters laid down by the Soviet political leadership. One important consequence of SALT may be the politicization of issues which traditionally have been perceived as narrowly technical and military. Thus the political leadership is likely to become involved more directly in structuring the Soviet strategic posture because of an increased awareness of the interdependence of Soviet and American decision-making. Such a change of perceptions would tend to reemphasize that interdependence in a sort of self-fulfilling prophecy.

The Soviets had a general negative reaction to the controlled response strategy which Robert S. McNamara made official American doctrine during his early years in the Pentagon. A major reason was probably the unavailability of much of the relevant technology for command and control. The first and second generation Soviet ICBMs were rather clumsy systems with low survivability, not very well suited for a firing doctrine involving controlled and flexible response. Soviet analysts divide the post-World War II "Revolution in Military Affairs" into three stages:

1. Fission and fusion weapons

---

[21] See, e.g., V. A. Bokarev, *Kiberneitika i voennoe delo (Cybernetics and Military Affairs),* 1969; Yu. S. Solnyshkov, *Optimizatsiaya vybora vooruzheniya (The Optimization of Weapons Selection),* 1968; Yu. V. Cheyev (ed.), *Osnovy Issledovaniya Operatsij v voennoy teknike (The Fundamentals of Operations Research in Military Equipment),* 1965; Yu. V. Chuyev, *Issledovanie Operatsilj v voennom dele (Operations Research in Military Affairs),* 1970.

2. Long-range missiles
3. Electronics and cybernetics

The Soviet Union is currently in the third stage. Hence Soviet spokesmen have paid increasing attention to problems of command and control, emphasizing such factors as hardening, avionics miniaturization, and retargeting capability. The absence of relevant technology may explain, for example, the fact that Soviet strategic forces never went on alert, even during the Cuban missile crisis, until the mid-to-late sixties. The Russians now claim that "the missiles are equipped with a reliable blocking system which can prevent any accident, mistake, or misunderstanding."[22]

As the former deputy commander of the strategic missile forces, V. F. Tolubko, described the Soviet missile force:

> They [ICBMs] are launched from shafts which afford protection against the effects of nuclear explosions, and the time required to prepare the rockets for launch and the launch itself is counted in tens of seconds. All preparatory operations are automated. The simultaneous launch of several rockets is performed by a crew of two to three men.[23]

Soviet arms control literature has increasingly stressed the problem of accidental war recently. Certain disturbing signals often accompany rather assertive statements about the military might of the Soviet Union, such as an implied pre-emption or launch on warning scenario. Here we may be up against doctrinal legacies reflecting technological constraints and incentives which no longer prevail. Some uncertainty prevails because of the recurrent theme that the Soviet Union will be able to strike at the aggressor before the latter can hit the Soviet Union.

Soviet targeting doctrine does not seem to reflect a basic preoccupation with population hostages for deterrence or

---

[22]Moscow broadcast in Hungarian, February 24, 1967.
[23]*Krasnaya Zvezda,* November 18, 1967.

with the deliberate destruction of population targets in a war. However, the targeting doctrine includes an approach which generally mixes counterforce, counter-industry, and counter-administration. Soviet strategists have tended to emphasize the effect of attacks upon the social organization and the control net of the adversary, an approach which reflects, perhaps, their own emphasis on administration and control. It is important here to notice that the concept of central war developing out of an escalation process in a local conflict is now part of official Soviet doctrine.

The SS-9 has caused considerable concern in the United States on two accounts: (1) the number of missiles seems very large compared to the number of urban targets in the U.S. which would require single 20MT warheads or multiple 5MT warheads; and (2) the SS-9 is more accurate than the other Soviet ICBMs. Why are the Russians putting their best accuracy into the system carrying the largest payload? These questions are obviously generated from an assured destruction perspective. The SS-9 program may be more comprehensible judged against the background of Soviet rather than American doctrinal perspectives! No quantitative descriptions of SS-9 accuracy are available. The figure of about one-fourth of a mile was frequently cited in official discussions of the U.S. strategic missiles. Some projections indicate that ICBM accuracies may be down to 30 meters by 1980. (The calculation has been made that 420 SS-9 missiles each equipped with three reentry vehicles of 5MT could destroy 95 per cent of a Minuteman force of 1,000 missiles [in silos hardened to withstand an overpressure of 300 psi], assuming retargeting capability and a ¼ n. mile C.E.P. (Circular Error Probability). It would seem reasonable to assume that in the mid-seventies the Russians could upgrade the guidance on the SS-11 force. We could not know whether Soviet objectives include the attainment of a credible first strike capacity, but a prudent American planner would naturally hedge against the possibility that the Russians may end up with a *de facto* first strike posture by either design or default. The dynamics of military technology make it quite possible for both superpowers to have a first strike capacity. The premium on striking first is thus likely to have an unsettling and exacerbating effect on international crises. I feel that a primary purpose of SALT ought to be for the two superpowers to work out the ground rules for that particular predicament.

Coping with a reciprocal first strike situation may involve some rather substantial doctrinal revisions, perhaps toward a restrained counterforce, with a no-cities emphasis, and away from the suffocating embrace of "mutual assured destruction." The feasibility of such a shift would of course depend on numbers—absolute and relative—and should have an ethical orientation to the "what happens if deterrence fails" problem. Such a shift may be more marginal for Russian strategists than for many Americans.[24]

The ground rules would also have to deal with racing or dynamic stability. In principle, one of the better ways to protect the deterrent forces against an obliterating first strike would be to deploy active defenses. But this cannot be resolved in principle; it has to be resolved concretely, with reference to specific technology, offense-defense cost exchange ratios, tactics (precursor and self-black-out techniques, shoot-look-shoot, etc.), and money. This is not the place to discuss the particular merits of the SAFEGUARD system. But I do think that active defense of missile silos will constitute an interesting and feasible option in the mid-to-late seventies.[25] It is particularly more cost-effective than

[24]For a quite sophisticated analysis see Chapter 9 by V. I. Voneev in A. M. Belyavskij (ed.), *Sovremennye Problemy Razoruzheniya (Contemporary Problems of Disarmament)*, 1970, pp. 198–226.

[25]The issues in the ABM debate are explored in: C. F. Barnaby and A. Boserup (eds.), *Implications of Anti-Ballistic Missile Systems*, Pugwash Monograph II; Souvenir Press, London, 1969; Abram Chayes and Jerome B. Wiesner (eds.), *ABM: An Evaluation of the Decision to Deploy an Antiballistic Missile System*, Harper and Row, 1969; Johan J. Holst and William Schneider, Jr. (eds.), *Why*

hardening by reinforcing the silos (generally considered to be hopelessly uncompetitive with the projected improvements in accuracy). The Russian decisions on hard-point defenses will probably reflect *inter alia* the value attributed to the protection of forces within the Soviet doctrinal framework.

Another alternative would be to make the ICBMs mobile or semi-mobile. The Russians seem interested in that option; they reportedly proposed that mobile land-based missiles be permitted under a SALT agreement.[26] Such options would pose some serious monitoring problems. And what sort of impact would mobile ICBMs have on offensive tactics? How would it be consistent with the objective of limiting damage to population and industry? A third alternative would be to increase the number of missiles in order to raise the second strike force to levels that could guarantee a certain level of destruction. The problem with that is that it would imply the buildup of a first strike capacity. It is difficult also to find stable cutoff points in the quantitative race which it might inaugurate. From a Soviet perspective, U.S. ABM for force protection would seem more desirable, as it would not imply a threat to Soviet values (except if a first strike option be among them).

The Russians have clearly tended to favor active defenses; the deployment of such systems is completely consistent for them. It is possible that some of the Soviet perspectives on active defenses have reflected perhaps a nostalgic desire to be released from the interdependence of a deterrent relationship, and a rather simple-minded "defense is defense" denial of interaction links. However, it may be just as irra-

---

ABM: Policy Issues in the Missile Defense Controversy, Pergamon Press, 1969; William Kintner (ed.), *SAFEGUARD: Why the ABM Makes Sense,* Hawthorne, 1969. The best discussion of SAFEGUARD and the issues involved in its systems evaluation is found in the *1971 Authorization Hearings* with testimonies by Donald F. Hornig, Lawrence H. O'Neill, Wofgang Panofsky, and Albert Wohlstetter, pp. 2212–2415.

[26] *International Herald Tribune,* December 28, 1970.

tional to be against active defense in principle on the grounds that it would undermine deterrence. Surely deterrence is a means to peace and security, not an end in itself. There are some reports that the Russians have changed their view on ABM at the SALT meetings. Their irritation about Western press reports that they had agreed to limit ABM to national capital areas (NCAs) may indicate that the issue has still not been settled in Moscow.

The Soviet strategic weapons program is sustained by very substantial research and development. According to official American estimates the Soviet effort is already 20 per cent larger than that of the U.S. and has been increasing from 10 to 13 per cent annually in recent years.[27] Defense-related outlays are estimated at about two-thirds of the total.[28]

The Soviet defense effort is exercising a considerable strain on the Soviet economy. The growth rate of the Soviet GNP has tended to flatten out and the capital-output ratio has been increasing. There appear also to be fewer spillovers from the Soviet military programs to the civilian sectors of the economy than in the U.S. To a large extent this is due to the gap in the technological level of the two sectors. As strategic systems become relatively more important, the choice between guns and growth (and there is a choice) becomes increasingly limited to investment rather than production, because the missile support industry is relatively nonconvertible to civilian production.

The official Soviet defense budget is 17.7 billion rubles for 1971. The real expenditures are probably in the neighborhood of 20–25 billion rubles. At the official exchange rate that would amount to only $22–28 billion; but at dollar costs, the budgeted goods and services would probably amount to

---

[27] *ABM, MIRV, SALT, and the Nuclear Arms Race*, p. 500 (John S. Foster, Jr.).
[28] The Limitation of Strategic Arms, Hearings before the Subcommittee on Strategic Arms Limitation Talks of the Committee on Armed Services, U.S. Senate, 91st Congress, 2nd Sess., Part 2, 1970, p. 60 (Thomas W. Wolfe).

some $60–70 billion. Since the military sector of the Soviet economy is thought to be relatively efficient, the output would be less expensive in terms of factor inputs (opportunity costs) than for a less efficient sector. In dollar terms, Soviet and American defense budgets are quite comparable. But the burden of defense to the Soviet economy measured in Soviet price terms amounts to some 10 per cent of the GNP. This calculation does not include the drain on the economy associated with allocating top resources and high priority people to the Soviet defense effort. In dollar terms the Soviet strategic force budget is on the order of $18 billion, some 25–30 percent of the defense budget.

The history of the American strategic posture is fairly well known; I shall touch only on some salient features. Through the middle and late fifties SAC (Strategic Air Command) came to dominate the U.S. strategic posture. Strategic power was not so central to the posture and doctrine of the 1940s. When SAC was established in 1946 it had only one unit capable of delivering nuclear weapons. In an exercise in May 1947, SAC sent 101 B-29s (Superfortress), all it could put in the air, against New York City. However, by 1949—following the crises of 1948—the force consisted of three heavy bombardment wings with B-36 (Peacemaker) and eleven medium bombardment wings consisting of B-29 and B-50 aircraft. SAC had begun some overseas rotation with B-29 squadrons in 1947 and by 1948, in response to the Berlin crisis, it started a regular system of rotation of bomber groups to England, Germany, and the Far East. The first jet bomber, the medium-range B-47 (Stratojet), became operational in 1951 and eventually replaced all B-29s and B-50s. Thus by 1954 SAC had 175 B-36s and more than 400 B-47s, at a time when the Russians first displayed their jet medium- and long-range bombers. After the Korean War there began a crash program on overseas bases to permit the bombers to reach targets in the Soviet Union. Runways were lengthened on the bases in England and Guam; bases were opened in French Morocco in 1951 and in Spain in 1954. Air-refuelling techniques, tested experimentally before 1950, became operational with the acquisition of a fleet of KC-97 (Stratofreighter) tankers after 1951. Following the development of the H-bomb, the Soviet demonstration of advanced bombers, and the subsequent debate over the presumed "bomber gap," Congressional support was mobilized behind the Air Force's request for an accelerated procurement program. To counter projections of the Soviet threat, some 700 long-range B-52s (Stratofortress) would be procured in addition to the 1,500 medium-range B-47s. The first B-52 entered service in 1955. In 1957 the first all-jet tanker for air-refuelling, KC-135 (Stratotanker), became operational and in 1959 the supersonic medium bomber B-58 (Hustler) entered the inventory; but the total production of this aircraft was limited to 116.

Today all the B-47s and B-58s have been phased out of their strategic nuclear role; SAC consists of 500 B-52s and two squadrons (35 aircraft) of the variable geometry FB-111. It includes also 500 KC-135 tankers and two strategic reconnaissance squadrons operating SR-71s. The force is dispersed on 28 main bases and some satellite bases. The later B-52 models carry the 700-mile air-to-surface cruise missile, Hound Dog. To improve the penetration capability of its bombers the U.S. is developing a supersonic Short-Range Attack Missile (SRAM) for use against terminal defenses. Work is in progress on the Subsonic Cruise Armed Decoy (SCAD), an advanced bomber penetration aid against area defenses. Engineering development on a new intercontinental jet bomber, the B-1, is also under way.

By 1959 fears of the bomber gap had subsided as it became clear that Moscow had not opted for a large-scale long-range bomber force. The U-2 flights provided more accurate intelligence about Soviet operational capabilities. In the meantime, attention shifted to missiles. The American missile program was not revived seriously until 1954–55, after the Von Neuman report concluded that the feasibility of a long-range ballistic missile was no longer in doubt. The availability of the hydrogen bomb made a C.E.P. of five miles quite acceptable. The Atlas program was overhauled and in 1955 development of the intermediate-range missiles, Thor and Jupiter, was approved. The Soviet Sputniks of 1957 produced a significant acceleration of the American missile program through fears of a missile gap developing in favor of the Russians. Intelligence estimated that the Soviet Union might have as many as 200 ICBMs by 1962, and possibly as early as 1960. The expenditures on strategic missiles rose from less than $160 million in 1955 to $3.3 billion in 1960.[29] Only 20–40 ICBMs were originally scheduled for deployment in the U.S. The first squadrons of Atlas D missiles were deployed by 1959 above ground in erect positions vulnerable to damage by only two psi overpressure. The Atlas E was emplaced in horizontal coffins and hardened to 25 psi and the Atlas F (1963) was deployed in underground silos hardened to withstand 100 psi. The 54 Titan Is were similarly deployed by 1961, as was the solid-fuel Minuteman I by 1962.

The NATO council in 1957 agreed in principle that medium-range missiles be emplaced in Europe as a stop-gap measure. The 60 Thors for the United Kingdom were, however, not operational until 1959 and the 30 Jupiters in Italy and 15 in Turkey not until 1961. They were phased out by 1963.

The incoming Kennedy Administration in 1961 initiated a substantial buildup of strategic missile forces with solid storable fuel permitting in-silo launching from hardened sites. Since 1965 there has been no increase in the established number of 1,710 missiles. By 1965 the U.S. had phased out all the first generation liquid-fuel missiles (including the 126 Atlas and 54 Titan I missiles). Thus the current force

---

[29] *Missiles, Space, and Other Defense Matters,* Hearings before the Preparedness Investigating Subcommittee of the Committee on Armed Services, U.S. Senate, 86th Congress, 2nd session, 1960, p. 444.

comprises 1,000 Minuteman IB II and III missiles, 54 Titan IIs, and 656 Polaris A-2 and A-3s in 41 submarines. At any one time, 20 submarines are deployed in the Arctic–North Atlantic–Mediterranean area, and 5 in the Pacific. Eventually all 500 Minuteman Is will be replaced by Minuteman IIIs, the first squadron of which is now deployed with the MK 12 MIRV warhead system containing two 200KT warheads and a decoy. The Polaris A-3 is equipped with a triplet MRV system. Eventually the SLBM force is scheduled to include 496 Poseidon C-3s with the MK-3 reentry system containing ten to fourteen 50KT warheads on 31 boats, and 160 Polaris A-3s on 10 boats. Design studies are under way on a follow-on system, ULMS (Underseas Long-Range Missile System), including a larger and quieter submarine and a longer range missile.

Since the early fifties the problem of vulnerability has been central to the posture and operational doctrine of U.S. strategic forces. As the U.S. had to adjust to bilateral nuclear deterrence, during the early and mid-fifties, the problem consisted in the fact that the deployment of the strategic bombing force presented a number of points of force concentration which was not very large compared to Soviet expected capabilities for attack in the late 1950s.[30] SAC tried to reduce its overseas vulnerability by abandoning its mobility plan in favor of basing the aircraft in the United States, with prestrike aerial refueling and poststrike staging overseas. Then it adopted a counterforce strategy in the hope of being able to knock out the Soviet Long Range Air Force. Subsequently, it attempted to reduce its vulnerability in North America by a combination of improved warning,

---

[30] See A. J. Wohlstetter, F. S. Hoffman, R. J. Lutz, and H. S. Rowen, *Selection and the Use of Strategic Air Bases,* R-266; The RAND Corporation, 1954; 2d declassified printing, 1962, and A. J. Wohlstetter, F. S. Hoffman, and H. S. Rowen, *Protecting U.S. Power to Strike Back in the 1950's and 1960's,* R-290; The RAND Corporation, 1956.

dispersal, ground alert, reflex, and airborne alert, while the target doctrine came to emphasize Soviet cities and population.

Paradoxically, as the objective vulnerability of the U.S. strategic deterrent grew as a function of Soviet capabilities, subjective assessments permitted the Eisenhower Administration to make strategic air power central to the U.S. posture. Previously, it had been viewed largely as an instrument for a holding operation permitting the mobilization and transportation of ground troops to Europe. In December 1954 NATO strategy was restructured to assure the early availability of nuclear weapons in a major military conflict. Presupposing a fairly automatic escalation to the nuclear level, the strategy transferred much of the burden of European defense to the North American continent. The new posture depended less on the large American mobilization base, more on ready forces, particularly nuclear forces. Hence the perceived vulnerability of the American deterrent has been basic to intra-alliance politics in NATO, being a major determinant of the credibility of the American guarantee in European eyes.

The problem of vulnerability "re-emerged" with the first generation strategic missiles, which were incapable of in-silo launching and did not permit on-board storage of propellants. They did not even permit quick firing on warning that a Soviet salvo was underway. More importantly, the soft configuration of the bases raised anew the problem of preemptive disarming strikes and the possibly explosive interactions of the reciprocal fears of surprise attack in an environment when both sides were relying on soft, vulnerable deterrent systems. This particular problem was "solved" by the introduction of the second generation solid-fuel and hardened Minuteman and Polaris systems.

However, no solutions are final; the improvements in accuracy are threatening to make the fixed ICBM vulnerable to preclusive first strikes. At the same time, the introduction of MIRVs raises the possibility of attack ratios favoring the attacker. The cancellation of the Hardrock silo program is a recognition of the fact that passive protection is no longer competitive with improvements in accuracy. Roughly speaking, improving the accuracy by a factor of two offsets a tenfold increase in overpressure resistance. A first strike scenario might then include depressed trajectory SLBM attacks against airfields, nuclear submarines in port, and command centers, as well as some strikes against the Minuteman fields, pinning down the missiles until the arrival of a second wave of accurate ICBMs. The American deterrent would come to rest rather heavily on the Polaris/Poseidon force. It has, however, for some time been thought imprudent to base deterrence on only one kind of weapon system, which like all systems will have its particular defects and vulnerabilities. Attacks become more complicated, and hence possibly more likely, as they have to cope with the destruction of different weapon systems with separate and different technological uncertainties. The option of active hard point defense here becomes particularly relevant as a means both of enhancing crisis stability and of stabilizing the arms race.

The history of the American BMD program needs no repetition here. The first phase of the SAFEGUARD deployment includes the emplacement of a one-face PAR (Perimeter Acquisition Radar) and one four-face MSR (Missile Site Radar) unit as well as long-range Spartan and short-range Sprint interceptors around the Minuteman fields at the Grand Forks (North Dakota) and Malmstrom (Montana) Air Force bases. The specific number of interceptors involved is not known, but it is understood that some 200 Spartan and Sprint missiles will be deployed at the two sites[31] when they become operational in 1974. The first in-

---

[31]*New York Times,* August 8, 1969.

stallment in Phase 2 will involve the deployment of Spartan and Sprint missiles at the Minuteman field at Whiteman AFB in Missouri and the initiation of work at another field at Warren AFB in Wyoming. Congress refused, however, to approve the acquisition of land for four more sites which were to be used primarily for area defense purposes. The U.S. has initiated Hardsite, a program which aims at generating a BMD system optimized for the task of protecting fixed ICBM installations. It would employ more but cheaper and smaller radar and computers than those in the Safeguard system.

Strategic analysts commonly assume greater coherence and consistency in strategic doctrine and its relationship to the strategic posture than actually prevails. To a considerable degree doctrine has to be discussed in terms of idealized principles. In the real world there are bureaucratic, economic, technological, and other kinds of constraints which conspire to make actual practice deviate rather irregularly from the ideal model.

"The basic task of the strategic forces is deterrence." Such a statement is too general to be useful as guidance for planning. The question of who is preventing whom from doing what in what circumstances and with what confidence of success is actually a very complicated set of subquestions.

In our context the "who's" are the United States and the Soviet Union. These are basically dissimilar actors not necessarily constrained by the same propensities, expectations, values, or priorities. It makes a difference whether decision-makers view the adversary through a mirror or a window pane.

The extent of deterrence has been the subject of much discussion and political activity. Should U.S. strategic forces be deployed and configured to deter contingencies other than a direct attack on the United States? And if so, what contingencies are covered by "extended deterrence?" What is the role of other capabilities such as conventional forces and tactical nuclear forces as elements of deterrence? What discontinuities, if any, should be emphasized in the spectrum of deterrence? How does one reconcile the deterrence value of precommitments with the value of maintaining political control and exercising judgment? Such issues have complicated the formulation and implementation of American strategic policy, particularly as they apply to U.S. alliance commitments. Former Secretary of Defense Clark Clifford describes qualifications which reflect the dilemmas:

> We must be prepared to maintain at all times strategic forces of such size and character, and exhibit so unquestionable a will to use them *in retaliation if needed,* that no nation could ever conceivably deem it to its advantage to launch a deliberate nuclear attack on the United States or its allies [emphasis added].[32]

One common dichotomy suggests a choice between strategies for deterring wars and strategies for fighting and terminating wars should they occur. This I find rather artificial. The two perspectives may be linked by the concept of credibility: strategies which it is deemed incredible that a particular actor would choose to carry out may not deter. Residual uncertainties will always remain, and a basic issue in strategic policy has been the *extent to* which one ought to hedge against the event that deterrence should fail by acquiring capabilities for escalation control and damage limitation.

Robert McNamara set out to provide for the United States a strategic posture which was explicitly designed for a bilateral deterrence environment. The strategic forces should provide decision-makers with the option of deliberate and measured response and not force them to precipitate action because of the unavailability of alternatives. The doctrine of flexible and controlled response in its first phase focused on

---

[32] *The 1970 Defense Budget and Defense Program for Fiscal Years 1970–74,* p. 47. A Statement by Secretary of Defense Clark M. Clifford, 1969.

city avoidance and damage limitation. However, by 1965 there was a discernible shift away from damage limitation, with the result that the U.S. was moving toward a Minimum or Finite Deterrence policy based on a capacity for "assured destruction." The shift of emphasis predated the Soviet acquisition of a large and secure missile force, although the buildup may have been considered likely to take place at that time.

A more plausible explanation is probably associated with the emergence of ABM as a serious issue in relation to the strategic posture. Robert McNamara appears to have viewed that issue primarily in terms of the dangers of an escalation of the arms race. The assured destruction concept served the function of suggesting upper (and lower) limits to the forces needed for deterrence. It provided a standard of sufficiency which was defensible against pressures for "more." Thus Mr. McNamara estimated that a second strike capability to destroy one-fourth to one-third of the Soviet population and two-thirds of the Soviet industrial capability would constitute a sufficient assured destruction potential for deterrence.[33] By 1968 he had lowered his requirements to one-fifth to one-fourth of the population, and one-half of the industrial capacity.[34] Such operational definitions of the "assured destruction" mission did not constitute a criterion for *deterrence* sufficiency. Deterrence is a psychological quantity which is a function of the adversary's estimate of the probability that one will act a certain way in a given situation, and his assessment of the consequences of such action. The "assured destruction" criterion was based primarily on an analysis of American marginal costs associated with the infliction of damage on the Soviet Union.

---

[33] *The Fiscal Years 1966–70 Defense Program and the 1966 Defense Budget.* A Statement by Secretary of Defense Robert S. McNamara, 1965, p. 39.

[34] *The Fiscal Years 1969–73 Defense Program and the 1969 Defense Budget.* A Statement by Secretary of Defense Robert S. McNamara, 1968, p. 50.

These costs will rise as the margin utility of strategic force increases diminishes, because of the need to attack smaller and smaller population centers and industrial complexes.

With this in mind, ballistic missile defense could be seen as a threat to deterrence, generating offsetting countermeasures which again would result in a quantitative and budgetary escalation of the arms race. United States doctrine came to reflect the model of a largely autonomous arms race with its own separate "mad momentum."

The Nixon Administration has changed the strategic outlook but the basic doctrinal perspective remains unclear. In regard to the action-reaction arms race model, Secretary Laird has said:

> Just as weapons in themselves are not the cause of wars, neither are a country's actions in weapons deployment—in themselves—the driving force in a so-called arms race. The fundamental driving force in an arms race is what one country perceives as possible objectives of another country's actions.[35]

It is interesting to note the similarity with the Soviet perspective which was quoted above.

The concept of "assured destruction" has been dropped; instead, sufficiency is related to a rather general objective which is pointedly ambiguous in regard to extended deterrence: "Our forces must be adequate to ensure that all potential aggressors are convinced that acts which *could* lead to nuclear attack or nuclear blackmail pose unacceptable risks to them."[36] President Nixon has mentioned the existence of "four basic criteria for strategic sufficiency,"[37] but

---

[35] Address by the Honorable Melvin R. Laird, Secretary of Defense, at the Annual Luncheon of the Associated Press, New York, April 20, 1970. *DOD News Release,* No. 316–70, p. 7.

[36] *Fiscal Year 1971 Defense Program and Budget.* A Statement by Secretary of Defense Melvin R. Laird, 1970, p. 39.

[37] *U. S. Foreign Policy for the 1970's: A New Strategy for Peace.* A Report to the Congress by Richard Nixon, President of the United States, February 18, 1970, p. 122.

he has not identified them publicly. This policy, he told the world, will be somewhere between unilateral force reduction and the pursuit of superiority. McNamara was, perhaps deliberately, somewhat ambiguous on the issue of superiority. He would couple his assertion that meaningful superiority was unattainable with a commitment to maintain a three or four to one numerical superiority over the Soviet Union in effective deliverable warheads. It may be a problem of having to talk to different audiences with different biases and concerns, but it may also to some extent be rooted in language. Thus it may be useful to distinguish between *stark superiority* in the sense of being able to initiate central war with impunity—which is clearly unattainable—and *relative superiority,* which involves the expectation of not being worse off than the adversary after a war. "Superiority" in this sense may have some important impact on both prewar and intrawar deterrence, while its convertibility into valid currency for peacetime political bargaining may be more problematical. Thus it would seem that the American Administration will have to formulate its strategic doctrine in relation to four alternatives:

1. Finite deterrence emphasis
2. Defensive emphasis (including substantial ABM and civil defense programs)
3. Deterrence plus insurance emphasis
4. Extended deterrence emphasis

The choice of alternative will in turn influence targeting and firing doctrine, numbers and explosive yields of weapons, size and character of the forces best suited to deliver the weapons. The current Administration is focusing particularly on insuring the preattack invulnerability of the American strategic forces. This could lead to increased interest in intrawar bargaining and deterrence, as well as war-termination and recuperation. Survival of the forces and command and control systems for extended periods in a wartime situation may be emphasized. The alternatives are likely to be considered also in relation to the dangers and burdens of the arms race.

It is perhaps necessary to arrest the common notion of the two superpowers being engaged in an unlimited arms race. Actually they have been exercising considerable restraint. SALT may come to both symbolize and expand such mutual restraints.

The level of expenditures on U.S. strategic forces indicates none of the exponential behavior that is often assumed to prevail. The strategic force budget in 1970 will amount to about $8 billion or a little less. Measured in 1971 dollars the 1962 force budget was a little less than $15 billion. Strategic forces accounted for 10.5 per cent of the defense budget in 1970 and 25.5 per cent in 1962. During the late fifties the comparable strategic force budgets were more than $18 billion in 1971 dollars.

It is not possible to unscramble the Soviet defense budget so that the profile or distribution on missions and programs emerges. There have probably been substantial increases since the early sixties, but the expenditures may be leveling off and, as we have noted, the Soviet decision to keep the total defense budget constant in current ruble values may symbolize a deliberate restraint. Budgetary restraints may be one important outcome from SALT, although it would seem to depend on restraints in other dimensions.

In regard to quantities, it is worth noting that the Soviet buildup since 1965 coincides with no increases in the U.S. established level of 1,710 strategic missile launchers and a reduction of the heavy bomber strength of 780 by over 200. The U.S. did build up substantially between 1961 and 1965. But the total number of strategic delivery vehicles did not change significantly from the established level of the late fifties, since the missile buildup coincided with the phasing out of some 1,500 B-47s. The number of warheads in the strategic force has gone down and the total megatonnage of the force has diminished substantially. The number of launchers is not the most useful criterion for measuring the effectiveness of a strategic force—the number and types of warheads correlated with the structure and extent of the target system would be more relevant—but it does have a symbolic value. The apparent leveling off of the Soviet SS-9 and SS-11 deployments in the context of SALT may, as I have noted, also constitute a symbolic gesture of restraint.

There have also been some important qualitative restraints. The U.S. MIRV program, for instance, does exhibit a certain quantitative restraint: not all Minuteman and Polaris submarines are to be converted to MIRV (the ten Polaris submarines that are not converted are the oldest and noisiest, which may be retained primarily for service interest reasons. The modern 31-boat SLBM force rounds off the number of launchers at the closest point to 500, while the Minuteman force remains at 1,000.) More important, however, the American MIRV warheads have relatively small yields and reasonably high accuracy. Such a configuration would make feasible various forms of restraint in war, permitting, for example, the destruction of military targets in ways which would minimize collateral damage to civilian areas. The technology would thus provide also the infrastructure for a strategy of deliberate avoidance of large civilian fatalities. The cancellation of the MK-17 reentry vehicle program for Minuteman, which would have provided a "big-bang" single reentry vehicle warhead, and of programs which would have produced a combination of accuracy and yield in the warheads which would have threatened the survivability of the Soviet strategic land-based force are also symbolic signals of intent and invitations to exercise restraint. United States MIRVed ICBMs are clearly less efficient against hard targets than un-MIRVed missiles. Over time, further improvements in accuracy are likely to further blur such distinctions.

Qualitative restraints are visible also in the design and

configuration of the ballistic missile programs. On the American side the distinction between area and hard-point defense has been emphasized, as has that between thin and thick coverage. The intent has clearly been to communicate to the Russians that the systems did not constitute a threat to the Soviet deterrent. Ambiguities are, of course, difficult to avoid and a Russian fear that Sentinel constituted a down-payment on a more comprehensive system, such as the $10 billion "Posture A" or $20 billion "Posture B" options, could be confirmed by observation that ten of the fifteen Sentinel bases would be deployed near large cities.

Safeguard reflects even more concern about Soviet sensitivities, both in overall design and in deployment. The choice of Phase II measures in fiscal 1971 does not emphasize the area defense aspect of the system, and Congress showed even more concern by refusing approval for preparations of sites with primarily area coverage capabilities. It is, to a large extent, a separate issue whether the Russians were ever really concerned about an American area defense BMD system.

Soviet reactions, mostly in the press, to the U.S. ABM decisions have presented the decisions as a concession to the pressure from the "military-industrial complex." They have expressed sympathy for the opposition to ABM in the U.S., which it is noted coincides largely also with opposition to the war in Vietnam, the power of the military, etc. However, there has been no official Soviet criticism of the Sentinel or Safeguard decisions. Though not discussing defense-offense arms race interactions, Soviet commentators have expressed fears that the American ABM will cause an arms race because of the increases in expenditures, suggesting that the Russians may be sensitive to budgetary restraints.[38]

The Russians themselves have shown restraint in not

---

[38] See Johan J. Holst, *The Russians and "Safeguard,"* H1-1176/4-P, April 18, 1969, Hudson Institute and *Some Observations on the Soviet Views of ABM and SALT,* H1-1301/2-DP, January 19, 1970, Hudson Institute.

expanding the ABM-1 system around Moscow. That, of course, may be related to their own technology and budgets. However, the American reaction to Soviet ABM deployment and the intensive communication of U.S. concern by high-level decision-makers is likely to have caused Soviet ABM decision-making to be treated as high-level policy with important ramifications for Soviet-American relations.

The negotiations at Helsinki and Vienna, though proceeding rather slowly, have not been accompanied by ideological or abusive language. Both sides have stressed the business-like quality of the exercise. Information has been very hard to come by, a state of affairs which complicates an outside assessment, making predictions extremely difficult. However, certain elements in the picture are visible.

First, it seems likely that the Soviet Union has postponed basic decisions in regard to the outcome of SALT. In part, this may be due to tactical considerations, but more important, it probably reflects the fact that decisions will be difficult because of the interests and perspectives involved. Some basic decisions will probably be made in connection with the Twenty-Fourth Party Congress in March, as future military claims on economic resources will have to be reflected in the five-year economic plan to be presented there. In such circumstances it has probably been good strategy for the United States to outline concrete proposals which, in the absence of a Soviet position, become focal points for the decisions which have to be made.

The U.S. proposal apparently suggests, first, an aggregate ceiling on strategic delivery vehicles (reportedly 1900). Second, it envisages a subceiling (250?) on strategic vehicles exceeding a certain cubic content. This part of the proposal is designed to minimize the first strike threat to fixed land-based missiles. Third, the plan evidently provides for a limitation of ABM to National Capital Areas.[39] This would be a

---

[39] *International Herald Tribune,* July 27, 1970; August 17, 1970; October 19, 1970; and November 27, 1970.

serious concession to the Soviet deployment pattern and would imply the dismantling of installations currently deployed under the Safeguard program. There may, however, be specific provisions in an agreement exempting hard-point defenses.

The issue of MIRV raises the whole complex matter of on-site inspection which the Soviet Union is unlikely to accept. The United States reportedly proposed a ban on MIRVs provided Moscow accepted on-site inspection in SALT, and the proposal was turned down. A MIRV test-ban would probably not prevent the deployment of multiple warheads, but it could conceivably affect their perfection. The Russians seemed uninterested in a MIRV test-ban when it might still have had a major impact on the deployment of MIRVs, probably because of unwillingness to be frozen in an inferior position vis-à-vis the United States, which was ahead in this technology.

There is, of course, the danger that if SALT should not succeed in producing agreements, the superpowers may accelerate the arms race as they might not otherwise have done, simply because so many decisions have been postponed, contingent on the outcome of SALT. Of course, SALT may not necessarily, and should not necessarily, result in a formal agreement. SALT could instead lay the basis for the tacit and interdependent exercise of restraint, which might avoid some of the difficulties of incorporating all relevant provisions in a treaty. Such an outcome might be associated also with the permanent institutionalization of SALT as an important mechanism for the management and alleviation of the arms race.

The issues in this connection are not simple. It is not a foregone conclusion that the influence would in fact be symmetrical, given the very different political cultures of the two superpowers. SALT can also provide the context for competitive interaction, as the disputes about the definition of strategic arms at SALT remind us. The Soviet Union has apparently insisted upon a definition which would include all nuclear delivery systems capable of reaching the heartland of the other superpower—such as the seven wings of 400 F-4 and F-110 forward-based aircraft in Western Europe and the 100 F-4s and A-6s with the Sixth Fleet in the Mediterranean—but would exclude Soviet M/IRBMs.

Such a definition seems tailored to divorcing the security of Western Europe from the American deterrent. It begs a whole set of issues of extended deterrence and could provide a basis for serious intra-alliance disputes in NATO. The West Europeans did for some time, rather ill-advisedly I think, insist on the M/IRBMs being included in a SALT agreement and on the need for the launch installations to be targeted by U.S. forces. An agreement from SALT could conceivably establish some constraints on the deployment of follow-on systems to the SS-4s and SS-5s. The United States may also be able to affect the issue unilaterally by hardening and dispersing some of the potential targets for the rather inaccurate M/IRBM force, such as the forward-based aircraft. In the longer run, it may be feasible for MIRVed strategic systems to take over some of the interdiction missions of the forward-based aircraft. It is very hard to conceive of a scenario where the United States would attack the M/IRBM force in the Soviet Union in a first strike. Absolute security is as unavailable for Western Europe as it is for the superpowers, and the nuclear threat to Europe is not limited to Soviet M/IRBMs. However, these issues which relate directly to European security are probably better discussed in the context of mutual and balanced force reductions in Europe. There the Europeans would be present at the bargaining table and the fears of being sold out by a Soviet-American condominium would presumably diminish, though they could never disappear. Thus we observe that SALT has connecting links to other areas of politics, reconstruction, and security.

Do the American SALT proposals provide us with clues

as to what the U.S. may be emphasizing in our four doctrinal alternatives? Not very good ones, I would submit. There are, however, several curious characteristics of the proposal. It would seem to foreclose moving toward a greater degree of defensive emphasis, as ABM would be limited to NCAs. In the long term, such foreclosure may come to exclude implementing fundamental changes away from exclusive reliance on revenge against civilians in case deterrence should fail. Indeed, wars may break out and nuclear weapons be brought to explode as a consequence of processes which are essentially "adeterrable."

Furthermore, it is hard to see how an agreement between the two superpowers would affect the potential threat for other countries so that the arguments arrayed in favor of a thin area defense in the U.S. would no longer apply. The simultaneous restriction on offensive and defensive systems in the kind of ratio which the U.S. apparently has suggested begs the question whether reciprocal first strike options would not become acute in the absence of hard-point defenses. The Soviet SS-9 force, already exceeding 250, could presumably be deployed with a reentry system containing more than three powerful and accurate warheads. Improved guidance accuracy for MIRVed SS-11s also seems to involve potential first strike threats to the U.S. Minuteman force. Thus, an ABM freeze which limits ABM to the pattern of the existing Soviet deployment, as does the U.S. proposals, may require less-preferred survival measures such as expensive airborn alerts, land-mobile ICBMs, and possibly even launching on warning, as some analysts and senators proposed during the American ABM debate. That would most certainly be retrogressive, increasing the dangers of inadvertent war and curtailing the exercise of political control over weapons and decisions about their use.

By leaving out the problem of MIRV and curbs on accuracy, while excluding hard-point defenses, a SALT agreement based on a parity freeze on strategic delivery vehicles could result in an arms agreement which focuses on the wrong elements of both dynamic stability and crisis stability.

In SALT the statesmen are indeed confronted with orchestration of a most complex relationship, but also with wide opportunities for man to reassert enlightened control over the Promethean powers he has so tragically acquired.

4 • Superpower Postures in SALT: An American View

Richard Garwin

There is neither necessity nor space to repeat here what has been presented in earlier chapters. From Hedley Bull's paper, "Strategic Arms Limitation: The Precedent of the Washington and London Naval Treaties," we learn some historical parallels to the questions of scope, quantitative limitations, and unilateral verification in SALT. Particularly interesting to me was his conclusion that "it is best to think of the task of SALT as that of producing over time not a single system of limitation but a series of agreements."

From Johan Holst's chapter, which summarizes weapons systems and deployment patterns on both sides, I would like to recall his judgment that SALT encompasses several levels of negotiation, the most important set taking place "inside the decision-making systems in Moscow and Washington." I also found of interest his conclusion that we just "do not have an explanatory model for the Soviet-American arms race." He judges that in addition to offense on one side competing with defense on the other and vice versa, there is a large component of "unilateral parallel racing, with offense competing against defense in the laboratories and in the minds of men." Further, his caution that strategic analysts commonly "assume greater coherence and consistency of strategic doctrine and its relationship to the strategic posture than actually prevails" explains some of the results obtained by detailed reasoning applied to an initial situation which is internally inconsistent. A simple desire for symmetry is a third reason for the arms race—thus, ABM tends to call forth ABM whether from fear of criticism for doing nothing in the field or from a more sophisticated view that the other side must regard it as important, if they spend resources on it, and that they would regard inaction on our side as a weakness.

In this chapter I discuss my views of SALT and my hopes therefrom.

The U.S. and the U.S.S.R. will shortly resume the SALT talks. On the side of the U.S., and presumably also the U.S.S.R., the initiation of SALT was preceded by long and intense analysis at the highest levels of the government. SALT is, in part, a consequence of the mutual interest of the two countries in avoiding strategic nuclear war. Other influences have helped to bring about SALT, such as the nuclear powers' responsibility, assumed under the nonproliferation pact, to proceed with other significant arms control measures.

The prevention of strategic nuclear war is, however, enough reason for SALT and is the focus of this chapter. It has been abundantly clear for years that strategic missiles and bombers are far more than sufficient to kill promptly one-third of the population on either side. Further, the possible use of the large number of warheads on either side in an attack on the land-based missiles of the other side would provide lethal doses of fallout over large fractions of the country.

The dangers associated with nuclear war have been underestimated by the "offense conservative" approach of ignoring deaths from fallout, fire, sickness, or starvation, thereby reducing the perceived danger to population from a counterforce attack. This conservatism, of course, also overstates the numbers of missiles required for effective deterrence. As all know, this mutual interest in avoiding nuclear war is not simply passive, but accounts to a large extent for the strategic posture on either side, since the primary means of avoidance is deterrence. Deterrence involves not only the capability to inflict mortal damage in response to a first strike, but requires the recognized and unswerving resolve to do so even if the actual employment of the strategic force results in a worsening of the absolute position of the country replying.

In strategic matters, the property of stability is all-important. However, electrical and chemical systems which can be modeled accurately show a substantial variety of stable and unstable behavior, some of quite unexpected nature. The more complex political-military-sociological system must surely be even less amenable to simplification and analysis. In physical systems we are familiar with small-signal stability and large-signal stability. Both these types are probably necessary for what has been called crisis stability, which is desirable to prevent the launch of the strategic force until a purposeful, large-scale nuclear strategic attack has in fact been launched by the other side. Contributing to instability are feedback loops of information of uncertain value and significant but uncertain delay.

It is in the interest of both sides to have a stable but responsive strategic posture, but our knowledge of the structure and behavior of military-political-sociological systems is by no means adequate to support detailed analyses. Our posture must be simple if we want to be sure that it is really understood by the other side.

The "time constant" associated with crisis stability is very short (hours to days), but there is another kind of stability involved in the strategic field: the preservation of the crisis-stable system against organizational, technical, or political change. This may be called "arms-race stability."

Thus the procurement of large numbers of weapons on one side could, through the imperfect view of the other as to effectiveness, schedule, and intent, lead to a perception of future first-strike capability on that one side.

Similarly, especially in the U.S., the complexities and public discussions attendant to the decision, authorization, and appropriation process for obtaining a multipurpose weapon system such as Sentinel or Safeguard ABM systems, supported by different factions for different reasons, can lead to a perception that influential and well-informed people regard such a defense as effective against a major attack, thereby perhaps requiring an offensive response by the other side. This latter could then be of such a nature and magnitude that it would threaten the second strike force on the one side, resulting in a clear net loss of security as a result of what might have seemed a reasonable initiative.

A similar ambiguity of perception, and indeed of reality, can be seen in MIRV, which has been supported by many as a sure means to penetrate even widely deployed and highly capable ABM systems. For this purpose, in the context of a finite deterrent strategy, MIRV is a stabilizing influence. But if the warheads might be thought to have sufficient accuracy, yield, and reliability to destroy the land-based strategic force on the other side, then in threatening an element of the other's deterrent, MIRV is destabilizing.[1] These well-known phenomena are particularly troublesome since decisions on each side are made as a consequence of contributions and pressures from different audiences and

---

[1] D. G. Hoag, "Ballistic-Missile Guidance," pp. 20–108 in B. T. Field, et al. (eds.), *Impact of New Technologies on the Arms Race,* MIT Press, 1971. In this excellent technical review of inertial guidance, Hoag "estimates an overall ICBM CEP of 30 meters may be expected with reasonable and practical application of science and technology to the task." An accuracy far worse than 30 meters would make our projected Minuteman III force a significant apparent threat to the Soviet land-based missiles, at least as great a threat as a future 3-MIRV SS-9 force is to our own.

groups of varying degrees of sophistication, prejudice, and knowledge.

The primary spur to SALT is the possibility thereby for each of the nations to increase its security. For instance, John S. Foster, the Director of Defense Research and Engineering, is quoted in an interview: "The fastest and cheapest way to provide for future security would be to have an equitable agreement emerge from our discussions with the Soviets." An additional incentive to SALT is the possibility of obtaining such security at lower cost than by the continued development, deployment, and operation of strategic weapons systems.

Proposals for arms or for arms limitations are judged differently according to one's aims. Thus the improvement of accuracy of U.S. MIRVs has not much value to a person whose goals are finite deterrence, but it is a matter of great urgency to one interested in counterforce capabilities. For instance, General John D. Ryan, Chief of Staff, U.S. Air Force, said on September 22, 1970: "We must have the capability of destroying the remaining strategic weapons which the enemy no doubt would hold in reserve."[2] Further, he says about the MIRVed Minuteman III: "This missile, with a multiple, independently targetable reentry vehicle, will be our best means of destroying time-urgent targets like the long-range weapons of the enemy."

The U.S. and U.S.S.R. have come to SALT in agreement on the desirability of strategic arms limitations beneficial to each side. Aside from that, the two countries are strong competitors and even enemies. Yet even if one side derives some pleasure from increased costs and decreased security on the other side, there appear to be SALT agreements which

---

[2]General John D. Ryan, address to Air Force Association Annual Convention, Washington, D.C., September 22, 1970 (excerpted in *Defense Industry Bulletin*, November 1970, pp. 3–5).

would improve security sufficiently such that they should have a reasonable chance of being negotiated in finite time.

Another difficulty to a SALT agreement is the differing posture of the U.S. and the U.S.S.R. The U.S. strategic missile launchers have been stable for years at 1,000 Minuteman, 54 Titan II, and 41 Polaris/Poseidon boats. At present, however, the Soviet Union has had a continuing deployment of the large SS-9 and the small SS-11 ICBMs. The Soviet Union has a wide network of space-track related radars which would be capable of detecting incoming missiles and continues to build highly capable radars which could be used for ABM. The U.S.S.R. also has operational 64 ABM launchers and associated first-generation ABM radars around Moscow, while the U.S. has no operational ABM.

On the other hand, the U.S. has quite thoroughly tested true MIRVs on both Minuteman and Poseidon and is in the process of deploying these MIRVs, with more than 50 Minuteman III operational. At the same time, the U.S. is deploying the first phase of Safeguard, an ABM system far more capable technically than the Soviet system, but located so that it will protect no large segment of U.S. population or industry. Further, the Soviet Y-class submarine fleet with 16 missiles each is growing rapidly. The U.S.S.R. has had for years many hundreds of IRBM targeted on Western Europe, and the U.S. has not only aircraft based in Europe and operated by U.S. and allied forces, but also aircraft carriers with airplanes capable of carrying nuclear weapons which might strike the Soviet Union. There is thus such asymmetry in the offensive and defensive forces on the two sides that it would seem impossible for SALT to mandate identical weapon systems.

Further, not only weapons but geography, history, and tradition contribute to the asymmetry. The United States is adequately supplied with all-season ports, while the Soviet Union has only restricted access to the sea. World War II is still fresh in the minds of Soviet leaders, and the powerful nations of Germany and China are not far away. Indeed, until very recent years, the Soviet view of strategic defense was that since it didn't threaten lives it could only be good. While one might argue the degree to which ABM contributes to the arms race and to instability, little progress could be made in the discussion of strategic arms until the existence of a connection was recognized on both sides.

Another impediment to the success of the SALT is the mythology of strategic arms. In particular, the annual U.S. budgetary process is not completely understood by either the American or Soviet public. What appear to be new initiatives are in many cases simply repeated testimony and justification for an ongoing program, necessitated by the constitutional bar to the appropriation of money for more than two years to the Armed Forces. Further, in the development of the Administration position and its support in testimony to the authorization and appropriation committees of the Congress, and in political appeals for support of one side or another, many persons occupying key positions make statements which analysts try to interpret as part of a coherent picture.

These statements are often descriptive rather than prescriptive. Thus, Robert McNamara made much of the Triad of the forces—land-based missiles, submarine-launched ballistic missiles, and bombers—as improving the robustness of our strategic force. Certainly it is more sure to have three forces than two, but do the bombers really contribute more as bombers than would an equal investment in a different type of land-based or sea-based missile? Alternatively, if the fixed-based Minuteman were replaced by a new type of sea-based system, say ULMS with a 5,000- or 7,000-mile range missile and hence with different prelaunch vulnerability from Polaris, might not the two sea-based systems and bombers provide a better strategic force than now exists? And no matter how favorable the outcome of SALT, is it desirable to retain the Triad to provide the best strategic force at a given level of expenditure?

In my view, the primary purpose of the strategic forces is deterrence, but there are other benefits, ranging from demonstration of advanced technological capability to possible use in limiting damage by destroying enemy forces before launch. This damage limitation capability is, of course, desirable if no liabilities arise from its existence, but unfortunately this latter assumption is not reasonable, since the other side might see the damage-limiting capability as a threat to his deterrent, especially if there is also a more-or-less capable area-defense ABM. It was quite natural for Secretary McNamara to explain to Congress that the U.S. strategic forces had a deterrent role, and that the excess over those required for deterrence would be valuable for their damage-limiting capability. Having assigned some (unstated) positive value to this damage-limiting capability, he thus set the stage for concern about the "erosion of the deterrent" as Soviet capabilities grew, although the deterrent could be restored to its previous strength in the face of such growth simply by a paper transfer of missiles from the previous bonus of damage-limiting to the deterrent target list.

A further contribution of the strategic mythology is seen in the requirement to have a single system to defend bombers and land-based missiles against a Soviet missile attack, and population and industry against a light accidental attack or a purposeful attack launched by the Chinese or another lesser nuclear power. Although cogent arguments were presented in Senate testimony that a far better system could be deployed to defend Minuteman against the stated threat, and although Air Force circles protest that the Air Force does not need to have bombers defended against either ICBMs or submarine-launched ballistic missiles, and although the Safeguard system was far from optimum in defending against a single warhead accidentally launched, Safeguard was chosen over a properly prescribed mix of separately optimized systems.

The Food and Drug Administration has recently moved against hundreds of prescription and nonprescription concoctions which are mixtures of drugs, in fixed ratio, maintaining that individually prescribed drugs do a better job with less chance of damage. Individual prescription for silo defense, bomber rebasing, and perhaps a super-light area defense (PAR and Spartan only) might have been in order here.

In the SALT context, the stress on Safeguard was prominent but ambiguous, since the Safeguard hardware is identical with Sentinel hardware, and the Safeguard program would have been a substantial beginning on production and basing for a nationwide but thin ABM system using the same hardware which had been supported by some in testimony as a start on a thick anti-Soviet system. This very ambiguity was presented later as an advantage, a bargaining chip to induce the other side to bargain in good faith, presumably in the hopes of being able to stop Safeguard.

My own view of the Safeguard decision of early 1969 is that it would not have been made in favor of Safeguard if the Department of Defense had done the exploratory and analytical work on true hard-point defense systems which would have been more effective and appropriate for Minuteman defense. Indeed, in the current budget, substantial funds are provided for this improved system, Safeguard being represented as inadequate and too expensive for that job if the threat does develop.

A further difficulty with SALT is that the strategic posture does not stand still while the talks are going on. Construction continues on Safeguard. The Soviet Union has tested multiple warheads on the SS-9, the MIRV tests for Minuteman and Poseidon have continued apace, and the first Minuteman III deployment has been accomplished. Clearly if it should require, say, five years to perceive the strategic situation in SALT and reach an agreement on the basis of that situation, the agreement would indeed always be out of date and hence impossible of conclusion. Two possibilities are evident: (1) to reach agreements limited in scope but which can be taken rapidly and so to achieve a step-by-step progression toward comprehensive strategic arms limitation, or (2) to freeze strategic arms for the period required to review, analyze, and reach agreement on a comprehensive scale.

Possible SALT agreements have three major parameters:

a. the degree to which the security of the nations would be increased if the agreement were in fact followed,

b. the degree to which compliance can be verified,

c. the negotiability of the agreement, i.e., the time to reach agreement.

In addition, contemplated postures differ in scope or degree of comprehensiveness, the possible savings which might be achieved in strategic expenditures, the degree to which agreements are regarded as final or as first steps toward additional measures such as mutual- and balanced-force reductions (MBFR) in NATO, extension to other nuclear powers, etc.

A spectrum of possible arms limitations has been described in a recent article.[3] It would take us too far afield here to analyze in detail all postures which have been proposed as objectives of SALT. We can, however, discuss in some detail what I believe are two promising examples.

First, since both sides likely regard the present panoply of strategic forces as crisis-stable, it is natural to consider a "freeze" of the present situation. The advantages of a freeze agreement are that it can be reached without extensive dis-

---

[3]Herbert Scoville, Jr., "The Limitation of Offensive Weapons," *Scientific American,* January 1971, pp. 15–25.

cussion of equivalence, in that it would by definition extend for some time the present reasonably satisfactory situation. Further, it is important to note that it is easier to verify compliance with the freeze than with some cookbook recipe of allowable changes.

The freeze proposal presents problems:

1. An inherent difficulty is definition of the word "freeze." Does it mean that all work stops on strategic systems, both offensive and defensive, or does it mean that construction work stops but that fitting of missiles and electronic equipment goes forward? Or does it mean that programs already authorized and begun can be completed, including construction and equipment? What does "authorization" mean in this sense, in view of the two-year constitutional rule in the U.S.? In the most rigid meaning of the term "freeze," one would be left with some holes operational but with no missiles therein, and with some missiles in operating shape but out of their silo. Would it not be allowable to put these together in the interests of economy?
2. Freeze can mean no more research and development firings, no test firings, or simply continued firings of precisely the same vehicle and payload types which have been fired in the past. Our own experience shows that relatively minor changes introduced into missiles or their basing structure can cause nonrandom malfunction, and that a continued test program is necessary to insure the workability of the entire missile system. Since a reasonably reliable missile force is regarded as necessary for deterrence, a complete ban on test firings has an ambiguous effect on deterrence.
3. Finally, if research and development and test firings are unrestricted under a freeze, new types of strategic weapons systems might be developed specifically so that they could be substituted for existing weapons systems without change in external observables. In the absence of arms limitation agreements, and especially of a freeze, this

would be an unnatural development program and would have high cost and performance penalties. It would also take several years to begin such a program specifically oriented toward achieving these types of weapons under the agreement. If a freeze were to stand alone for, say, two years, then the participants must be concerned not only with deterioration of their security during the period of the freeze, but with what might follow the expiration of a temporary freeze. Thus, a two-year freeze on deployment might lead in analogy to the "safeguards" accompanying U.S. ratification of the Limited Nuclear Weapon Test Ban, to an energetic program not only in research and development but also in production, in order to have a "readiness to deploy" at the expiration of the freeze.

On balance, I think that a freeze is viable only in connection with some permanent agreement as a first step of the strategic arms limitation process.

We now discuss agreements more specific than a simple freeze.

1. *A "No-ABM Agreement":* An agreement to eliminate ballistic missile defense would have a very powerful dampening effect on the arms race and would help to insure the preservation of the deterrent capability of land- and sea-based missiles. Indeed, this "no ABM" agreement seems to be necessary as a component of any larger agreement. The agreement might call for

a. a ban on production and deployment of ABM systems,

b. the elimination of current systems with significant ABM capability,

c. a ban on testing of surface-to-air missile systems in an ABM role.

We conclude that for any reasonable level of strategic offensive force, even a few hundred missiles, a no-ABM posture will preserve the capability for deterrence.

So far as verifiability is concerned, it is a simple task to confirm the complete absence of large high-power radar and interceptor missile installations such as accompany the U.S. Safeguard system or the Soviet-Moscow ABM system. As one considers poorer and poorer ABM systems, such as the residual ABM capability of an existing surface-to-air missile (SAM), verification that a system lacks any ABM capability becomes more and more difficult. Indeed, the ABM capabilities of as yet nonexistent SAM systems are the most difficult to assess. There is thus a question not only of definition of ABM or ABM-related radars, but also the necessity to some extent to control SAMs as well.

Fortunately, a strategic philosophy which leads a nation to accept a "no-ABM" agreement is quite compatible with the imposition of mild requirements on SAM. Thus, ancillary agreements might be proposed to preclude the deployment of SAM systems in numbers and locations where they might have a strategically significant ABM system capability. It should be noted that the strategic offensive force can be modified (without, incidentally, the necessity to use MIRVs) to have a good capability to penetrate even advanced SAM systems.

In principle, the negotiability of a no-ABM ban would seem to be high. The Soviet Union possesses a small operational ABM (64 interceptors, according to Secretary Laird) around Moscow, but the system is easily penetrated and of little value. The U.S. is building a Safeguard ABM system without any area defense capability. A no-ABM posture on the Soviet side, together with the continued operation of Minuteman and Polaris-Poseidon on the U.S. side, would allow the preservation of an adequate deterrent capability. A symmetric agreement would provide the same benefit for the U.S.S.R.

Further, it has not generally been recognized that a "no-ABM" agreement would respond to a deep-felt desire to have more flexibility than is inherent in a massive deterrent response. For instance, in the 1970 State of the World Message, the President asked:

> Should a President, in the event of nuclear attack, be left with the single option of ordering the mass destruction of enemy civilians, in the face of the certainty that it would be followed by the mass slaughter of Americans?

In his 1971 message, President Nixon states:

> We must insure that we have the forces and procedures that provide us with alternatives appropriate to the nature and level of the provocation. . . . This means having the plans and command-and-control capabilities necessary to enable us to select and carry out the appropriate response without necessarily having to resort to mass destruction.

In the absence of any ABM system, a single Minuteman missile could be used to destroy a military post, a dam, a small town, or any other chosen target. I can see no better or surer way to obtain the capability sought by the President than to conclude a "no-ABM" agreement, whether or not this is accompanied by an agreement on offensive forces.

The force necessary for finite deterrence is tremendously robust. It is resistant to developments in Soviet technology and forces which might threaten Polaris submarines cruising in their operating area. In many operating areas the submarines could for instance be withheld in the open oceans and move in only to launch their missiles. If the Soviet Union should develop and deploy the MIRVed SS-9 which, Secretary Laird feared, threatened the existence of Minuteman, it is technically feasible to adopt a posture, as needed, under which Minuteman will no longer be withheld after some number—say 10 or 100—Minuteman silos have been destroyed. Whether or not this rapid firing posture is actually adopted would depend, of course, upon the evaluation at that time of the current threat to Polaris, the status of warning radars and satellites, etc.

Offense-conservative analysis of the capability of an ABM system, experience shows, can so far exaggerate its real capability that large investments in strategic forces may be provoked by a very small ABM system. Further, since the residual strategic force required after a first strike to penetrate this worst-case analyzed ABM system may appear to be quite high, uncertainties arise as to the adequacy of the deterrent, in addition to the cost of the offensive force. For these reasons, I regard a no-ABM agreement as the cornerstone of meaningful strategic arms limitations.

In principle, there is no strategic disadvantage to the defense of offensive missile silos. In fact, such silo defense would benefit the strategic balance. Unfortunately, the United States defense of Minuteman, Safeguard, uses very long-range radars and some very long-range interceptors, identical with those previously proposed for area and even city defense. Silo defense equipment could in principle be very different from city defense, but this would require a system completely different from Safeguard. I believe that a system which is both less costly and more effective than Safeguard for this purpose should be developed, although not necessarily deployed.

In general, the significant ambiguity of most of the proposed ballistic missile defense schemes for the offensive force would seem to have a more negative impact on the strategic picture than their actual capability would contribute on the positive side. For this reason, I believe a no-ABM agreement is more readily negotiable and has more value than one which attempts to permit ABM for the defense of the offensive force. There would be no bar at a later time to a modification of the agreement to permit specific silo defense schemes which truly and apparently had no capability for threatening the deterrent.

2. *"No-ABM" plus Limitations on Offensive Missiles:* Another possible arms limitation proposal would augment the no-ABM agreement with restrictions designed to ease

fears about the vulnerability of the land-based forces. Thus a proposal could seek effectively to ban MIRVs and at the same time to limit the number of launchers. In devising such a scheme, the problem is one of comparability and thus negotiability. For instance, the Soviet Union has for the last four or five years been deploying the large modern SS-9, while the United States has no large modern missiles. Similarly, the U.S. has operational truly independently targeted multiple warheads on its Minuteman III, while it is believed the Soviet Union has no such systems in operation. A limitation on offensive forces must either include or exclude such problem elements as the Soviet IRBMs and the United States forward-based aircraft. In general, the problem is far more complicated than a no-ABM agreement.

The situation is further complicated by the closed nature of the Soviet society as contrasted with the open nature of the U.S. Thus, a simple undertaking not to increase the size or payload of missiles in silos could be monitored very well by the U.S. political and budgetary mechanism, whereas no such clear evidence would be available on the Soviet side. Such a proposal would therefore be undesirable because of the difficulty in verifying compliance.

Similarly, an agreement simply to ban MIRVs from operational missiles would, if actually complied with, have a very good effect on the survivability of the land-based component of the deterrent. However, it is perfectly possible to design "MIRV front ends" for specially designed missiles which are interchangeable within a short time for single warhead front ends, and which could be stored near the missiles in properly prepared receptacles. Thus, if MIRV R&D testing, operational proof testing, and manufacture were permitted, either side could comply with the agreement and still have a MIRV capability available.

As I indicated above, MIRV is truly ambivalent. The substitution of many small warheads for one large one, with a resulting smaller total yield, is beneficial to the deterrent role and reduces the worldwide threat from fallout. However, high-accuracy MIRVs which can be used against the land-based element of a strategic force are highly destabilizing.

There is a distinction between these two types of MIRVs beyond the largely unobservable parameter of accuracy. That further distinction is reliability. Particularly in the absence of ABM, a MIRV for use against the Minuteman would have to have extremely good reliability, which can be preserved in the face of maintenance actions, block changes, etc., only by an intensive and continuing flight test program of operational missiles. A limitation of all missile launches to a small total number annually would thus allow adequate demonstration of reliability, adequate for the deterrent role but not for the counterforce role. This limitation would be further strengthened if the flight tests were restricted to missiles carrying single reentry vehicles into known and observable test ranges.

Thus a meaningful agreement could be proposed which would

a. set some overall limit on the number of missile launchers,

b. forbid the flight test, manufacture, or deployment of MIRVs,

c. forbid the enlargement of existing missile launchers,

d. set some overall annual limitation on missile launches, the total to include both R&D and operational test firings,

e. require test missile launches to be conducted on known and observable test ranges,

f. ban or strictly limit ABM.

Although such an agreement would be symmetric in its construction, it would not be symmetric in its application, given the different natures of the two forces. Further, the MIRV ban would bind differently the United States and the Soviet Union—the United States being most restricted by the ban on manufacturing and deployment, since it has had much more extensive flight testing of MIRVs, while United States verification of compliance of the Soviet Union would be obtained more readily from the ban on flight testing.

In order to prevent the surreptitious flight testing of MIRVs as individual warheads, a limitation on overall launches, say 40 per year, would put such launches into competition with other weapon and nonweapon purposes and would, in my opinion, further inhibit the contemplation of transforming a significant fraction of the offensive force to a counterforce MIRV capability. After all, who wants to change a tested system for an untested and possibly ineffective system, when the chief application of that system requires very high reliability?

An agreement restricting offensive forces as well as defensive forces is stronger and inherently more desirable. Such an agreement is clearly more difficult to negotiate either within a government or with another government, and the question then arises as to how much delay one should pay for reaching the more comprehensive agreement as contrasted with a potentially earlier implementation of a no-ABM agreement, if that were possible. My own view is that it would be better to have an immediate no-ABM agreement and to leave limitations on the offensive forces for near-term and urgent further action in a continuing SALT environment.

The elimination of ABM would break a positive feedback loop leading to the arms race. A simple no-ABM agreement would do nothing to prevent either side from fully MIRVing the offensive force. It would do nothing to prevent a very great increase in overall force level. On the other hand, the Soviet heavy bomber force has remained static for many years in the absence of any agreement to control numbers of bombers. It would be reasonable for the normal economic forces on the two sides to slow the deployment of more offensive missiles if they could not be justified on the basis of penetrating some future ABM system. Similarly, a system whose only value depended upon the opposing land-based forces remaining in their holes to be destroyed would seem not to be a very good candidate for expenditures in the face of the technical possibility that those forces need not so remain. The resulting savings might be applied to other military goals, or they might be made available for the civilian sector.

In discussing overall strategic capability, Secretary Laird said in 1970 to the Senate Foreign Relations Committee:

> There are certain things that as a defense planner one must take into consideration:
>
> First, we have to maintain, as far as our deterrent force is concerned, an adequate second strike capability to deter an all-out surprise attack.
>
> Second, we must see to it that there is no incentive for the Soviet Union to strike the United States first or on a surprise basis in any crisis.
>
> Third, I think it is important in our defense planning to prevent the Soviets from gaining the ability to cause considerably greater destruction than the United States could inflict in any type of nuclear exchange.
>
> Fourth, I think it is most important in our defense planning to defend against the major damage which could be caused by small attacks or accidental launches.
>
> . . . I think that all of these criteria must be considered in planning the strategic sufficiency of the United States. . . .

These appear to be reasonable and important goals, so important that they might be accepted without question except for the possibilities of conflict among these goals and the question of the response of the other side. In fact, the difficulty is a *combination* of internal inconsistency and response of the other side. Specifically, if the U.S.S.R. strategic forces were fixed, there would be no difficulty in the U.S. achievement of these goals. We could build a full ABM system, which would not in fact work very well against a major onslaught by the Soviet Union. We could build a much larger strategic force and thereby guarantee under all conceivable circumstances a second-strike capability as well as a counterforce capability and the possibility for the United States to cause considerably greater destruction on the Soviet Union than vice versa. In fact, while we are at it, we could get a first-strike capability as well (to the extent that a first-strike capability can be equated to the capability of destroying the other side's land-based missiles). Obviously, this U.S. capability would be unacceptable to the Soviet Union, and the hypothesis that the Soviet Union force would be static is in error. Indeed, an ABM system which would truly defend against small attacks or accidental launches, no matter where targeted, would be an area defense system with capabilities readily overestimated by the other side. The second and third criteria have as much to do with targeting doctrine as with force composition. The first criterion presumably can be satisfied for the United States and for the Soviet Union at the same time, and it is of overwhelming importance, in my opinion.

In this regard, it is of the greatest interest to reproduce a statement issued simultaneously by the governments of the United States and of the U.S.S.R. on May 20, 1971:

> The Governments of the United States and the Soviet Union, after reviewing the course of their talks on the limitation of strategic armaments, have agreed to concentrate this year on working out an agreement for the limitation of the deployment of antiballistic missile systems—ABMs.
>
> They have also agreed that together with concluding an agreement to limit ABMs, they will agree on certain measures with respect to the limitation of offensive strategic weapons.
>
> The two sides are taking this course in the conviction that it will create more favorable conditions for further negotiations to limit all strategic arms.
>
> These negotiations will be actively pursued.

> This agreement is a major step in breaking the stalemate on nuclear-arms talks. Intensive negotiations, however, will be required to translate this understanding into a concrete agreement.

It seems far simpler to reach effective arms limitation agreements that will strengthen a strategy of finite deterrence than to reach agreements that will permit both sides to maintain a posture of strategic sufficiency as defined by Secretary Laird. The problem lies with the estimation on the two sides of the relative destruction which might be caused in "any type" of nuclear exchange. Such a policy risks attempting greater *relative* security for the U.S. at the price of lesser *absolute* security. An analogy might be drawn to the unilateral renunciation by the Nixon Administration of *any* biological warfare capability, an act which evidently reduces (to some extent) our overall offensive military capability but does so in order to *increase* our actual national security. A firm espousal of the limited deterrent strategy would have a similar effect and seems to me to be the key to improving the national security.

I have emphasized here that the banning of ABM either as the initial arms limitation agreement or as part of a larger agreement provides the utmost in flexible military capability, in addition to the preservation of the effectiveness of the deterrent force. As noted by the President, attention must be given to plans and command-and-control capabilities, but the "no-ABM" agreement which I support here is the key to retaining these options.

In concentrating here on the limitation and control of strategic arms, I do not want to slight those positive measures which I think should be taken in weapons technology and systems. I believe it desirable to develop a much less expensive and more effective system for defense of Minuteman silos and to carry this development through the testing of a functional prototype. If the system selected is not the autonomous defense of individual silos, then I believe that technology development and exploratory systems development should be done in the attempt to define a system which can defend Minuteman silos and which would evidently and unambiguously have no capability for the defense of soft targets. Further, I believe that continuous attention must be given to the improvement of the national capabilities for verification.

The strategic offensive forces need attention also. MIRV is an excellent penetration aid, but it will not be needed in the absence of ABM, and it may not be permitted in a SALT agreement. Therefore, and in any case, it is desirable to have a greater variety of penetration aids developed, tested, and partially deployed, in order to complicate the task of a prospective defender. The command and control system for monitoring and reporting the status of the offensive and defensive forces and of the warning systems must continually be refined and tested. The unauthorized, but properly authenticated, nationwide alert broadcast by the commercial network on February 20, 1971, is a rather benign example of the potential of a system which depends on people within the loop rather than in an alert, multistage monitoring capacity. I believe it valuable to have the technical capability to support a decision to move rapidly to a posture in which the Minutemen would not wait out a highly MIRVed counterforce attack, but could be launched while most of them were yet undestroyed. The existence of this technical capability does not mean that the Minuteman would be launched on warning under normal circumstances. It is, rather, a posture to which we could fall back if confronted with highly unlikely capabilities and schedules on the part of the Soviet Union.

In taking this overall position on SALT, I believe I am in accord with the views expressed by both sides that there should be no unfair advantage to either side as a result of SALT. What I suggest for the United States, the U.S.S.R. would also be free to do.

It is as fruitless to discuss here all details of a possible SALT proposal as for a chess player to write down in advance not only his own but his opponent's moves to the end of the game. The negotiability of an agreement with the U.S.S.R., and even within our own government, is dependent to a large extent on unknowable and even random influences. Discussion of specific examples, as contrasted with an attempt to perfect a fixed position, is clearly of value in understanding the influences at work.

5 • Superpower Postures in SALT: The Language of Arms Control

Richard Perle

Karl von Clausewitz once asked: "Is not War merely another kind of writing and language for political thoughts?" And he answered: "It has certainly a grammar of its own, but its logic is not peculiar to itself."

Had Clausewitz observed the SALT meetings in Vienna or Helsinki or, perhaps more to the point, the preparation for them in Washington and Moscow, he might have asked: "Is not arms control merely another kind of writing and language for thoughts about national security?"

The "logic" of arms control lies in its potential contribution to strategic stability, a purpose "not peculiar to itself" but shared with defense planning in general. In this sense the deployment of the Safeguard ABM at our Minuteman fields and the deliberations at the SALT talks are both part of the logic of national security.

But while the logic of secretaries of defense and arms control negotiators is a common one, their grammars are diverse. I have tried here to look at some arms control issues from the point of view of a conception of strategic stability that recognizes the primacy of stable deterrence. I believe that the underlying logic is one to which both the Secretary of Defense and the Director of the Arms Control and Disarmament Agency could subscribe.

Narrowing the difference between a first and second strike should be the central objective of American arms control policy. Where the difference between a first and second nuclear strike is large, the temptation to pre-empt in crisis is a major source of instability. Where not only one side, but both can minimize damage by striking first, the resulting instability becomes the mechanism by which a nuclear war could break out.

Let's assume a strategic balance in which the Soviets, by striking first, could expect to destroy a large fraction of our strategic forces and thereby limit to, say, 20 million the number of fatalities resulting from U.S. retaliation. Assuming that they would suffer losses on the order of 100 million if they were to sustain rather than strike the first blow, in a severe crisis they would have a clear incentive to initiate thermonuclear war.

But suppose, on the other hand, that the balance is such that the Soviets expect 100 million fatalities, whether they strike first or wait and strike second. In this case there is no incentive for them to strike first, however severe the crisis and however deep their anxieties about our intentions. Where both sides possess strategic forces incapable of limiting damage by being used in a first strike, and where the level of damage from a nuclear exchange is great, a high degree of stability exists.

In my view we should welcome arms control agreements that narrow the difference between striking first and second, while rejecting those that widen this difference—and we ought to base our strategic weapons procurement decisions on precisely the same central criterion.

There are three assumptions underlying this view of strategic stability that it is well to make explicit. It assumes, first, that the men who have their fingers on the button in both countries are rational: They will not initiate a nuclear war whose outcome is certain to be a level of destruction at least as great as if it is initiated by the other side. (A rational leader will always prefer the chance of nuclear war to the certainty of it, if the consequences are equally catastrophic.) Alternatively, national leaders are assumed to prefer a *certainty* of a low level of damage to the *near-certainty* of a much higher level of damage.

This assumption is actually quite common. The prosecutor who agrees to accept a guilty plea to a lesser crime rather than press for conviction on a more serious offense is exhibiting this behavior.

Second, this view of strategic stability assumes that the Soviets are indifferent to the relative outcome of a nuclear war involving very high levels of damage. They would not sacrifice large numbers of Russians in order to increase the number of American casualties. To put it positively, I am assuming that a Soviet leader will act to minimize Soviet casualties even if, in order to do so, he must refrain from adding to the number of American casualties and therefore to the relative outcome of the war. Clearly this second assumption holds true only for expected levels of destruction that are very large indeed.

Third, I assume that there is no foreign policy objective that would justify initiating an all-out nuclear war. This assumption, too, is obviously sensitive to the level of destruction expected to result from an all-out nuclear war. It has been our policy to maintain strategic forces capable of inflicting an overwhelming number of casualties on any potential adversary. Mr. McNamara's judgment of this requirement, known as "assured destruction," called for the capability to destroy more than a third of the Soviet population and more than half of Soviet industry.

Precisely what the numbers should be—whether we must promise to destroy half the Soviet population or a quarter or a tenth to make the first strike option unattractive—is a matter of judgment, subjective and somewhat arbitrary. The choice of any number inevitably involves a trade-off between reducing the likelihood of war and reducing the level of destruction should it occur. Thus, at least one goal of arms control: that we take reasonable steps, including international agreements, to minimize the destruction resulting from war should deterrence fail.

The only circumstance in which I can envision the deliberate initiation of full-scale nuclear war between nuclear superpowers would involve a desperate effort by one side to pre-empt in a crisis in the hope of preventing its own destruction. It becomes clear with respect to this contingency, however remote, that the gap between the consequences of striking first and striking second must be kept as close to zero as possible. For if the strategic balance is such that one side feels its only hope for survival lies in striking first in an effort to pre-empt—especially if both sides believe this to be the case—the resulting instability makes nuclear war a real possibility.

If, on the other hand, it is impossible to guarantee national survival by striking first, and if no lesser objective is worth the costs of nuclear war, then even crises are likely to be stable.

I emphasize the importance of stability in a crisis because the extent of crisis stability should be the acid test for both strategic force planning and arms control proposals. Far too much analytical attention has been paid to the "Pearl Harbor" scenario, which is perhaps the least plausible of contingencies. Yet thinking about the "out-of-the-blue" Sunday morning attack may encourage much of the arms control community to dismiss the importance of the strategic balance and the difficulty of maintaining it.

Consider the following statement from an article by McGeorge Bundy in *Foreign Affairs* (October 1969):

> In all the real world of real political leaders—whether here or in the Soviet Union—a decision that would bring even one

> hydrogen bomb on one city of one's own country would be recognized in advance as a catastrophic blunder; ten bombs on ten cities would be a disaster beyond history; and a hundred bombs on a hundred cities are unthinkable. . . . In sane politics, therefore, there is no level of superiority which will make a strategic first strike between the two great states anything but an act of utter folly.

Certainly, a decision that would bring "even one hydrogen bomb on one city" would be a terrible one to make, and the destruction of that city would be a terrible catastrophe. But does it follow that the decision would inevitably be a "catastrophic blunder?" Is it not possible that even so terrible a decision could, in some circumstances, be seen as the least destructive course of action open to a national leader faced with a set of dismal alternatives? Is there really no difference between the loss of a dozen cities and the loss of a hundred? In my view, all nuclear catastrophes are tragic, but some are more tragic than others.

One can share McGeorge Bundy's horror at the prospect of a nuclear exchange and even believe that he echoes the sentiments of those men whose fingers are closer to the button than his, yet still reject the facile conclusion that there is for the foreseeable future "literally no chance at all that any sane political authority, in either the Soviet Union or the United States, would consciously choose to start a nuclear war."

It is, of course, very tempting to accept such extreme versions of the doctrine of minimum deterrence. McGeorge Bundy is not alone. Indeed, nine out of ten voices speaking the grammar of arms control believe, consciously or not, that deterrence is relatively easy to achieve, if not indeed automatic. Curiously enough, a remarkable number of people simultaneously hold the view that arms control to end the "spiraling arms race" is essential if we are to avert nuclear war.

Those of us who believe that deterrence is not automatic

—that it is hard rather than easy—are sensitive to the importance of maintaining strategic forces that exhibit a high degree of crisis stability. Largely for this reason, defense planners have tended to reject the notion that a few nuclear weapons delivered on a few Soviet cities constitute a sufficient deterrent.

The word "overkill," which has been used to describe a strategic force capable of delivering more than a handful of weapons on the Soviet Union, has had an unfortunate effect on public discussion of arms control issues. It conveys the notion that some fixed (and generally small) number of weapons constitutes an adequate retaliatory force, and that once we have deployed this number, nuclear war has been deterred.

The word "overkill" obscures the fact that a constant effort is required to assure that the gap between striking first and second is kept narrow.

There is another common and equally unfortunate use of the word "overkill," where it is taken to mean the possesson of retaliatory forces sufficient to destroy the Soviet Union "many times over." This view commonly suffers from two major errors. It implies, first, that the capability of a deterrent can be determined by merely counting the number of weapons in the force, failing to take account of the size of the force that will survive a first strike and penetrate Soviet defenses. This latter figure, the relevant one, is a small and declining fraction of the total force available before a first strike.

Second, the accounting that leads some critics of U.S. defense policy to describe it as having a capacity to "overkill" the Soviet Union results from adding together the inventories of each type of strategic weapons system: manned bombers, land-based, and sea-based missiles. It is, however, the policy of this country to maintain a deterrent capability in *each* of these three systems, not to enable us to destroy the Soviet Union three times over, but rather to insure that even the loss of two strategic systems would leave our retaliatory capability unimpaired.

Contemporary arms control literature is full of articles in which technology is identified as the villain of the arms race. Much of the pressure for a U.S. SALT posture based on a total freeze of strategic forces on both sides originates with a concern to stop the development of weapons technology. Technology has replaced the arms manufacturers of the 1930s as the devil in the new devil theory of the arms race. (I might mention an outstanding exception: John Kenneth Galbraith, whose political education ceased in the 1930s, is still fixated on the armaments industry as the source of war. The only thing that saves Galbraith from an oversimplification is the prior selection of an even more sweeping oversimplification.)

The stability of the strategic balance is undeniably affected by the rapid pace of technological development. Improvements in missile accuracy on the offense side and the perfection of phased array radars and associated data processing equipment on the defense side are two among many current examples of problematic technological developments that may threaten the strategic balance.

New technologies in and of themselves, however, are not necessarily destabilizing, although many proposals to limit strategic weapons systems development are marked by an implicit acceptance of this belief. The list of technologies whose development has contributed to the stability of the strategic balance is formidable: nuclear submarines and their undersea-launched missiles, early warning radar systems, hardened missile silos, solid propellants and some storable liquid rocket fuels capable of instant ignition, and sophisticated communications for command and control, as well as those developments in warhead design and fusing mechanisms that reduce to near zero the probability of a technical or mechanical accidental detonation. What these developments have in common—and what makes them sources of stability—is their contribution to the relative invulnerability of our (as well as Soviet) strategic forces. Prior to these developments numbers were of the essence. The side possessing overwhelming superiority of numbers of, say, ICBMs, in a world where strategic systems on both sides were soft and slow to respond, threatened the very existence of the numerically inferior opponent. Uncertain and unreliable intelligence, combined with the vulnerable nature of these forces, generated requirements on both sides for comfortably large numbers of relatively invulnerable strategic systems. It was, and still is, generally true that technological developments making possible measures to reduce the vulnerability of strategic forces contribute positively to stability.

There are, to be sure, technologies whose impact is destabilizing; these are, as one would expect, developments that increase the vulnerability of strategic forces. Large-scale programs of population defense coupled with highly accurate or high-yield ballistic missiles may threaten the opponent's retaliatory capability, and because they admit of possible differences between the consequences of striking first and striking second, are highly destabilizing. Penetration aids effective against hard-point ABM systems, combined with other elements of an offensive force (such as large numbers of delivery vehicles, high accuracy, and large yield) are destabilizing. An effort to constrain area defenses while leaving hard-point defense uncontrolled might prove an important stabilizing element of an arms control agreement. The point is that for analytical purposes it is essential to evaluate weapons systems and the technologies they employ in terms of whether they are stabilizing or destabilizing.

The sense in which some advanced technology is in general destabilizing has to do with the requirements for dynamic, as opposed to static, stability. Static stability has to do with the absence of an incentive to strike first, a condition that is a function of the size of the gap between striking first and second, the absolute level of anticipated destruction, and the value of the objective in support of which a strike might be contemplated. At any given point in time, these conditions define the extent of strategic stability. But maintaining that stability is a major concern of defense planners, and much of their activity has to do with measures to guarantee that the balance of the moment, if favorable, can be maintained or, if unfavorable, can be favorably altered. It is in this sense possible for the strategic balance to be characterized by a high degree of static stability and, simultaneously, a low degree of dynamic stability.

Dynamic stability is a function of the rate at which the conditions leading to static stability can be changed, the rate at which countermeasures to possible changes can be developed, the quantity and quality (reliability) of available information about the enemy's capabilities and intentions, and, finally, the magnitude and visibility of the effort required to change the fundamental conditions on which static stability is based. All of these factors affect and are affected by technology.

If we assume a distribution of forces exhibiting a high degree of static stability, then we can formulate agreed controls to give us a high confidence that dynamic stability is likely; provided that a major, long-lead-time, and visible effort would be required for one side to acquire a force capable of striking the other's retaliatory capability with a high chance of success. How large the effort must be, how time-consuming, and how visible, will depend partly on how vital the constrained system is to maintaining the balance, partly on the numbers in the affected system, and partly on its technological characteristics.

The control of improvements in missile accuracy, for example, comes out poorly on all three measures. It is vital to the strategic balance that accuracies not improve to the point where our strategic forces are vulnerable; the required effort to accomplish improvements is relatively small; and it is, finally, of relatively low visibility.

There is some disagreement about how visible the testing program required for substantial improvements in missile accuracy is likely to be. The judgment that it is of relatively low visibility is based on the difficulty, under *ideal* conditions, of assessing accuracy, and on the usual resort to secondary phenomena to make the necessary estimates. Moreover, the history of prediction of accuracy is not a very impressive one.

For planning purposes, some judgment must be made today about Soviet missile accuracy several years hence. The uncertainties that surround this estimate are not, in themselves, a source of dynamic instability, but the tendency to make defense-conservative assumptions, and then to base force requirements on those assumptions, does contribute to dynamic instability. There is an inevitable tendency to overcompensate, which in turn may invite overcompensation by the Soviet Union.

The important point is that in the absence of an agreement, both sides are free to take such measures and countermeasures as they deem necessary within the relevant lead times. In the best case, this acts in mitigation of dynamic instability—the continuing flexibility of response by unilateral development programs.

But if one refrains from "self-help" measures (to use the international legal term), then an important corrective to potential shifts in the strategic balance is lost. The dilemma results from an inability to constrain enemy developments with high confidence, on the one hand, and an inability to counter them, as the result of adherence on our side to the terms of agreement, on the other. The potential of a technological constraint (such as limiting improvements in accuracy) to exacerbate tensions, promote a sense of insecurity, and perhaps even lead to abrogation is considerable. A ban on MIRV would seem to have similar problems: It is a central element in the balance, a moderate effort is required to attain a MIRV capability, and the necessary development and deployment program is of low visibility.

More promising candidates for arms control are those systems that require large, long-lead-time, and visible development and deployment programs. The construction (or retention) of missile systems and ships, for example, would seem to fall into this category.

If stability is our central criterion, it is clear that our approach to the limitation of technology will be surgical, aimed at control of potentially destabilizing technology and promotion of technologies contributing to stability. Unfortunately, it is not always possible to make such clear-cut distinctions. The technology for ballistic missile defense, for example, may be stabilizing or destabilizing depending on the configuration of the resulting system.[1] Moreover, in a world of multiple nuclear powers one can imagine systems that are stabilizing vis-à-vis one country and destabilizing with respect to another. As the Chinese develop their nuclear potential this is likely to get worse rather than better. Some years from now, the force size we need to deter the Chinese and the Soviets simultaneously may threaten each of them individually. The potential for an earnest arms race in a three-power nuclear world is considerable.

Historical efforts to constrain the development of new weapons systems have had little success. Not only have nations shown themselves extraordinarily resourceful in circumventing temporary constraints, but the constraints attempted have themselves broken down in time.

Arms control agreements have in the past stimulated development of new technologies to compensate for those limited by agreement. The art of underground nuclear testing, for example, has been rapidly advanced in both

---

[1]Current proposals for the defense of U.S. Minuteman silos are in my view, highly stabilizing.

the United States and the Soviet Union since the partial nuclear test ban was signed in 1961. Techniques thought unfeasible a mere decade ago are now in common use.

A more general problem has to do with channeling technology into one area by prohibiting its development in another. The other day I received two packages of cigarettes in the mail, part of an industry campaign to compensate for the removal of cigarette advertising from television. I predict that we will soon see cigarette advertising in the most unlikely places. Moreover, we shall very likely see the tobacco industry employing advertising techniques which would have been considered too costly in the days when cheap television advertising was available.

In the same way we should expect arms control agreements to lead to changes in the development and deployment of weapons systems, particularly those based upon emerging technologies. With an agreement, systems may well be deployed whose deployment was considered wasteful before the agreement was signed. To take a current example: Assume that the United States has made clear its intention to deploy defenses at its missile sites in such a way as to offset any increase to the Soviet offensive force. Soviet defense planners, realizing the futility of further increments to its offense, may well decide to abandon their program of offensive expansion.

At this point an arms control agreement is reached in which defenses at Minuteman sites are prohibited. The same Soviet planners who were impressed earlier with the futility of offensive expansion now find that such deployments make sense because they cannot be easily countered by the United States. The end result is a lessening of stability, increased American anxieties, and a frantic search for some response.

An agreement freezing the current balance by prohibiting the introduction of weapons systems reflecting developing technologies may purchase static stability dangerously—

at the price of dynamic instability. The danger is acute during periods when the central adversaries are on the verge of technological developments that may degrade the effectiveness of the frozen forces. The incentive to proceed with prohibited developments or at some time in the future to abrogate the agreement is immense, not least of all because each side, doubtful of the compliance of the other, is tempted to hedge against violation by violations of its own.

Where violation is not possible, as in an open society such as our own, pressures for abrogation are likely to mount as new developments by the other side are thought to be possible. Uncertain information suggesting possible violations by the other side, *even information that is without foundation,* only contributes to the pressures for abrogation. Notably, discussion of verification has tended to focus on the likelihood of discovering clandestine activity, although the probability of incorrect information suggesting a violation is of equal importance; an unwillingness to enter into a limitation whose probability of detection is low should be matched by an unwillingness to sign an agreement in which the probability of a mistaken detection is high.

For the United States the most likely response to mounting pressures generated by uncertainty is abrogation, with all that implies in the post-agreement international environment: adverse international opinion, crash programs to restore the balance, and a level of tension seldom reached in the absence of an agreement where unilateral corrective measures are part of day-to-day defense policy, undertaken at a relatively unhurried pace in full view of Soviet planners.

Particularly because of the problem of dynamic stability, it is important that systems constrained under an agreement be highly visible, either by national means or through forms of cooperative inspection that are adequate to give assurance to both sides that no violations are taking place. Of the two, reliance on national means of inspection is preferable, since the potential for abrasive and unsettling disputes associated with intrusive inspection is considerable. Disagreements arising out of application of on-site inspection prerogatives are a constant danger of such schemes, and even innocent failures of the system can cause great concern where on-site inspection is vital to maintain the necessary assurances of compliance with the terms of agreement. The familiar case in which an inspection party is unable to proceed to a selected destination because weather conditions will not permit aircraft landings and overland routes are many hours away can cause grave concern on the part of the state whose inspection efforts are so frustrated. Even if the excuse is valid, such situations can exacerbate the very doubts that initially led to the inspection requirement.

Too much inspection can be as destabilizing as not enough, a notion that is anathema to agencies charged with the collection of strategic intelligence. Too close an inspection of the opponent's flight test program, for example, may inadvertently reveal system reliabilities far from the expected norm, with the result that both sides' perception of the strategic balance is precipitously altered. Inspection that adds degrees of confidence to the information required for a first strike also may prove highly destabilizing.

Although the point is seldom acknowledged, uncertainty may, under some circumstances, contribute to stability. Not surprisingly, it is the uncertainty of the other side that is held to be stabilizing, while we, on our side, strive to acquire as much information as possible.

The most readily visible components of a strategic force are fixed installations (ICBM silos, for example) and large mobile systems such as submarines (while under construction). Both can be observed by national means, although there would seem to be some possibility for clandestine production of a submarine or two.

It is thus tempting, but perilous, to consider seriously only those limitations that involve systems of high visibility like fixed-based ICBMs and submarines. The danger is that in an effort to obtain the required degree of confidence of a change in the status of a constrained system, we shall prohibit the wrong (i.e., stabilizing) systems. Mobile missiles, for example, while of low visibility and therefore unattractive to analysts concerned with verification, may contribute more to stability than easily observable, undefended fixed systems that are becoming increasingly vulnerable precisely because they are highly visible and completely undefended.

The problem of verification is critically related to the sensitivity of the monitored system as a variable affecting the strategic balance. We would naturally wish to be extremely confident of detecting a change in capabilities in a weapons system, either of numbers or quality, if it were believed that a change in that system might upset the balance. But we have already seen that there are many and good reasons for concentrating on limitations whose violation would not, in and of itself, materially affect the difference in consequences between striking first and second. If this condition is achieved, the level of confidence required for verification is much diminished, and we can live more comfortably with the inherent uncertainties that affect any program of intelligence collection.

Low visibility systems, then, may be usefully constrained only if their potential impact on the strategic balance is slight, or if the lead times necessary to derive material advantages from clandestine activity (e.g., deployment following clandestine testing) are long enough to enable us to make a timely response. High visibility systems contribute to stability only if improved detectability is not accompanied by increased vulnerability. We must be careful, however, to insure that the response required is not itself a violation of the agreement, or we run the risk of having to choose between abrogation to build a case before world opinion in those cases where the evidence of violation is not adequate (or cannot be made public), or no response at all.

To some extent the first alternative, abrogation, can be hedged by writing an agreement of short duration. However, agreements of short duration stabilize the strategic balance, if at all, for correspondingly brief intervals. There is a trade-off here between the greater likelihood of adherence to a short-term agreement, with its relatively lower incentive for violation, and the more permanent effects of a long-term agreement that is also more likely to be violated or abrogated. To some extent a balance can be struck between the comparative advantages by providing at the outset for periodic review and renegotiation during the period covered by a lengthy agreement.

In comprehensive, far-reaching agreements involving substantial force reductions, the problem of visibility takes on a new and seriously complicated form. Low-visibility systems are better controlled at the periphery than at the center of the strategic balance. For the same reasons, the control of low-visibility systems comprised of large numbers of weapons is less problematic than the same controls exercised over small numbers. The inherent risks are far greater when prohibiting increments to a force of, say, 50 ICBMs than, to a force of, say 500: Assuming that the probability of detecting a clandestinely added missile is the same in both cases, the impact on the strategic balance is profound if the total allowed force is 50, and trivial if the allowed force is 500. For as the number declines, the importance of each unit increases. Moreover, as the number of units declines, other factors increase in importance.

The reliability of the force may become critical when the force size is small. Doubts that were tolerable to both sides when they were in possession of comfortably large forces may become intolerable as force size declines, unless there are confidence-building improvements to the smaller residual force. Such upgrading of existing forces, especially of forces declining in number, presumes freedom to pursue advanced technologies. Thus, to some extent at least, the absence of constraints on developing technology may offset potential sources of insecurity resulting from force reductions.

6 • U.S., Europe, SALT, and Strategy

Frederick S. Wyle

Profound doubts have persisted among the European allies over the "nuclear guarantee" of the U.S. ever since Sputnik, and certainly since the Russians attained an assured destruction capacity against the West some years ago. A discussion of Strategic Arms Limitation Talks (SALT) and Europe must be set in the general context of strategic issues in the Alliance over the last decade and more, relating to the balance between relying on nuclear weapons and preparing to fight conventionally, that is, without nuclear weapons being used by either side.

The way to avoid serious trouble within the Atlantic Alliance over these issues is to put them in perspective.

The fact is that the situations in which Alliance solidarity is dependent wholly upon the willingness of the U.S. to involve itself in a nuclear war are extremely unlikely. The overwhelming majority of imaginable contingencies are those in which nuclear weapons will be involved only with respect to their one clear and obvious function: to deter their use by the other side. It is hardly an overstatement that in the equation of confrontation in Europe the nuclear weapons of the U.S. and the U.S.S.R. cancel each other out.

If the security situation in Europe were otherwise, that is, if it were really what it is sometimes pictured as being, wholly a case of Europe being dependent upon the U.S. making good its commitment to European defense by instant nuclear war, the U.S. commitment would not long be credible.

The fact is, fortunately, that no such dependence upon nuclear weapons exists in Europe or elsewhere. Professional military pessimism to the contrary notwithstanding, there is a balance of conventional forces in Europe. Indeed, most of the quantitative and qualitative physical properties of the opposing forces, so far as these can be "objectively" examined, favor NATO rather than the Warsaw Pact.

Nevertheless, a wide and persistent myth of Soviet conventional superiority persists, perpetuating a false and unnecessary dependence on nuclear war as the only available answer to any substantial Soviet conventional aggression.

In their recently published book, *How Much Is Enough?*, Alain Enthoven and K. Wayne Smith make a complete presentation of this myth of Soviet superiority in conventional forces, how it grew, and why it is false (see Chapter 4). The Soviets are most assuredly reading it.

The crucial point is that in terms of overall resources of men and equipment, in terms of measurable combat effectiveness (bomb carrying capacity, ammunition moving capacity, loiter time of aircraft, fire power, engineer support, communications), indeed in almost every category of equipment other than tanks (but including anti-tank weapons and the killing capacity of aircraft against tanks), the NATO Alliance is not only well balanced, but richer and better supplied than the Warsaw Pact. (Many uncertainties remain, and "asymmetries" abound, but these cut in both directions, and neither the Soviets nor we can be sure which of us is more advantaged by these "asymmetries" taken as a whole.)

In the face of the facts, most argumentation that the Soviets must nevertheless be superior is reduced to asserting

TABLE 1
COMPARISON—NATO/WARSAW PACT

	Total Reg. Armed Forces	Army	Navy	Air Force	Para. Mil.
NATO	6,158,025	3,690,400	1,064,447	1,388,250	388,35[illegible]
WARSAW PACT	4,280,500	2,822,000	529,500	914,000	635,50[illegible]
NATO/EUR	2,903,700	1,998,050	353,472	537,250	388,35[illegible]
WP/EUR	975,500	822,000	54,500	94,000	405,5[illegible]
NATO/EUR/CENT	1,630,150	1,221,000	220,100	405,750	150,50[illegible]
WP/EUR/CENT	539,000	437,000	38,000	64,000	153,50[illegible]
NATO/EUR/CENT + US	4,791,150	2,878,000	916,100	1,215,750	150,5[illegible]
WP/EUR/CENT + USSR	3,844,000	2,437,000‡	513,000	884,000	383,5[illegible]

SOURCE: ISS, The Military Balance, 1970–71†
* Estimated
† Tables 2, 3, and 4 contain country-by-country analyses for NATO, neutrals, and Warswa Pact.
‡ Includes Air Defense Command, 500,000.
NATO/EUR/CENT = Bel. Den. Fr. Ger. Neth. UK.
WP/EUR/CENT = E.Ger. Pol. Cze.

(1) that they can mobilize forces faster, and thus win the day; or (2) that the Warsaw Pact is monolithic and that the Soviets can therefore command their allies as if they were their own forces; and (3) that they are certain to be the aggressors, thus being able to choose the placè of attack and to enjoy the advantage of surprise.

Each of these propositions is at least highly debatable (mobilization of *trained, ready, equipped* forces?!) (Czechs more reliable in attacking Western Europe than French in defending it?!) (Soviets being able to keep secret an enormous buildup of forces for a massed, sudden attack?!).

The fact is that no one can prove what the outcome of a substantial conventional war in Europe would be. Arguments over such matters rarely clarify the assumptions on

eserve	Men of Mil. Age (millions)	Populations (millions)	1970 Def. Exp. ($ millions)	1969 GNP ($ millions)	1969 % of GNP for Def.	% of Men of Elig. Age in Reg. Forces
524,900	199.400	532.210	99,375,000	1,582.09	4.2*	3.1**
740,000	67.570	347.200	47,203,000	608.60	4.8*	6.3**
501,400	58.160	305.483	23,234,000	582.69	3.6*	5.1**
540,000	19.970	103.200	7,425,000	142.60	4.1*	4.8**
565,500	36.740	193.150	19,263,000	462.22	3.7*	4.4**
150,000	12.160	64.425	5,845,000	100.80	5.5*	4.4**
589,000	73.840	398.475	93,663,000	1,394.22	6.1*	6.4**
250,000	59.760	308.425	45,623,000	566.80	7.0*	6.4**

which they are based. The outcome depends, usually, on the assumption that the other fellow gets all the breaks and is spectacularly successful in all the subsidiary elements, and that one's own side suffers the worst imaginable handicaps. That is not the real world.

The point is that it would be irrational for the Russians to think that they could easily overcome NATO's conventional forces on the Central Front, forces equaling them in numbers, and mostly surpassing them in quality and supporting equipment. Whatever deficiencies NATO forces—including, yes, the French—have, and they are legion, and even assuming that the Russians do not suffer from comparable deficiencies of their own, there is not in Europe an imbalance in conventional forces of a kind that could re-

TABLE 2
NORTH ATLANTIC TREATY FORCES & COUNTRY DATA

	Armed Forces Total Reg.	Army	Navy	Air Force	Par Mi
Belgium	102,400	70,000	4,400	20,500	13,[illegible]
Canada	93,325	35,350	16,975	41,000	. . .
Denmark	44,500	27,000	7,000	. . . . .	54,[illegible]
France	506,000	328,000	72,000	106,000	75,[illegible]
Germany	466,000	326,000	36,000	104,000	18,[illegible]
Greece	159,000	118,000	18,000	23,000	23,[illegible]
Italy	413,000	295,000	45,000	73,000	76,[illegible]
Luxembourg	550	550	. . . . .	. . . . .	[illegible]
Netherlands	121,250	80,000	20,000	21,250	3,[illegible]
Norway	38,000	23,500	8,600	9,000	70,[illegible]
Portugal	185,500	150,000	18,000	17,500	15,[illegible]
Turkey	477,500	390,000	37,500	50,000	40,[illegible]
United Kingdom	390,000	190,000	87,000	113,000	. . .
United States	3,161,000	1,657,000‡	694,000	810,000	. . .
NATO TOTAL	6,158,025	3,690,400	1,064,447	1,388,250	388,[illegible]
NATO EUROPE	2,903,700	1,998,050	353,472	537,250	388,[illegible]
NATO EUROPE CENTER	1,630,150	1,221,000	220,100	405,750	150,[illegible]
NATO EUR. CENTER & US	4,791,150	2,878,000	916,100	1,215,750	150,[illegible]

SOURCE: The Military Balance, 1970–71, ISS, LONDON
Estimates: "*", by F. S. Wyle, by comparison w. similar countries
NATO EUR. CENTER = Bel., Den., Fr., Ger., Neth., UK
* = estimated
‡ = includes Marines—294,000
** = average

motely justify the view that we are dependent upon rapid nuclear weapons use in Europe in the event of even a large Soviet attack.

Fortunately, it may be expected that the Soviet military bureaucracy is quite as prone to exaggerating the opposing NATO forces as the NATO bureaucracy is to exaggerating

(December 23, 1970)

				1969			
serve	Men of Mil. Age (millions)	Populations (millions)	1970 Def. Exp. ($ millions)	GNP ($ millions)	% of GNP for Def.	Per Cap Def. Exp ($)	% of Men of Elig. Age in Reg. Forces
. . . .	1.820	9.700	677	22,000	3.0	67	5.6
22,900	4.040	21.400	1,741	67,400	2.5	85	2.4
15,500	.900*	4.950	365	13,500	2.6	72	4.9*
30,000	9.800	50.725	5,874	140,000	4.4	123	5.2
63,000	11.500	59.000	5,560	150,000	3.5	90	4.1
00,000	1.775	8.975	420	8,370	5.1	47	9.0
30,000	10.775	54.300	2,416	82,300	2.9	44	3.8
. . . .	. . . . .	.340	8	860	.9	23	. .
90,000	2.520	13.000	1,075	25,500	3.7	80	5.0
10,000	.700*	3.885	370	9,700	3.8	95	5.4*
00,000	1.770	9.635	356	5,460	6.1	35	10.5
70,000	6.500	35.200	401	14,000	4.6	19	7.3
70,000	10.200	55.775	5,712	109,000	5.1	100	3.8
23,500	37.100	205.325	74,400	932,000	8.6	393	8.5
24,900	199.400	532.210	99,375	1,582,090	4.2**	. . .	3.1**
01,400	58.260	305.483	23,234	582,690	3.6**	. . .	5.1**
65,500	36.740	193.150	19,263	462,220	3.7**	. . .	4.4**
89,000	73.840	398.475	93,663	1,394,220	6.1**	. . .	6.4**

the Soviet Forces.[1] It is highly unlikely under current circumstances, therefore, that either side will feel at all con-

[1]The tables beginning on page 138 demonstrate that how you present data is important. They also suggest that NATO's problem cannot be the size of forces in being, nor can it be reserves, or other potential sources of strength.

TABLE 3
NEUTRAL FORCES AND COUNTRY DATA

	Total Reg. Armed Forces	Army	Navy	Air Force	Para. Mil.	Reserv
Austria	50,000	45,000	.....	4,000	12,000	......
Finland	39,000	34,000	2,000	3,000	3,250	......
Spain	281,950	210,000	39,350	32,600	65,000	......
Sweden (includes mobilized)	627,500	600,000	12,100	15,400	300,000	..(m).
Switzerland (includes mobilized—48 hrs.)	656,000	603,000	.....	53,000	.....	..(m).
Yugoslavia	238,000	200,000	18,000	20,000	19,000	......
TOTAL NEUTRALS	1,891,450	1,692,000	71,450	128,000	399,250	......

SOURCE: The Military Balance, 1970–71, ISS, LONDON
Estimates: "*", by F. S. Wyle, by comparison w. similar countries
NATO EUR. CENTER = Bel., Den., Fr., Ger., Neth., UK
* = estimated
** = Average
(m) includes those mobilizable in one or two days

fident that it could win a quick and easy victory with conventional forces. Only such a quick and easy victory could place before the opponent the choice of yielding its interests or going to nuclear war. Neither side is confident that it will be the opponent who will have to make the choice. This lack of confidence creates stability.

To understand the strategic discussion within the alliance, the difference in approach between Americans and Europeans to defense should be noted.

Broadly speaking, Americans approach the problems of defense as essentially technical tasks, to be mastered by the application of energy, physical resources, planning, and organization. Europeans approach the problem of defense as

						(December 23, 1970)
			1969			
en of l. Age illions)	Populations (millions)	1970 Def. Exp. ($ millions)	GNP ($ millions)	% of GNP for Def.	Per Cap Def. Exp ($)	% of Men of Elig. Age in Reg. Forces
.875*	7.410	.....	11,300	1.2	...	5.7*
.750*	4.720	.....	8,800	1.6	...	5.2*
.400*	33.275	.....	27,100	2.1	...	4.4*
.500*	8.020	.....	27,100	4.0	...	41.8*
.000*	6.300	.....	18,800	2.2	...	65.6*
.140	20.550	.....	11,000	5.3	...	5.7*
.665*	80.275	.....	104,100	2.7	...	12.9**

essentially political, to be solved by calculations of interest and political purpose, and to be decided in large part by structuring political relationships and interests.

The difference in approach was well demonstrated in the debate of the sixties over the effort necessary to bring NATO forces to a level of quality that would eliminate any possible remaining doubt in the Soviet mind that NATO could meet any attack.

The U.S. View: The U.S. argued that improvements in training, equipment, and supplies would make it clear to all that there was no point whatever in the Soviets threatening a conventional attack or pressure, because any such pres-

TABLE 4
WARSAW PACT FORCES AND COUNTRY DATA

	Total Reg. Armed Forces	Army	Navy	Air Force	Par[illegible] Mi[illegible]
Bulgaria	154,000	130,000	7,000	12,000	167,[illegible]
Hungary	101,500	90,000	1,500	10,000	35,[illegible]
Rumania	181,000	165,000	8,000	8,000	50,[illegible]
East Germany	129,000	92,000	16,000	21,000	73,[illegible]
Poland	242,000	195,000	22,000	25,000	45,[illegible]
Czechoslovakia	168,000	150,000	.....	18,000	35,[illegible]
Soviet Union	3,305,000	2,000,000‡	475,000	820,000	230,[illegible]
WARSAW P. TOTAL	4,280,500	2,822,000	529,500	914,000	635,[illegible]
WARS. P. EUROPE	975,500	822,000	54,500	94,000	405,[illegible]
WARS. P. EUR. CENTER	539,000	437,000	38,000	64,000	153,[illegible]
WARS. P. EUR. CENT. & USSR	3,844,000	2,437,000‡	513,000	884,000	383,[illegible]

SOURCE: The Military Balance, 1970–71, ISS, LONDON
Estimates: "*" F. S. Wyle, by comparison w. similar countries
NATO EUR. CENTER = Bel., Den., Fr., Ger., Neth., UK
WARS. P. EUR. CENTER = E. Ger., Pol., Cze.
* = estimated
‡ = includes Marines
** = Average
‡ = includes Air Defense Command, 500,000

sure could obviously and easily be withstood and matched. The U.S. kept pointing out how little was required to make clear that at any point whatever in the spectrum of possible hostilities, the NATO powers could hold their own very well. Having that strength across the whole range of possible hostilities, so that an enemy's aggression could be met at any level, the U.S. argued, was the most certain deterrent to any such maneuvers or experiments, without having to base our defense on such awful political dilemmas as "nuclear suicide" to respond to a border crossing. For the remote contingency

(December 23, 1970)

					1969		
serve	Men of Mil. Age (millions)	Populations (millions)	1970 Def. Exp. ($ millions)	GNP ($ millions)	% of GNP for Def.	Per Cap Def. Exp ($)	% of Men of Elig. Age in Reg. Forces
5,000	1.600*	8.450	.....	8,300	2.8	28	9.6*
5,000	2.070*	10.325	.....	13,500	2.7	44	4.9*
0,000	4.140	20.000	.....	20,000	2.9	29	4.4*
0,000	2.960	17.150	.....	32,000	5.9	116	4.1
0,000	2.800	32.800	.....	40,500	5.0	62	3.6
0,000	2.800	14.475	.....	28,300	5.6	109	6.0
0,000	47.600	244.000	.....	466,000	8.5	164	6.9
0,000	67.570	347.200	.....	608,600	4.8**	...	6.3**
0,000	19.970	103.200	.....	142,600	4.1**	...	4.8**
0,000	12.160	64.425	.....	100,800	5.5**	...	4.4**
0,000	59.760	308.425	.....	566,800	7.0**	...	6.4**

that the Soviets could somehow manage secretly to mass the whole of the Warsaw Pact, and then one day mount a sudden, explosive, mass attack, unexpected and unforeseen, driving to the Channel with the whole of the Warsaw Pact armies, we would have to acknowledge the probable necessity of nuclear weapons use to stop the attack. But this wholly unlikely contingency should not make us muscle-bound with nuclear weapons, depriving ourselves of the flexibility and efficiency of our conventional forces for the really likely contingencies by burdening them with the priority for the special care and custody required by nuclear weapons and by training and planning primarily for nuclear war.

In the argument, the U.S. insistently tried to focus the discussion on the most probably real events, and how governments would most probably wish to meet these events, and what sorts of forces and plans they would then wish to have

TABLE 5
M-DAY LAND FORCES IN THE CENTER REGION IN MID-1968[a]

	NATO	Warsaw Pact
Divisions	28⅔[b]	46[c]
Manpower in divisions	389,000	368,000
Manpower in division forces	677,000	619,000
Riflemen (NATO as percentage of pact)	100	
Equipment (NATO as percentage of pact):		
Tanks	55	
Antitank weapons	150	
Armored personnel carriers (APCs)	130	
Artillery and mortars (number of tubes)	100	
Divisional logistic lift	150	
Total vehicles	135	
Engineers	137	

SOURCE: Alain C. Enthoven, "Arms and Men: The Military Balance in Europe," *Interplay,* May 1969, reprinted in *Hearings before the Subcommittee on Europe of the Committee on Foreign Affairs,* U.S. House of Representatives (91st Cong., 2nd Session, May 17, 1970).

[a] Center region includes West Germany, Belgium, Netherlands and France for NATO; East Germany, Poland and Czechoslovakia for the pact countries.

[b] Includes 5 French divisions.

[c] 20 of which are Soviet, and 24 of which are East European, including 8 Czechoslovak.

at hand. Real warfighting capacity, for the most likely situations, was the goal of the U.S. government.

The European View: From the European point of view, most of the U.S. argumentation was sheer unrealism. Either the Soviets understood that the U.S. was committed to European defense, and would under no circumstances yield vital interests in Europe—and of Europe—to Soviet pressure, or they did not. The test of vital interests was whether the U.S. would not shrink back in protecting those interests even if it should become involved in nuclear war.

In the fifties, the U.S. had made these propositions plain to the Soviets. Its nuclear forces were certainly adequate to the task. The large-scale deployment of U.S. nuclear weapons to Europe in the late fifties and early sixties seemed to serve further notice to the Soviets that they could not crunch across Europe without hitting all those nuclear weapons. If this fact were clear, and were kept clear, that was sufficient to deter the Soviets.

TABLE 6
WORLDWIDE NATO AND WARSAW PACT MANPOWER, MID-1968[a]

	NATO	Warsaw Pact
Army/Marines	3,000,000	2,850,000
Navy	1,070,000	470,000
Air Force	1,400,000	880,000
Total men	5,470,000	4,200,000

SOURCE: Alain C. Enthoven, "Arms and Men: The Military Balance in Europe," *Interplay,* May 1969, reprinted in *Hearings before the Subcommittee on Europe of the Committee on Foreign Affairs,* U.S. House of Representatives (91st Cong., 2nd Session, May 17, 1970).
[a] Excluding U.S. increases for Vietnam.

U.S. forces in Europe were physical hostages to the policy, the guarantee that U.S. military forces would have to be attacked by any Soviet aggression. Soviet belief that no government in the U.S. would suffer U.S. forces in Europe to be decimated without going to nuclear war would keep the peace.

It followed that from the European point of view the exact size, quality, and cost of NATO's conventional forces were distinctly secondary. What counted was not the number of days of supplies of some regiment, but the U.S. political presence and commitment in Europe, the determination of its government, and the clarity of its political posture.

TABLE 7
NATO AND WARSAW PACT TACTICAL AIR FORCES IN THE CENTER REGION IN MID-1968

	NATO	Warsaw Pact
Number of deployed aircraft	2,100	2,900
Percentage of total inventory (of center region countries)	20	40
Percentage of force by mission capability (center region):		
Primary interceptors	10	42
Multipurpose fighter/attack	48	15
Primary attack	9	6
Reconnaissance	13	8
Low performance	20	29
Total	100	100
Effectiveness indicators (NATO as percentage of pact):		
Average payload	240	
Typical loiter time	250–500	
Crew training	200	

SOURCE: Alain C. Enthoven, "Arms and Men: The Military Balance in Europe," *Interplay,* May 1969, reprinted in *Hearings before the Subcommittee on Europe of the Committee on Foreign Affairs,* U.S. House of Representatives (91st Cong., 2nd Session, May 17, 1970).

Two further factors supported this essentially political approach to strategy:

a. the strong conviction by European politicians that anything suggesting a repetition of World War II—that is, a large conventional war—was simply unacceptable to their people; and

b. the general belief, based on statements by NATO military sources and unquestioningly accepted by the

Europeans, that the Soviets were so hopelessly superior in conventional forces that no remotely possible effort by the European countries could ever match them. If no amount of effort that the Europeans could undertake would make any substantial difference in any event, why attempt such a domestically difficult policy as the Americans were asking?

Nuclear threats thus seemed the only "militarily" and budgetarily feasible strategy, and the stance of the U.S., not the efforts of Europeans, seemed to the Europeans the decisive element in deterring the Soviets.

These two different approaches on the part of the U.S. government and the European allies obtained through most of the sixties, and to a large part they obtain today.

At the same time, in view of the Soviets' assured destruction capacity against both the U.S. and Europe, the validity of the heavily nuclear reliant strategy of the NATO of the fifties eroded more and more. Indeed, even a "local" or "limited" nuclear war in Europe—referred to by the Americans, but not the Europeans, as "theater war" or "tactical" nuclear war—seemed to offer no more advantages to the defender than to the attacker.

In 1967 the NATO Defense Ministers formally adopted substantially the U.S. position as the official NATO strategy. Little followed by way of concrete action, however, to change the basic structure of the NATO forces, or to move NATO military posture very far away from a heavy nuclear reliance. An additional restraint on costly improvements of the conventional forces was the fact that in the later sixties the political focus in NATO shifted even further from improving military preparedness. The new focus was on holding the line militarily while exploring possible steps to political detente with the Soviets. The prospects of a Soviet attack seemed less and less likely to the Europeans, provided always that the U.S. maintained its firm stance.

What then of SALT?

There is, in this area too, a difference in attitudes between Europeans and Americans.

First, there is a lower perception of Soviet military aggressiveness in Europe than there is in the U.S. Most Europeans simply do not perceive any Soviet interest in marching to the Channel. The length of the Soviet military shadow is a political phenomenon, not a direct military threat. Likewise, interest in the precise numbers of intercontinental launchers, nuclear delivery vehicles, megatonnage, penetration capabilities, and the like, is far less intense in Europe than in the U.S. There is general recognition that this is the superpowers' game, not in a large way that of the middle powers.

Second, there is considerable disapproval of the seemingly mindless and endless technological race to nowhere by the superpowers.

In particular, the U.S. gets a good share of the blame for the spiraling arms race, with its continuous political campaigns about "missile gaps" that turn out more often than not to be fictional; with its decision to go ahead with an ABM that was admittedly "marginal," and that clearly could not work against the Soviets, yet impelled the Soviets to another round of the arms race; and with its decision to dash forward with the MIRV, though the U.S. was clearly substantially ahead of the Soviets in the technology involved, and though the original justification of MIRV seems to have gone by the board.

The Soviets, of course, get their share of the blame. But to Americans it is often surprising that Europeans seem to be so calm about the Soviet MRBM/IRBMs poised on their doorstep, about Soviet expansion of their Polaris-style submarine fleet, and even about the general Soviet expansion in North Africa, the Middle East, and the Mediterranean. Perhaps what one can't do anything about, one learns to live with at a lower level of anxiety and tension.

One strong attitude in Europe, then, so far as SALT is concerned, is a feeling that the more SALT, the better, and the sooner the limitations are agreed, and the more of them, the better.

At the same time, there is profound concern over the fact that the two superpowers are bargaining on a subject of such vast importance, and perhaps dealing with the interests of Europe, in the absence of the Europeans.

There is not total faith in the U.S. capacity to perceive European interests as Europeans would perceive them. Nor is there total faith in the U.S. ability to resist subordinating European interests to achieve a bargain with the Soviets. There is also the underlying conviction that sooner or later the U.S. will recede from Europe, and that when that day comes, the Europeans will be left face to face with their Soviet neighbor.

The fear is that the U.S. will at some future time significantly diminish its military presence, interest, and political presence in Europe; that it is torn by internal dissension and doubt as a result of the Vietnam disaster and domestic social problems; and that these forces set up a considerable pressure on the U.S. to seek, as one means of relieving such pressure, to "make a deal" with the Soviets—and perhaps a deal that would in some fashion be unfavorable for Europe.

The short description, then, of European attitudes on SALT is schizophrenia—pressure to wind down the arms race and move to detente coexists in the same breasts with profound concern about the potential sacrifices of European interests in SALT or their sequels.

So much for *attitudes.* What about the strategic *interests* of Europeans in SALT, and possible European reactions to possible future strategic and defense developments?

First, it should be acknowledged that, as in previous debates such as the Multilateral force (MLF) subculture, it seems to be the case that European strategic interests arouse more heated discussion and debate among Americans than among Europeans. This contribution should be taken subject to the same caution.

My own view is that European interests in security (as distinct from political sensitivities) are relatively unaffected by either SALT itself or by any foreseeable outcome of the SALT process over the coming years. The strategic interests of Europeans are in any event based upon a *global* strategic balance, made up of the totality of the two opposing threat systems, and not upon a nonexistent European or "regional" strategic balance. The *global* balance is exactly what will be preserved by any SALT agreement or continuing SALT process.

Thus, supposing ultimate agreement between the U.S. and the U.S.S.R. to limit major intercontinental offensive and defensive weapons systems, or ABMs alone, or a policy of tacit restraint parallel to SALT, it must logically be a part of any such agreed limitations or process of restraint that the global strategic balance is not upset by radical changes in any substantial part of the two threats systems, including the European-based components of the two threat systems, to the extent that these could upset the global balance.

It should be noted at once that it is difficult to see what changes in European-based systems could in fact bring about a strategic imbalance globally. As a "purely strategic" matter, a doubling, or hardening, or total replacement of Soviet MRBM/IRBMs with new longer-range missiles, based deeper in Russia, would not create any new end result so far as European safety is concerned. The threat to Europe would not materially change. The current total Soviet threat system to Europe (MRBMs, mobile missiles, bombers, sub-launched missiles, and retargeted ICBMs) cannot under any foreseeable circumstances be reliably disabled by a first strike by present or foreseeable U.S.

forces or by any combination of foreseeable European forces, or by both together.

In other words, the Soviets now have an assured destruction capability against Europe. They will keep it.

If there should ever be a voluntary dismantling of Soviet MRBMs, highly unlikely for the near future, it would by its occurrence prove that the Soviets had available more efficient, or least equally capable, assured destruction threats against Europe: ICBMs, Polaris, mobile missiles, or other systems. Their dismantling of the MRBMs, therefore, in or out of SALT or other security or disarmament conferences, would change nothing from a military point of view.

On the NATO side, it is equally impossible that the global strategic balance could be upset by changes limited to European deployments or systems. Suppose, for example, that one day the U.S. and NATO made formal acknowledgement of what most experts have known all along, that devoting the NATO fighter-bombers based in Europe to nuclear delivery roles yields little additional benefit to the global NATO nuclear system. Let us suppose an outright and exclusive commitment of all NATO fighter-bombers in Europe exclusively to the role of conventional ground support and interdiction, where they can do the most good in any event.

Such a stance, arising from SALT or not, would leave the European exposure to the Soviet threat system unaffected. Neither the current total of NATO fighter-bombers based in Europe, nor double their number, nor triple their number, even if all devoted to attacks on the MRBMs, or on MRBMs and medium bombers, would be able to avoid the assured destruction capacity of the total Soviet threat system against Europe. Thus, a change of numbers, or missions, or ranges, of NATO fighter-bombers would not affect European interests from a nuclear strategic point of view.

But politically, if such a change were made by U.S.-Soviet agreement alone, there would be the devil to pay. The *strategic* interests of Europe would not be affected by marginal tinkering with two very large opposing threat systems. But the European perception of the *political meaning* of such tinkering would depend on the method of the tinkering. The means is the message.

There is, as one observer has called it, a sense of "community property" about the U.S. fighter-bombers in Europe capable of carrying nuclear weapons. That sense is even stronger regarding the potential for delivering nuclear weapons of the allied fighter-bombers. The way to preserve European interests in SALT, therefore, is to pay close attention to their political instincts. This, fortunately, the U.S. seems to have done.

The most likely outcome of the current SALT is more SALT. But assuming that some limitation is agreed, sooner or later, on the gross definitions of systems such as launchers or vehicles, it is likely that any first agreement will be restricted to more or less freezing the current size of intercontinental missile inventories and Polaris systems and ABMs. Perhaps these freeze limitations could be accompanied with a logical and implicit or explicit corollary proposition that the rough freeze so achieved implies at least no sudden and drastic changes in collateral systems that might in sum amount to an upset of the general freeze or balance.

The Soviets seem to be arguing that in any attempt to establish a count of vehicles that can constitute a threat to the U.S.S.R., all vehicles with adequate range from their normal places of deployment must be counted, and that this must include the European-based fighter-bombers. It is hard to fault the logic, but this argument, too, has little to do with the assured destruction capability of either side, and may be more political than strategic. An agreement that sought to limit deployments of bombers, and mobile missiles, and submarines, to areas beyond range of the superpowers would involve hopeless complexities. How could it be controlled? Would a simple redeployment of aircraft from one base to another violate it? Since a large redeployment could occur in a few days, would either power ever put itself at the mercy of such a situation, if the redeployment would upset the balance? Clearly not.

The U.S. response to the Soviet view on fighter-bombers appears to be based not on the strategic significance or lack of significance of these systems, but on the political view that these systems are so much a matter of European concern that it is simply impossible to discuss them and the MRBMs in the absence of the Europeans; and that these systems are therefore more properly to be discussed in a different forum. (That stance also avoids adding the fighter-bombers to the U.S. side of the ledger, but this would appear, again, to be a secondary consideration.)

Thus, the current rounds of SALT, despite recently voiced concerns of some Europeans, are unlikely to reach a serious discussion of the fighter-bombers or the MRBMs.

Some Europeans have also voiced concern that the U.S.-Soviet talks may result in a "no first use of nuclear weapons" pledge. To the extent that this fear relates to a strategic weapons exchange, it deals with a *fait accompli.* An assured destruction capability on one side is for all practical purposes the same thing as a "no first use" pledge by the other side, so long as rational decisions are made by governments.

To the extent that the concern relates to a pledge limited to the "European theater," or to Europe only, it seems wholly improbable that this subject would be raised seriously in any foreseeable round of SALT. The SALT, of course, include some general mutual education. To the extent that the inutility and dangers of exchanges of strategic weapons are mirrored by the inutility—for all concerned—of "theater" weapons, this flows from logical propositions and thoughts, not a separate discussion of "theater" weapons as a subject in SALT.

If any attempt by the Russians is made to discuss seriously some sort of restraints on war-fighting decisions—like the Geneva convention against gas, for example, applied to nuclear weapons—it seems certain that the effort would be referred to later discussions including Europeans.

No conceivable outcome of SALT is likely, in my view, to involve any considerable effect upon either the current global strategic balance, or European defense arrangements, or NATO, or any significant European cooperation or independent national steps in defense. SALT is simply the wrong framework for speculating about the future of Europe's defense.

Leaving aside the narrow framework of SALT, however, what are the conceivable changes that might involve major departures from current European defense postures, strategies, or organizations?

The difficulty in answering these questions is that they generally presuppose that there is a third force option, a "third nuclear superpower" possibility that is available to Europe if the U.S. commitment should appear at any point to become unreliable. Some voices in Europe have advocated, as a matter of plain prudence, that Europeans should begin to build a hedge, or an option, however unwillingly, that would give them most of the substance of the sort of protection that they have been enjoying from the U.S. commitment to European security for the past generation.

In my own view, there is no such option. Under foreseeable circumstances, no political entity in Europe is likely to emerge that could create, control, and credibly threaten to use through the ultimate power of decision of one man, a nuclear weapons arsenal of the same order of magnitude, that is, "sufficiency," as the two superpowers. The existing nations of Europe are wholly unlikely to be able to surrender to any one person the power of decision over their existing forces, or to combine their financial resources and decision-making processes sufficiently even to build an adequate force, much less control it.

The only choice open to Europeans, if the U.S. commitment really begins to weaken substantially, in my view, is:

a. whether to try to revive it, that is, to support it with a genuine attempt at sharing the burden of it; or

b. whether to proceed instead with some conscious plan of accommodating to a status of neutrality of sorts—armed after a fashion, but unmistakably neutral and withdrawn from any sort of confrontation.

That sort of neutrality may be for most of the European countries a status closer to Sweden than to Austria, or to Switzerland rather than to Finland, but it may be questioned what the status of West Germany would be.

Even such a state of neutralism would depend in the last analysis upon U.S. determination to preserve at least some independence for Europeans, that is, to avoid outright and open Soviet control. It would certainly involve at least some process of political accommodation to the Soviets over contested issues such as the legal, and eventually political, status and role of Berlin; the degree and quality of commercial and political contact between East and West European countries; the sorts of associations among West Europeans, and between them and the U.S., that would be tolerable to the Soviets and those that would be considered aggressive, hostile, or even just plain unfriendly; and similar issues.

I do not see any real choice for Western European countries between continued alliance with the U.S. and neutralism of some sort. The attempt, therefore, to devise particular weapons systems or strategies appropriate to the regional concept of Europe, without any political reality to which to refer that attempt, is not very meaningful.

Nevertheless, possible approaches often mentioned are:

a. to associate the existing U.K. and French forces in some new manner, or

b. to create a joint force of some kind from these two forces.

In either case there would have to be a choice between inventing some appropriate nexus of West Germany to the effort, or ignoring West Germany.

It is often argued that the independent national nuclear forces of the U.K. and France may be the embryo of a future "European" force that could take over the task of deterring the Soviets from a progressively disinterested U.S.

This suggestion is in my view a version of the recurrent yearning for a European superpower. That yearning does not seem to me to have any basis in political fact. There is no Western European superpower in the process of being born. In the last few years the trend has been going away from such a goal rather than toward it. Whatever the economic arrangements in the EEC over the next five or ten years, it seems clear that no single political sovereignty will be forged of the three countries of West Germany, France, and the U.K. and without such a single sovereignty as a core, there can be no military superpower in Europe. (It is important to distinguish this military side from the enlargement of the EEC, and the generally expected beneficial political consequences from the U.K.'s joining the Common Market.)

As to the U.K. and French nuclear forces cooperating as a "joint force" or "independent European force," a strategic argument is at first plausible. Why could not these two small national forces in time be built up to a respectable force size, perhaps consisting of twice the projected Polaris forces of the U.K. and France, and, let us say, twice the projected IRBM force of France, and twice the projected bomber forces of the U.K. and France?

Such an economic effort is not, after all, beyond the strength of the two countries. With a reasonable pooling of efforts, supported by a benevolent U.S. policy on release of atomic secrets to the French, a good start within some four or five years, could be made on such a force. And would not a force of some ten Polaris ships at sea, each with sixteen missiles, backed up by some surviving IRBMs in the French mountains, and a variety of bombing aircraft to complicate the Soviet defense problem further, constitute at least a very serious deterrent to the Soviets?

Thoughts of this kind seem to tantalize some European observers and politicians, but they seem to me largely devoid of political reality.

The balance of power in Western Europe is based upon a more or less equal position among Western Germany, France, and the U.K. The discrimination against Germany in the nuclear field—the "special situation in which Germany finds herself," as the French sometimes put it—is made tolerable over time only by the fact of the U.S. presence and the NATO organization within which the diverse political interests of the NATO members can find a "neutral" defense framework, without having to be confronted or reconciled.

To attempt to leave the Germans out of a new future European nuclear superpower upon which the security of Germany would rest would be to court disaster. To attempt to include them in a clearly discriminatory manner, as was attempted in the MLF episode, would be to ask the Germans to trust the French and the British rather than the Americans to defend their interests against the Soviets. To state that proposition is to demonstrate its lack of prospects.

To attempt to build a nuclear superpower with Germany as an equal partner would result in a prolonged crisis in Europe with uncertain outcomes in Eastern and Western Europe both, and in a divisive debate within Western Europe and the U.S., and within Germany, as to how far the Germans can be trusted with nuclear weapons.

The result of any effort at a "European" force would almost certainly be a situation in which the Germans could under no circumstances have a major influence in the decision to fire nuclear weapons, and in which the powers of decision would be divided between the other two powers in such a way as to ensure the sovereign right of each to commit national suicide only pursuant to a purely national decision. In other words, there would be no single force with a single decision, but only a structure, a joint organization, a great deal of consultation and joint planning, and talk. Far from being positively sufficient, it would be decidedly negative.

It would not be a force that could be launched by a single man, and would therefore not be credible. Whether it would not be far more destabilizing than the current situation is an open question. It would seem likely to help convince the American people that the Europeans now have "their own force," that they can therefore "hack it" on their own, and that there is no further need for the American people to maintain a risky, expensive, and exhaustive commitment. The pressures for U.S. disengagement from European security would thus be greatly strengthened by the very attempt to provide an alternative for it. This dilemma is, I believe, fully recognized by the governments most concerned.

In sum, while there is a vast field for intellectual effort at new defense organizations, doctrines, multilateral forces, groups, and theories on European defense, none of these seem to me to be very substantive. The real possibilities seem to me to be a continuing substantial U.S. engagement and participation in European defense (the most likely consequence), or a sufficiently clear U.S. disengagement to bring about a progressive drift into neutralism.

The situation in Europe today contains elements of both prospects. Probably Europe will continue to drift slightly in the direction of neutralism, but in my view the drift will stop well short of dissolving NATO, or of encouraging the withdrawal of the U.S. by reason of any policy decision of the Europeans. The continuing slow erosion of mutual confidence and commitment between Western Europe and the U.S. (caused above all by Vietnam) is the problem to address. It is the response to this problem, not to the notion of devising some sort of new organizational structure or defense doctrine, which will determine the future orientation of Europe.

Some specific questions remain to be considered:

Question 1: Are there organizational alternatives in a joint force or independent European force that SALT settlement may cause governments to suggest?

Answer: I think not, for the reasons given above. Although there is a persistent strain of wishful thinking in British policy that perhaps its nuclear capacity can somehow be converted into a dowry for a marriage to EEC/France, the practical difficulty of bringing about any significant merger of U.K. and French forces while satisfying the German sense of equality and dignity, preserving the U.S. commitment, and, indeed, inducing the Germans to expose themselves once more to the consequences of deep concern about a German nuclear role, in both East and West Europe, make the prospects exceedingly dim.

The last such attempt, an enthusiastic idea conceived by the U.S. State Department for a joint force, including the Germans in a safe but dignified fashion (the Multilateral Force Proposal), was a fiasco. It was opposed outright by the French, who give no sign of having changed their minds; covertly by the British, who diverted the proposal into a procedural and organizational swamp; and by the U.S. Congress —not to speak of the Russians, the East Europeans, and the smaller Western European powers. Any joint force idea that did not include the Americans as a guarantor of stability and safety would meet a much more concerned, and at least equally negative, reaction. The Germans themselves are not about to risk their standing as a peaceful citizen and neighbor in Europe in pursuit of a chimera.

For the purposes of this conclusion, it does not matter whether the organizational form of a joint force is *(a)* a joint targeting of two forces with a council to decide on firing; or *(b)* a joint force with the right of the two constituent nations to withdraw their components in time of ultimate danger for the execution of separate national plans; or *(c)* any other variety of cooperation falling short of ultimate decision power by a single man.

The most positive effect that could be expected from any such effort is that the U.K. and the French would save some money through sharing the production or development of some items.

Question 2: Under what conditions do new arrangements become feasible, reasonable, or necessary?

Answer: U.S. withdrawal from European defense would create a need for new arrangements, but the new arrangements would within the foreseeable time be an accommodation to some form of neutralism—Swedish, Swiss, Austrian, or Finnish are the usual models mentioned—as a matter of real policy, whatever the pretense. The question of what, under such circumstances, would become of the small national forces of the U.K. and France is an interesting one. The chances are that they would for a long time continue in being, without any clear or convincing rationale, more or less as at present. The shock of giving up the hallmark of ultramodernity would probably be too great for any French or U.K. government, unless a very glamorous supranational basket could be created into which to drop these forces. But any such basket would be as much a formula for preserving and continuing these forces, as for abandoning them.

Question 3: Under what nuclear postures and declaratory policies might NATO become obsolete or require major reorganization?

Answer: The only postures of which I can conceive are unlikely. They would be attempts to articulate clearly the extent of reliance upon nuclear weapons. If there were an attempt to return to the "nuclear retaliation" doctrine of the fifties, I believe that the Alliance would fall apart at a somewhat more rapid pace than under any other nuclear defense strategy. The total reliance on nuclear weapons was a doctrine of desperation, hardly credible even in the early and middle fifties, when it was developed in response to the mistaken impression that the Soviets had an immense conventional superiority over NATO. Since nothing else was apparently available at that time, it was the best that NATO could offer. We are living with that heritage in large part even today. In the last ten years, however, two decisive developments have occurred: (1) the Soviets have now acquired a nuclear arsenal which would assure that any nuclear war would be two-sided, and thus would destroy NATO territory in whatever degree the Soviets chose (for example, by a strict retaliatory policy, whatever the level and scope of nuclear hostilities); and (2) a close analysis of the actual balance of conventional forces between NATO and the Warsaw Pact has disclosed that the assertion of Soviet superiority in conventional forces is false.

The myth of Warsaw Pact superiority is still widespread, and it will die hard, for various psychological, political, budgetary, and bureaucratic reasons. But the facts with which to question the myth have now been put on the table (see Chapter 4 of *How Much is Enough?* by Enthoven and Smith). The impact of the availability of the facts will hopefully be to convince those who seek an alternative to complete reliance on nuclear weapons that there is indeed a perfectly feasible alternative.

These two developments cannot be reversed. As more and more Europeans contemplate the prospect of a nuclear war being waged on their territory to defend them, more and more of them will decide that nuclear weapons of any kind are useful in the end only to deter their use by the other side, but not for much else. Professor Weizsäcker's *Kriegsfolgen und Kriegsverhutung* is an interesting beginning in that process. Defense Minister Helmut Schmidt of Germany has recommended that each member of the Bundestag read the introduction of that volume. Some of them may do so.

The option of returning to a policy of nuclear bluff is not available, even with the Americans doing the bluffing. Without the Americans, there is little prospect that bluffing with U.K. and French weapons will work.

The relative impotence of new doctrine or organization to touch fundamental strategic conditions does not suggest, however, that there might not be some major rearrangements in NATO in the coming decade. The whole question of the relationship of the flanks to the Center Region, of Turkey, Greece, and Italy, and perhaps even of the Norwegian and Danish flanks, not to mention Portugal, may assume a very different posture. It would be possible to restructure the NATO command systems or other parts of the organizational structure to take account of the very different outlooks as between the flanks and the Central Front. But there is probably little to be gained by such steps in practice, and perhaps much to be lost.

Changes of this kind may become in time the lesser of several evils, but in terms of replacing any sort of strength lost by U.S. withdrawals or changes of posture they would be of minimal effect. The positive political effects of a single NATO alliance with a single organizational structure are considerable. The flank countries themselves probably value these advantages of being in the big political league of the West, of having some sort of contact with central decisions about Germany and the continent, as highly as the more direct security protections against the East that they derive from the Alliance.

Question 4: How might U.S. and Soviet postures and policy change the strategic balance, and with what implications for NATO? For instance, might tactical nuclear weapons, or nuclear mining, come to be viewed as reasonable?

Answer: The day of doctrinal reliance on tactical nuclear weapons, so-called, is gone. It cannot come again in its original form; nor is there a promising new version.

U.S., British, French Military Manpower Stationed in Germany, and Bundeswehr Manpower

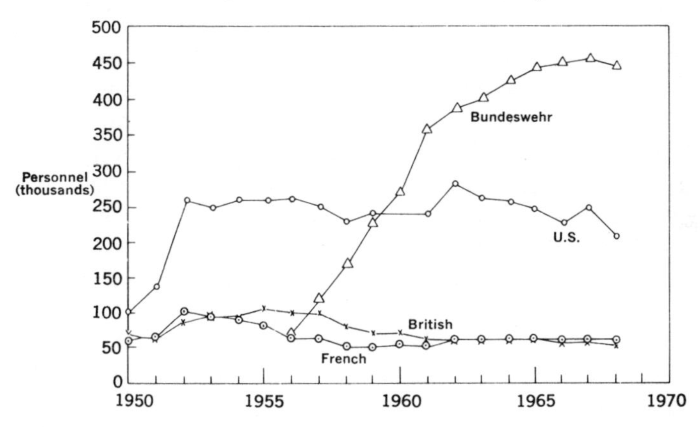

SOURCE: Horst Mandershausen, *Troop Stationing in Germany: Value and Cost,* Memorandum RM-5881-PR. RAND Corporation, Santa Monica, Cal., December 1968, p. 8.

The original idea in the fifties seems to have been that if the Soviets (thought to have larger conventional forces but no nuclear weapons), were to attack in a mass, the smaller NATO forces would use nuclear weapons to destroy the attacking masses. That theory was a fine theory while the Soviets had nothing with which to answer the use of nuclear weapons on their forces or installations in Europe. They now do. Any theory of "tactical" nuclear warfare must now be based on expectations of two-sided use of nuclear weapons.

There is no satisfactory theory of two-sided nuclear war

in any limited land area, whether Europe or elsewhere. As a war-fighting doctrine it makes little or no sense. In theory, both sides could very quickly destroy the opposing units and installations. Assuming that they could do so without escalating the hostilities to general nuclear war, the most they could therefore achieve would be an impasse within the "battle zone," where all the forces thrown into the combat zone would be destroyed by the nuclear weapons of the other side. In pure theory, the side with the most reserve forces—that is, reserve forces that would outlast the other side's supply of "tactical" nuclear weapons and capability to deliver them effectively—should win the day, i.e., inherit the charred battlefield.

A number of factors will disappoint that theory. In the first place, such an extensive nuclear war will be in practice indistinguishable in the affected area from general nuclear war. The pressures to destroy the supporting infrastructure of engaged combat forces—bridges, bases, railroad yards, roads, staging areas, depots, etc., in ever-increasing depths from the front—will almost certainly force the war to expand beyond imagined limited frontal "battle zone" of fifty kilometers or a hundred kilometers in depth.[2]

---

[2]Such a "pencil-sharpener" concept of war, with each side contentedly feeding its forces into the frontal death zone, there to be chewed up, and with the rear areas being totally unaffected, is a pipedream. It can be understood, perhaps, by considering the strong pressure to find something useful for nuclear weapons to do. Other versions of the consequence of this intellectual effort are miracle weapons: (*a*) nuclear weapons so small as to be non-escalatory and politically unexciting, but somehow effective enough to distinguish them from conventional munitions in effect—weapons, that is, of the Buck Rogers variety, killing only people in uniform, but leaving civilians unaffected, material property unaffected, etc.; or (*b*) weapons of miracular accuracy, which can be tiny in their nuclear yield because they are so enormously accurate.

It is never explained what the advantage is of nuclear weapons that are so small that they cannot be escalatory, and so accurate that conventional munitions would be almost as effective, without the escalatory risk. Most of these ideas derive from civilian sources, such as politicians or nuclear physicists. Very few military men seem to have become beguiled by either miracle theories or miracle gadgets.

The expansion of the war would then become, for the larger region in question, the same as general nuclear war. It seems wholly out of the question that any European ally of the U.S. would agree to a war-fighting strategy that limited nuclear destruction to Europe, or that contemplated more or less total destruction in an undefined but perhaps rapidly adjustable "combat zone," or any other variant of what has been called "tactical" nuclear war. (The best definition yet of the difference between tactical and strategic nuclear war is that if it is on someone else's soil, it is tactical; if it is on your soil, it is strategic.)

In the second place, the theory of substituting "tactical" nuclear weapons for missing conventional manpower is bound to fail because the conduct of "tactical" nuclear war requires more conventional manpower, not less, for the single reason that it uses up that manpower at a vastly greater rate. Thus, to follow the theory of tactical nuclear warfare to a successful conclusion, it requires so much conventional manpower that you would not have had to resort to tactical nuclear weapons in the first place.

The function of nuclear weapons of any kind and in any location seems to assume more and more the same character: that of deterrence of the use of nuclear weapons by the other side. Beyond that use, there is the further general deterrence that is exercised by the obvious and strong determination by any power not to surrender its interests, coupled with the availability of nuclear weapons. In effect, this stance, which is the current stance of the West, amounts to saying that whatever the outcome, rather than yield vital interests, the power possessing nuclear weapons will commence to use them, even though there is no satisfactory theory for how to fight a nuclear war, or stop one, or any experience whatever with the consequences of such a war on the social systems, the governmental structures, and the military forces involved. It is a stance more than a strategy, and it amounts very much to the same thing as declaring that some things are so dear to us that they leave the realm of the rational, and if you push us beyond rational action, you'd better be prepared for the worst.

Most governments might not in fact find this stance a restful one in an extreme emergency, but it appears to be the only one available for the most extreme circumstances. The U.S. government took a stance not too dissimilar from this description during the Cuba missile crisis. The interpretation often made of that crisis, that it was a victory for the nuclear superiority of the United States, is in my view wholly wrong. The U.S. prevailed in that confrontation because of its conventional superiority in the area, *once the nuclear element had been taken out of the equation by a stand-off of terror.* With President Kennedy's statement, the nuclear weapons were almost by definition kept out of any confrontation around Cuba. The remaining means of confrontation, the conventional forces, were so obviously and overwhelmingly in favor of the U.S. that they could have brought about any outcome that the U.S. insisted upon. Therefore they were not tested. The incident proves the essentiality of conventional forces in the nuclear environment of our times, not the reverse.

I believe that eventually the "tactical" nuclear weapons will play the same role, and there are many who argue that they have already achieved exactly that role today. For these reasons, I do not think that the French Pluto, or any future "tactical" or "short-range" or "limited" nuclear weapons systems produced by any European country, or deployed in Europe by the U.S. can have much effect on the strategic dilemmas and problems as we find them today.

Given the inutility of nuclear weapons except for the most extreme imaginable situations, the balance of power depends upon other elements of strength. These the U.S. and its allies now have, and should retain. There is no substitute.

7 • Secondary and "Almost-Nuclear" Powers: How Do They Affect Strategic Arms Limitations?

Leonard Beaton

No one dealing with the Strategic Arms Limitation Talks has given any impression at any time that he thought the problems involved were simple. To engage jointly in the management of a radical and advancing military technology whose implications are spectacular beyond all military experience is ambitious enough. To do so between two powers with a continental sense of self-sufficiency, a historic distrust of foreigners, differing political instincts and a long record of suspicion and hostility seems almost incredible. Yet this bilateral arrangment, with all its difficulties, is only the beginning of the problem.

Strategic nuclear arms are not and will not be a Soviet-American monopoly. Much effort in the American strategic community has gone into demonstrating that all other nuclear forces except these two (and it is noticeable that the Chinese are now assumed to have a manifest nuclear destiny) are—in the classic McNamara formulation from the high days of counterforce doctrine—"dangerous, expensive, prone to obsolescence, and lacking in credibility as a deterrent." Those who bore the brunt of this long and elaborate campaign, notably the British and French, have responded as allies must when their principal partner attempts to use the alliance relationship to circumscribe their freedom of action. They have ignored it. Those who do not matter have admittedly tended to use the American doctrines as a useful addition to domestic political debate. Those who have mattered have ignored the argumentation as politely as possible, or turned it back with whatever convenient explanations might lie to hand. On the whole, however, they have declined to make the central point: that all nuclear forces (not just "limited" nuclear forces) are dangerous, expensive and prone to obsolescence; and that when Mr. McNamara said that forces targeted on cities were lacking in credibility as a deterrent, he was suggesting not only that the British force and the coming French force were in this category, but also that this was true of the Soviet forces then targeted on the United States. As the deterrent effect of these on Mr. McNamara himself seemed all too evident, the allies could be forgiven for concluding that inferior nuclear forces were not entirely irrelevant. They also understood that things change; that no alignments have ever proved to be immutable, that the United States is prone to insist on the temporary character of its European involvement; and that nuclear weapons have been so little used in the confrontations of states that theoretical conclusions about what they can or cannot accomplish are premature.

These things were difficult to say when RAND and the State Department were watering places for a British Labour Party in search of a moralistic defense doctrine and when the broad, articulate range of French anti-Gaullist opinion was confident that anything which meant so much to de Gaulle as the *force de frappe* was almost certainly vain and foolish. We have not yet had a truly non-Gaullist regime in France to show that the nuclear program will go on; but we have had Mr. Wilson's five and a half years in which abdication was well represented in defense doctrine, but not abdication from the possession of nuclear weapons.

In my view, these nuclear programs will go on. There are critical questions to be answered about targeting and procurement, and some politicians may plan European nuclear arrangements of various kinds. Among countries which are using the term "political union" to refer to coordination of policies, there will be strong temptations to international nuclear arrangements, actual or demonstrative.

We should not forget how active the U.S. was over many years in exploring nuclear proliferation without loss of control for political purposes—in the Thor and Jupiter arrangements, in the two-key system, and in building up nuclear systems in allied countries. We can also be grateful that in the ultimate MLF adventure many people came to understand that there was a simple question—"Who can fire these weapons?"—which was the only one that really mattered.

In procurement, the British and Americans must make a major decision about the future of their nuclear arms sales and purchases. The French face a similar range of decisions. We can expect tension between the organization of an Anglo-French weapons development program and the virtual certainty that the U.S. will try to head this off by making her own systems available. Similar arguments will emerge over targeting, although here it is cheaper and easier to practice ambiguity and indecision.

All of this will provide plenty of activity for the public and strategic debate. If to some of us it seems to take on the quality of a *déjà vu* illusion, there are legions of keen-eyed young European activists from the Hebrides to the Elbe who can be expected to launch a nuclear debate every bit as naive as that sponsored by the State Department and the Bonn government in the early 1960s.

China is beyond the scope of this paper, and so is the broad prospect of nuclear proliferation. Clearly, however, nuclear weapons will continue to be important and will come slowly within the technical and financial resources of an increasing number of countries. The flirtations of Japan, Israel, India and Australia are already obvious. In other countries such as the Federal Republic of Germany, Sweden, Switzerland and South Africa, changing circumstances will be watched and debates once settled may well be revived. Neither nuclear technology nor insecurity is going to disappear. What may happen to strategic nuclear arrangements between the U.S. and Soviet Union will therefore have a direct bearing on the thinking about nuclear weapons both in the countries that possess them and in the countries that might ultimately possess them.

The reaction to SALT in Britain, France and Germany, to take the three leading European cases, has not yet been either profound or important. All three have adopted familiar stances which reflect standard attitudes rather than close analysis. The British are not going to be caught opposing something that matters to the U.S., nor are they disposed to impede the cause of righteousness, which SALT is widely assumed to represent. So the British are watching affirmatively, but keeping their counsel. The French see the outlines of a Soviet-American effort toward condominium as confirmation of the accuracy of their view of the world in contrast with the residual pro-Americanism of most of the rest of Western Europe. The Germans are somewhat confused and potentially suspicious, believing that any agreement with the Russians will have German clauses in it one way or another. The European unionists, for what they may be worth, appear to share in appropriate proportions the amiable sentiments of the British, the suspicions of the Germans and the cynicism of the French.

These reactions are visibly political or even instinctive. They are part of a broad conception of relations with the United States and Soviet Union and of traditional attitudes to disarmament. They are not at this stage derived from any clear analysis of the type of force levels or deployments which might emerge from SALT. Undoubtedly such analyses are being done in establishments that work on these problems. The politicians, however, are not now asking for their conclusions and a sound instinct is directing America's European allies to allow the U.S. for the present to make its own way in SALT. I say "sound" because I am sure there is no other policy, yet I am conscious that the last time America's allies allowed themselves to be ruled by such modesty, the issue was Vietnam.

In SALT, as in so many things, it is possible to suspect that the American objective is essentially technical and the Soviet objective political. Since the Americans are thinking in technical terms, they will be particularly insensitive to the political hesitations which are likely to be developed among secondary powers. In any case, the technical and the political are inextricably mixed.

Before examining the detailed conflicts of interest which might emerge, it should be stated that there is a clear and broad international interest in a soundly conceived American-Soviet strategic arrangement. This is easy to neglect because it is so obvious.

Every country has a powerful and decisive interest in the avoidance of nuclear war and thus in the avoidance of weapons deployments which might make war more likely. If a particular structure of weapons means that governments will decide to fire on warning, the chances of war are proportionately increased and the possible consequences of war are made more terrible. To avoid such a situation is clearly a general interest. If SALT is serving this interest, SALT is acting as an agency of the world as a whole and not just of the United States and the Soviet Union. A sense of alienation from the negotiation could conceal this from normally intelligent governments. The U.S. and the Soviet Union, however, will be powerfully placed in dealing with others to the extent that they are eliminating such dangerous elements from their arrangements. There is also a general interest in achieving a system under which responses remain controlled and directed toward traditional military objectives rather than the uncontrolled destruction of human life. These propositions are obvious, but they should precede any consideration of the complexities which SALT agreements might create.

Specific objectives which may be formulated by American and Soviet teams in SALT over a period of time are difficult to forecast. It is possible to say, however, that the American approach derives from the doctrines of deterrence and assured destruction capability. The United States would like recognition of her determination to maintain an effective countercity force in connection with the future construction and deployment of Soviet forces. She does not want a big and complex Soviet ballistic missile defense of cities. She does not want the Soviet armed forces to acquire a substantial number of reentry vehicles capable of destroying large numbers of the U.S. rocket forces. No doubt (though this has been less emphasized) she would like to see restraint in the development and deployment of anti-submarine forces in areas where missile-firing submarines operate.

Such objectives may be shared by the Soviet Union. But if they are, they are by no means new. Her equivalent of Mr. Laird's SS-9 crisis—the creation of an American force capable of doing great damage to her heavy strategic weapons on the ground—came with the deployment of 1,000 Minuteman missiles in the early 1960s. She became highly vulnerable to an American first strike. Being unwilling to bargain real objectives for such (to the Soviet Army mind) essentially secondary issues, she simply lived with this vulnerability.

If the United States is unwilling to face the same dangers and wants to talk, the Soviet government has been given clear proof of the advantages of pushing on vigorously where sound strategic arguments might have encouraged restraint. I am no authority on Soviet strategic or political thought, but if I were in the position in which they find themselves,

I would view SALT as the foundation of a political relationship of potentially great importance. To have achieved a dialogue with the United States on a central strategic issue is a bridgehead to a permanent relationship. This will be still more obvious if working understandings are established on certain matters of special importance to the U.S. The nature of strategic nuclear weapons is such that these understandings could remain valid only in the presence of a continuing and virtually permanent dialogue in which both sides would have extended opportunities for applying pressure.

It is already noticeable that U.S. anxiety for SALT encouraged the U.S. authorities to bury the Czechoslovakian issue at the earliest moment consistent with propriety and decency. (This is not one-sided; it also forced a modification in the flow of Soviet abuse over Vietnam). If the Soviet Union can enter some SALT agreements with the U.S. which are important to the U.S. but which the Soviet Union itself can take or leave (a direct consequence of the U.S. having technical objectives while the Soviet Union quite possibly does not), an important flexibility can be introduced into the Washington-Moscow relationship.

We must ask in this context what the nature of the U.S. relationship with her principal allies is, and on what it depends. Traditionally, it has been assumed that the alliance was one of dependence in which those who were threatened in Europe looked to their mighty defender across the seas for security. This view of the matter is historically misleading, but it has been important in the minds of most of those concerned. Many in Western Europe and the United States believe that their relationship depends in decisive respects on the threat of war and the unique capacity of the United States to deter the Soviet Union. Thus Europe must have the U.S. and the U.S. is trapped because she knows that she alone can maintain the vast reality of Western Europe outside the Soviet sphere of influence.

A new Soviet-American strategic relationship does not

necessarily cut across this state of affairs. It can be evolved on the sort of rivalries which were understood to lie behind the Washington naval agreements. Nevertheless, the American position in Western Europe has been linked in many people's minds to a readiness to respond with nuclear destruction on a great scale in the event of major war. In the early postwar years, the safety of the American continent from major Soviet nuclear attack was thought to be a significant source of assurance. The evolution of a substantial Soviet intercontinental force did not undermine the American commitment, but it led to the attempt to develop a counterforce capability yielding assurance that a western first strike would be disastrous for the Soviet Union.

We need not concern ourselves here with the valiant efforts of Mr. McNamara to justify his first strike capability at a time when strategic theory—which was tied to strategic nuclear war—was quite clear about how evil this was. His *obiter dicta* about hitting silos and bomber bases after the Soviet attack had landed because of the immense (and presumably decisive) unexpended power which would still be there sounded rather like some of the official reasons why Britain needed a nuclear force in addition to that of the U.S. But the European allies understood Mr. McNamara very well, indeed. They were interested in the first strike case much more than they were in the purity of the second strike forces. The reason for this is that they were primarily interested in the Soviet calculation of what would happen in a European conflict. The obvious case of this was Berlin, but generally Soviet doctrine for Europe had to be evolved in the face of what they could expect in battle situations of various kinds. If the Soviet forces proved inferior, nobody in the West would have any problems. But the real insecurity case for Europe is the one in which the Soviet forces prove superior. Here, the decisive question becomes the West's nuclear response. Unless NATO or the U.S. proclaims a doctrine (which was tried at Ann Arbor and abandoned after the comprehensible European outcry), the Soviet planners must calculate on a worst reasonable case. The West's first strike capability goes straight into this calculation. It thus plays, or is believed to play, a powerful role in the security of Europe.

The liquidation of counterforce options in a series of SALT agreements would thus return us to the problem which was avoided at the time when the Soviet Union acquired its capacity to hit the United States with thermonuclear weapons in substantial numbers. Those who had predicted that this would be the end of the American nuclear commitment to Europe—a view most prominently advocated in France, where national guarantees were nevertheless liberally handed out to the rest of Western Europe—were, in effect, sidetracked by the American first strike counterforce capability. What happens now if that is liquidated? The answer to this is more political than strategic. A readiness to respond is in the mind as much as in the forces.

The reduction of much or all of the U.S. counterforce capability as the price of restraint and reduction in the Soviet Union will demand strong American commitments to the security of Europe to match the rising price of nuclear war. Many are already saying that it implies a conventional option, although if this is so it would be best if the matter were settled first and not left to the familiar wishful thinking which dominates NATO discussion of this point. It might also be useful for the U.S. to ask itself realistically what part of a conventional option it might be expected to bear and whether it has any intention of doing so. Nothing is more pernicious in the affairs of the western alliance than the transfer of Puritan morality (and hypocrisy) by the senior member of the alliance to the security policy of the junior members. The fact is that nobody anywhere has any intention of producing the necessary forces at this stage. A SALT negotiation conducted in the early 1970s had better be conducted on this assumption.

We may therefore conclude that a far-reaching series of arrangements will have two important effects for the major European powers. It will create an American-Soviet relationship to which the United States may find itself committed in a significant way, and it will force NATO to construct its deterrent without the convenient weight of the American first strike threat. (It might be added that this second element is undoubtedly disappearing in any case with the increase in numbers, mobility and hardening of the Soviet missile forces).

I wish to examine the specific implications for the two Western lesser nuclear powers, Britain and France. Certain general questions suggest themselves to which the answers are by no means necessarily the same for both countries:

1. Have they an interest in getting into the negotiation at some stage?
2. What agreements can the U.S. and Soviet Union make without them?
3. To what extent might these agreements be discriminatory against them and to what extent do they become free beneficiaries because they cannot be asked for concessions?
4. Would the end of American-Soviet strategic counterforce options greatly increase their vulnerability by freeing forces for targeting on Anglo-French forces?
5. To what extent have Britain and France an interest in ABM restraint in the Soviet Union in order to retain a penetration capability?
6. How important is American nuclear cooperation and to what extent would it be affected by the kind of agreements SALT might achieve?

The question of broadening negotiation is likely to be a difficult one for the Soviet Union. One of the attractions of SALT to the Russians is that it proclaims Soviet-American parity and allows them to persuade themselves that they are half of some kind of world condominium. But it will obviously be an unattractive situation for the Soviets if they get American agreement to forms of restraint and then find that other members of NATO can go on unchecked in these technologies.

The Soviet instinct will be to insist that it is the Americans' business to control their clients. They assumed that the Americans would control Israel in 1967. The fact is that the Americans cannot control Britain and France without dealing with them (many would say that they cannot control France even then). It is the Soviets who do not want them in, and Moscow is thus pursuing a double policy. But its contradiction could be shifted to Washington if the U.S. could be persuaded that the allies should be threatened with a withdrawal of guarantees if they do not fall into line.

It may be doubted whether any U.S. administration would be so foolish as to play with this sort of fire. If the SALT agreements need others, we may therefore assume that the base of the negotiation will have to be broadened. The probability is that the Russians will be prepared to do without Anglo-French commitments rather than sacrifice the essential political objective of SALT, which is the unique bilateral link with the United States. In the present phase, most of the important agreements can probably be made without Britain or France, which do not possess and are not planning a significant counterforce capability. Any restraint in the deployment of anti-submarine forces would affect them, but their own nuclear forces are such obvious beneficiaries of such an arrangement that they could be expected to give tacit cooperation.

The decisions about ballistic missile defenses are important for Britain and France and both Washington and Moscow will obviously be conscious of this. The Americans have developed the doctrine of city defenses against the secondary nuclear power (China), but not the primary. It may be asked whether the Soviets have not as well, and if so whether this is not the logical line down which to find an American-Soviet agreement. There are obvious difficulties in this. Above all, there is the problem of where you draw the line, especially when dealing with the substantial and possibly coordinated nuclear forces which Britain and France could well be deploying later in the decade.

The evolution of a counterforce capability against minor nuclear powers would be a probable consequence of its abandonment by the major powers. But here again there is a difficulty. Both Britain and France (especially Britain) are putting their main efforts into missile-firing submarines. It is difficult to see how a counterforce capability could be mounted specifically against these submarines. The choice of this particular weapons base makes the forces of each fade into the environment of the other and removes all prospect of discrimination. The same could not be said of the French land-based missile forces which must be regarded now, as then, as first strike forces.

The prospect of ABM restraint by the Soviets is immensely important for both Britain and France. They will no doubt be forced into a substantial expansion of their forces if they face a major Soviet ABM buildup. But so will the Americans, with all the familiar objections about mutual overreaction which have led to SALT. It is going to be difficult for the SALT partners to have it both ways, and even if the British and French are brought into the negotiation they cannot be expected to agree to give up their ability to strike Soviet cities.

Finally, there is the question of U.S. nuclear cooperation. This has saved the United Kingdom a great deal of money, although it has forced her to spend substantial sums outside the country which might have maintained her own nuclear industries. Disarmament by embrace has worked to a significant extent with the British, although not, of course, with de Gaulle's France. U.S. nuclear cooperation may be much more reluctant in the future if Britain sustains her European ambitions and continues to give evidence that she understands the implications of these. Nevertheless, the need to sustain the Atlantic system will remain overriding under all but the most foolish of leaders. This will impose unavoidable conclusions on the Americans in the future as it has in the past.

One of the subtle implications of SALT is that it could greatly increase the identification of nuclear weapons with status. The naval agreements had this effect on capital ships. The 5-5-3 ratio was a kind of proclamation of status. When the rising power wanted to challenge the system, he reached out for the military option specifically because it had a political standing. Such considerations of prestige are still exceedingly important. They will become more important if the world order as a whole has to act more to protect itself and so has to achieve a means of reaching decisions. The assemblage of a political consensus depends on a pre-existing consensus about how important each of the actors is.

The desire for influence is a powerful element in making a world order possible. But the 1930s demonstrated how destructive can be the notion that one's country is not accorded its proper place. Ambitious politicians will make their challenge at the point they consider important. The attempt to construct nuclear limits founded on a narrow range of powers could itself be a major stimulus to those who think they do not have an important enough place in the world order. In this regard, the makers of SALT will have to take care that they do not add to the prestige of strategic nuclear arms and so add to the incentive to acquire them.

8 • Nuclear Weapons, The Pacific, and SALT

Harry G. Gelber

During 1971, the SALT talks between the U.S. and the Soviet Union became an accepted part of the international landscape. Since they are in mid-stream, it seems useful to consider their impact on a number of minor nuclear and some nonnuclear nations around the Pacific. These states are not parties to the talks. They do not have the intimate relationship with Washington and its strategic thinking of America's NATO allies. But a part of their future, too, is being decided. This paper will, after a few general introductory remarks, briefly discuss the SALT talks themselves and then China, Japan and Australia.

One of the basic concerns of many medium and smaller states is the fragmentation of the international system. Modern diplomatic history has usually veered between seeking security in alliances or seeking it in isolation from the troubles of others. The first can prevent or damp down conflicts, but at the cost of engagements in faraway disputes that new generations of voters find too burdensome. Isolation, or ring-holding, on the other hand, avoids such early involvement but sometimes at the cost of facing large-scale conflicts in more unfavorable circumstances later on, conflicts whose eruption an earlier engagement might have helped to prevent. In 1918–19 a grand alliance imposed peace upon a defeated Germany and sentenced the Austro-Hungarian Empire to dismemberment in the name of a self-determination which the peoples of that Empire had not initially sought. A mere twenty years later a British Prime Minister, responding to voters with instincts very similar to those of many American liberals of 1970–71, dismissed Czechoslovakia as "a faraway country of which we know nothing."

Public opinion in many countries is clearly impatient with problems of foreign affairs, let alone the burdens of alliance. At the same time the technological and economic gap between the advanced powers and others is, if anything, increasing. This produces a dilemma. Many nations desire freedom of maneuver, independence, and shedding of costs as a result of limiting their commitments. But smaller nations also desire continued protection, at least at the nuclear level, from their superpower allies, while those allies have been forced to recognize the limitations on the independent defense capacities of their smaller friends.

The fact that these wishes, for security and disarmament, for independence and protection, are often incompatible does not prevent them from being simultaneously pursued, usually with passion. This ambivalence is also apparent in the smaller powers' attitude to SALT. Its results will determine an important part of the framework for their own political lives. Yet they are mere spectators. It is, perhaps, inevitable that many of them prefer to concentrate their attention on issues where they can act, not merely look on. To this there is one important exception. They will watch SALT not for its details but for the emerging evidence as to the will of the great powers, especially the U.S., to go on protecting their allies. Will has become more interesting, because more doubtful, than hardware.

Two other points should, perhaps, be made about foreign perspectives on much of the American public and academic debate on arms control. Governments, as distinct from academics, find it hard to take seriously the kind of approach which discusses policy as if U.S. and Soviet interests and ambitions were somehow equal or equivalent or mirror images of each other; as if their political and strategic concerns could be usefully analyzed in the same way and by using the same criteria. The details of strategic postures on each side owe much to internal political and administrative debates in which the position of the opponent abroad is only marginally relevant. American and Soviet views are based on different geographic, ethnic, and economic circumstances, different alliance concerns, different ideologies and assumptions of many kinds. Neither morally nor politically are they comparable quantities, except in particular and carefully defined senses. There is no sign that they have identical strategic aims or similar nuclear weapons policies.

The other point is that the views of various powers on nuclear strategy cannot usefully be measured on some linear scale. There has been some disposition in the U.S. to imagine that all nuclear weapons concerns are similar in kind, and that other nations are sophisticated in proportion as they appreciate or can take part in the technicalities of the nuclear debate as defined in the U.S. This is a fallacy. Many of them are more concerned with dangers, to them more realistic, which involve less complex nuclear devices in the hands of smaller nuclear powers. All of them have different geographic, technological, political, and therefore strategic concerns. The relationships between domestic politics and international stability, the character of foreign threats, the details of force structure and its economic and technical determinants, are for them not simpler, but simply different.

First, then, the SALT talks themselves. Though it is pointless at this stage to try to predict exactly what will emerge, the aims of both sides in pursuing the talks can be summarized as follows: Each side wishes to increase its control over the political consequences of technical developments by both sides, and to reduce the dangers of accidents or miscalculation. Each side wishes to reduce the uncertainties which new weapons systems threaten to introduce into their strategic relationship. Each would like to be able to spend less money on strategic arms.

Second, each side will wish to make maximum propaganda use of the talks and to avoid the political costs of not seeming to pursue them in good faith.

Third, each side has more specific aims vis-à-vis the other. The Soviet Union wishes to use the talks, and the Congressional pressures created in Washington by the fact that they are going on, to prevent the U.S. from spurting ahead in weapons technology. Moscow may yet aim at strategic superiority. Doubtless the Soviets also want to use the talks to create as much disunity as possible between America and her allies. The U.S. wishes to combine the achievement of some control over weapons developments with the prevention of a Soviet achievement of genuine strategic equality. Since a measure of parity in some weapons systems cannot be prevented, the U.S. will further wish to minimize the Soviet political gains which are likely to result.

Fourth, each side probably wishes to insulate the strategic relationship between them from disruption by third parties. Whatever else the Soviet and American governments have agreed to discuss, it is not the abandonment of their superpower status or the accession of other nations to their club. It has seemed in recent years that the U.S. was pursuing this aim (as well as others) by such means as the Nuclear Non-Proliferation Treaty, intended to pursuade other states to abstain from developing nuclear weapons. But the smaller powers asked that, as the price for their abstention, the U.S. and the U.S.S.R. should gradually abandon their nuclear dominance. This was, of course, a quite dubious suggestion. There could be no guarantee that, even if Soviet and American nuclear arms were reduced, others would actually abstain from producing weapons of their own. Still less was it spelled out how such reductions were to be made compatible with the maintenance of credible superpower protection for allies, or how they would make war less likely. This seems to be one reason for the more recent shift of emphasis to vertical proliferation as a way of denying to third powers the option of entering the great power club and of making minor nuclear capabilities more innocuous from the point of view of the great power balance.

But the more important reason may be the potential danger of allowing any third power to gain an effective retaliatory capability against both the Soviet Union and the U.S. Most obviously, this means China.

The point is not that China is likely to welcome great nuclear risks. It is rather that any Chinese miscalculation—and the absence of a strategic dialogue with Peking by either Moscow or Washington makes such miscalculation more possible—may in some circumstances increase the danger of war between America and Russia themselves. If the United States, for example, abstained from all forms of thin BMD cover for its population, the creation of a Chinese ICBM force would greatly increase the compulsion to launch a U.S. pre-emptive strike in times of crisis. The more vulnerable such a Chinese force was, the greater the assumed temptation for its commanders to launch it; therefore, the more acute the U.S. need to pre-empt in a crisis. It would, however, remain necessary to maintain, throughout such a period, the American deterrent posture vis-à-vis the Soviet Union. Such deterrence might become doubtful either as a result of a partially effective Chinese strike against the U.S. or if too great a proportion of some American weapons systems (perhaps numerically limited by then under a SALT-type agreement) had been used up against China.

The problem could be still more acute if, as a result of withdrawals from East Asia, the U.S. had lost the facilities needed to launch an effective strike against China by land or carrier-based aircraft, or by medium-range weapons, and had therefore been compelled to use up a greater proportion of her land-based missiles and SLBMs. A significant diminution of the American capabilities is of itself equivalent to an increase in the Soviet first-strike potential.

The question for U.S. decision-makers would therefore be whether Moscow would remain adequately deterred by the reduced U.S. weapons capability. The question for Moscow would be how the U.S. would react to the change, what risks she felt able to tolerate in the new situation, and whether the U.S. would continue to feel able to avoid forward and pre-emptive action. In any case, both sides would regard the risks of the nuclear confrontation as significantly increased. From the point of view of both Moscow and Washington the fact that the Chinese action which could trigger such a process is highly improbable is much less important than the notion that their own political control over the course of events would be significantly decreased.

It therefore seems safe to list some other things which SALT will not do. It will not end the arms race. Insofar as it is effective, it will redirect weapons research into new channels not covered by SALT agreements. It already seems likely that the types of weaponry on which discussion has centered—land-based launchers, ABM systems, MIRVs—have a useful life whose end may be visible on the horizon. That is presumably one reason why the two sides could agree to limit them. But research and development, and probably deployment, of such technologies as submarine-borne ballistic missile defenses, long-range submarines, orbital reconnaissance, strike and defense systems, perhaps quite new BMD concepts, will go on.

It is also possible that there will be swifter progress with the miniaturization of nuclear weapons, with yields in the single-figure kiloton range and short-term radiation effects. Such weapons, for tactical use by forces in the field, would tend to close any but the psychological gap between nuclear and other forms of weapons. They would be much less calamitous and need not imply uncontrolled escalation to higher levels of weaponry. Their use might therefore be subject to fewer hesitations.

SALT cannot, irrespective of the wishes of the two parties, result in an agreement which would disbar the two sides from weapons developments in fully reliable fashion. The reasons are obvious. The increasing complexity of technical developments makes it almost impossible to draft any legal document which could wholly contain them. An agreement not laid down in writing, on the other hand, might be effective in many ways but not in preventing progress in weapons technology. And in any case no agreement, formal or informal, can by definition anticipate discoveries which have not yet been made.

Nor, again, will SALT necessarily lower hostility between the two sides. It may limit hostility. But a general lessening of tension is a different matter which depends on much broader political changes. One reason is perhaps sufficient. Hostility to the West in general and the United States in particular is essential to the Soviet government for legitimization of the Soviet system itself. Hostility is required for domestic purposes and will persist, irrespective therefore of rhetoric, until that domestic need no longer exists. But that hostility will not be uncontrolled; there is no reason to suppose that, even in the absence of a SALT agreement, the two sides would engage in an open-ended arms race. There is equally no reason to think that the absence of such agreement need make war more likely. It is doubtful whether there is any simple link between the success of SALT and the likelihood of a Soviet-American conflict.

What, then, is SALT likely to achieve? Currently the most probable outcome seems to be an agreement to limit the number of ICBM launchers or to limit ABM deployment by each side, or both. Somewhat further away, but apparently still possible, would be a limitation of other offensive systems, including forward-based systems capable of reaching the national territory of either of the two powers; and perhaps a limitation on the throw-weight of existing launchers as a way of tackling the MIRV problem.

Many variations of such agreements might be feasible. A special limit on large launchers like the Soviet SS-9 has been mentioned. ABM might be limited as to area covered, as in the suggestion that cover be confined to the national command and control center on each side. Or else point defense capabilities might be confined to the Minuteman fields. Such forms of agreement may well create important political pressures, especially within the U.S., for a slowing down of other arms developments. But apart from this it would encourage rather than discourage research and development on systems which remained outside the ambit of the SALT agreement. This would include research on novel concepts about thin area cover defenses, useful against a first-generation force in the hands of a third party, about which Defense Secretary Melvin Laird has spoken.

For other and smaller nations, novel political considerations would arise. The greater the technical complexities of the strategic balance between the superpowers, the greater the range of performance uncertainties and of risks which face any political leadership contemplating the use of such weapons. The closer the two sides appear to get to a rough parity of capabilities, the more its implications will be equivalent to a mutual pledge of no first use. Such a pledge the U.S. has so far refused to give. The achievement of parity by the Soviet Union would amount to conceding it. In consequence, there would be decreased risks for an opponent that American nuclear weapons would be used in response to anything less than a direct attack upon U.S. troops or territory.

From the point of view of America's allies, doubts about the credibility of American nuclear protection would grow. Insofar as U.S. nuclear protection continued to function at all, it could be expected to result merely in a mutual standoff at the strategic level. For a number of small nations this might actually increase the danger of conflict at lesser and subnuclear levels. Smaller nations may therefore face novel difficulties whatever the result of SALT. If the two great powers approach parity, the nuclear guarantee which each offers to its allies will become more doubtful. If they slow down weapons developments to the point where some third power achieves a credible second strike capability against one or both of them, the situation might be even worse. It would combine reduced credibility for great power guarantees for their smaller allies with greater risks and dangers in the relations among the great powers themselves.

To summarize: smaller nations will watch with care three types of consequence of the SALT talks. First, the conclusions to be drawn from any agreement, from the way it is reached, and from the surrounding circumstances as to the general will and determination of the great powers to maintain strategic stability, including their own commitments. Second, the extent to which the great powers are willing to risk the development by additional powers of effective deterrents against one or both of them. Small allies will watch the extent to which the great powers slow down technical developments in the weapons field, though there will be a genuine conflict between their strategic concern for protection and their public and political protestations calling for a slowdown in the general arms race. Such a slowdown, they will argue, was implied by the spirit of both SALT and previous agreements in the field, like the NPT and the partial test ban treaty. Third, they will be interested in any new family of miniaturized weapons which may be developed and in the appropriate scientific information which the U.S. may make available to selected friendly nations. This would present fewest problems in the cases of France and Britain, which already possess nuclear capabilities. But if the information is made available at all, pressures will inevitably arise for its dissemination to others, notably to Japan.

China's broad aims in the world remain connected with general recognition of her as one of the world's great powers. She wishes the discrepancy between her actual and her potential influence to be eliminated. Western influence is to be largely removed from East and Southern Asia, two areas where Peking wishes to exercise a general dominance. A united front has been organized with "progressive" Asians from North Korea to Indo-China. Peking will continue, at least for the time being, to encourage the development of what she regards as genuine Marxist-Leninist-Maoist parties and movements elsewhere. She will continue her leadership of, and support for, revolution abroad so long as this does not involve important dangers for China herself. The struggle against capitalism and revisionism will be maintained for the time being, though this will not prevent particular accommodations and interstate agreements where these are felt to be to China's benefit. Peking will seek to be the "elder brother" of smaller nations, not least with a view to redressing the balance against both superpowers. Mr. Chou's more flexible diplomacy has, during 1970–71, greatly improved Peking's posture and included some gains of substance. Entry into the U.N. has been something of a diplomatic triumph for China.

She is developing strategic arms for a variety of purposes. She has joined the nuclear club as part of her claim to great power status. She wants a measure of deterrence against threats from the U.S. or the U.S.S.R. and, perhaps, Japan. But that deterrence is intended as much to insulate China from outside interference and to allow her to concentrate on her enormous domestic problems, as to give her freedom of movement abroad.

Peking must be very conscious of the smallness and relative vulnerability of her initial nuclear force. There is so far little sign that the caution which has characterized Chinese strategic policies over the last decade is being abandoned. One would certainly expect that in the face of physical threats to national security that caution will continue, that China will be reluctant to take high risks or engage in forward military action rather than politically and strategically more ambiguous enterprises. Apart, therefore, from the strategic deterrence of potential attacks upon China, one would expect an emerging Chinese nuclear weapons capability to be employed in oblique and low-level ways so as to exercise political pressure and influence rather than as a way of openly threatening her neighbors.

For some time to come, that capability is in any case likely to be comparatively small and vulnerable. A few ICBMs, or even a second-generation force with a 6,000-mile range using a solid propellant, will not amount to a first-class force. And though a Chinese development of multiple warheads and penetration aids has been publicly discussed, it seems in fact doubtful whether China yet commands the electronic and computer capabilities required to close the technological gap between herself and the U.S. At the same time there is no suggestion that China would fail to take advantage of the removal of past constraints, whether internal or external. There has been no indication as yet that China might be prepared to slow down or amend her arms program in order to accommodate herself to general schemes of arms control. Indeed, virtually every one of the Soviet or American approaches to such control over the last decade has been attacked as another step toward consolidating the Soviet-American nuclear duopoly. The Chinese have detected anti-Chinese elements in almost all measures of arms control so far proposed, including SALT.

The difficulty is that they are right. Insofar as an arms agreement may be directed against third powers, it will be directed also against China. Insofar as SALT limits long-range delivery systems, it will do nothing about the IRBMs, MRBMs or the aircraft stationed in Soviet Asia and capable of striking at most of North and Central China including Manchuria and Peking. Nor will it affect American bases, sea-based systems, or medium-range strike capabilities in Korea, Japan, or the seas between Japan and the Philippines —not to mention U.S. bomber bases in such places as Thailand.

China cannot be expected to welcome a SALT agreement which limits threats to the Soviet and U.S. homelands, but leaves all these systems unaffected. In addition it seems likely that even if the two superpowers limit ABM systems, they will retain protection for their national command centers (and perhaps construct some forms of light cover for other populated areas). This will have a particular role in preventing small first-generation forces in the hands of third powers such as China from achieving a useful measure of direct or triangular deterrence against the great powers. It is true that some forms of arms control agreement could be in China's interest, at least in preventing a widening of the weapons technology gap between China and the superpowers. But for the time being China seems content to use her exclusion from arms control discussions to secure diplomatic leverage against the two great powers. Peking may calculate that in the longer run any stable Indo-Pacific balance, and any significant arms control agreement, must secure China's consent if it is to be effective. At any rate Peking has as yet given no sign that it regards any of the more likely outcomes of SALT as acceptable or that it will interpret a SALT agreement otherwise than as a concerted Soviet-American attempt to keep China in her place.

There is a further concern: about Japan. Here, Peking faces a dilemma. The diminishing U.S. presence in East Asia is welcome. But it also involves an increase in Japan's forces. Indeed, China claims to fear that the U.S. is actively urging Japan to acquire nuclear weapons and that, in any case, the decreased credibility attaching to a U.S. guarantee of Japan against the U.S.S.R. which may result from a SALT agreement will push Japan in this direction.

Such a Japanese force, once created, might be a greater threat to China than that previously posed by U.S. containment. As against this, Japanese accession to nuclear status would tend to create a four-cornered nuclear situation in North East Asia. This might result in an increasingly rigid standoff at the nuclear level with still greater freedom to wage conventional conflict at lower levels of violence. In that case China might benefit from the resulting upgrading in conventional military forces and therefore of her vast manpower reserves.

Very different are the nuclear defense concerns of Japan. Threats have been perceived as coming from the Soviet Union and, to some extent, from a nuclear-armed China. But it is nonnuclear or doubtfully nuclear conflicts which have seemed more likely to occur and therefore to require most attention. These have involved such matters as the security of Japan's trade and shipping routes and perhaps the disputes which surround claims to the natural resources of the East Asian continental shelf. There has been the problem of Taiwan and above all that of the politico-military balance in Korea.

Many Japanese doubt whether a real nuclear threat to their home islands exists. In so far as it may, the first line of defense is the U.S. guarantee. And they do not perceive a serious threat to the survivability of the U.S. deterrent. They seem to assume that the U.S. will retain, whether by increased dispersal or mobility of American ICBMs in the United States, or BMD, or through building new and longer-range submarines, the physical capability required for strategic deterrence of the Soviet Union.

Of greater concern than the details of SALT, therefore, seem to be some other groups of questions whose answers depend not only on strategic force developments but on the whole spectrum of U.S. activities in the Pacific and East Asia. There is a fear that strategic deterrence, even if it is available and technically effective, will not be usable against indirect and lower level threats. American tactical and nonnuclear deterrence, on the other hand, has lost some credibility not as a result of SALT but in consequence of the U.S. withdrawal from Japan, Okinawa, and Korea, not to mention U.S. political overtures toward China.

Some Japanese argue, for example, that the U.S. is losing the ability adequately to deter a North Korean attack southwards. U.S. ICBMs pointed at Moscow, it is argued, would not be relevant to such a development, given the increasing power of the Soviet second-strike capability. Local deterrence, however, would require the maintenance of precisely those bases in Japan which the U.S., acting under obvious political pressures both in America and Japan, is progressively abandoning. The circumstances under which Japanese air bases would in future emergencies be available to the U.S. Air Force are not clear. South Korean bases, on the other hand, would all be within reach of North Korean ground-to-ground missiles, of fighter bombers, and in some cases even of conventional artillery.

The alternative would be carrier-based air cover. But for sustained operations in Korean waters, U.S. carriers would probably need access to Japanese harbors and certainly the visible tolerance (implying non-neutrality in conflict situations) of the Japanese government.

There are other doubts. What would the U.S. promise, to provide a nuclear shield for her allies, mean in practice once U.S. forces—which represent a hostage in case of conflict—have been removed from Japan? The U.S. has announced that its future involvements in the region will not be automatic. If a threat to Japan were to arise, the U.S. would have to decide whether to respond by making a demonstrative counter-threat or by a precautionary forward deployment of forces. Either would require a major exercise of political will which cannot be taken for granted. A renewed forward deployment would encounter political and legal difficulties both in Japan and the U.S. The modalities of crisis reentry by the U.S. are not clear. Another possibility might be the threat of a pre-emptive strike, at a low level of violence, at the bases from which Japan was being threatened. But the U.S. is removing from the region much of the capability for mounting just such lower-level threats. All these doubts must be reinforced by the political impact of U.S. moves toward China and the economic measures in defense of the dollar, with their profound impact upon Japan.

It is therefore not surprising that Japan has been reluctant to accept the Non-Proliferation Treaty. She has signed, for a variety of reasons connected with domestic politics, the maintenance of U.S. goodwill, a wish not to encourage general proliferation and a desire not to appear threatening to her neighbors. But signature need not imply eventual ratification. Japan's nuclear capabilities are being refined. Her dilemma is real. She is concerned not to provoke others, especially the Soviet Union. She is conscious of her vulnerability as a small island nation where dispersal of population or of forces is not feasible. The government would hardly wish to court the domestic political problems involved in openly abandoning Japan's nonnuclear policies. It may also fear that the acquisition of a nuclear capability could lead to some Sino-Soviet combination against Japan, without necessarily leading to closer strategic cooperation with the U.S. One way of preventing this danger, as well as others, would be through closer Japanese political ties with the U.S.S.R.

On the other hand, the partial U.S. withdrawal faces Tokyo with real potential problems. Except for reentry vehicle technology Japan possesses many of the techniques required to construct a nuclear force. She could acquire a second-strike capacity, even in great power terms, by building submarines. Or she could concentrate on defensive systems such as ABM, which would give some sense of security and also have implications for the refinement of a strike capability in case of need.

It is not yet obvious where the solution of these conundrums will lie. But it seems likely that the combination of the Nixon doctrine, American domestic political disenchantment with security commitments, and the SALT evidence for America's future strategic intentions will cause some serious reappraisals of the situation in Tokyo.

Australians are also asking themselves whether a nuclear weapons option needs to be created or refined, and if so over what time period. But the parameters, as well as the contents, of the Australian argument are very different from the concerns of Japan.

Australians are very conscious of the fact that, in a period of fragmenting international responsibilities and emphasis on noncommitment, the old guidelines for policy may not serve. Nuclear weapons questions are subordinate, in terms of urgency, to a whole variety of matters concerned with the Soviet conventional presence in the Indian Ocean, the stability of Malaysia, the security of Singapore, the internal development of Indonesia, and the relationship between that populous nation and her neighbors.

But at the core of the Australian concern lies the maintenance of the U.S. alliance. This involves maintaining American interest, credibility, and a continuing U.S. influence upon the political balance of the Indo-Pacific region.

For Australia, therefore, the growth of China's nuclear capacity is less important than the relationship between it and both America and Japan. The character and extent of the U.S. interest in Australia, the ability of China to acquire an effective second-strike capability against the U.S., the influence of these matters on the exercise of nuclear weapons options in Japan—these are the sorts of matters which will determine the Australian outlook.

There are at least three reasons for regarding the American commitment to Australia as, at present, credible. The alliance between the two countries has been repeatedly reaffirmed by successive administrations and not yet seriously questioned by anyone. Partly in consequence, a visible abandoning of Australia would create important problems for U.S. credibility in most other areas of the globe. And, in any case, Australia's geographic position makes direct threats to her unlikely and an indirect and low-level military approach extremely difficult.

But other dangers remain. U.S. ability to protect Australia might diminish if her weapons technology lagged. American commitments might be gradually redefined in ways unfavorable to Australia. Other nations in Southern and Eastern Asia—Japan, India, and Indonesia are obvious possibilities—might acquire independent nuclear capabilities. Australia would probably not wish to be debarred from exercising a weapons option as part of her response to such developments. For the time being, however, there is no reason for her to incur the heavy diplomatic and political costs of doing so. Nor does Australia yet have the ability to launch a weapons program. She has no source of weapons-grade fissile material, for instance, and the diversion of resources to a weapons program, especially of scarce scientific and technological manpower, would have very serious consequences for the economy.

On the other hand, Australia is planning to acquire her first—foreign-built—power reactor, as the opening move in a reactor program which is likely to be needed for a variety of legitimate economic purposes. The whole future development of the Australian continent is likely to be bound up with various peaceful applications of nuclear power. The processing of Australian uranium resources offers glittering commercial prizes. Australia is a party to the partial test ban treaty. Her two existing experimental reactors operate under IAEA safeguards. She has signed, though not yet ratified, the Non-Proliferation Treaty. It is clear that the speedy and efficient acquisition of nuclear technology from the U.S., Britain, Canada, or Europe depends to some extent upon the confidence of those nations that Australia will not use their help to produce weapons. Yet in the longer term the growth of her general capabilities in these fields will inevitably make it possible for Australia to produce reactors, fissile material, and bombs of her own, even if she should not have access to special categories of scientific information from her military allies. It seems likely that Australia could be in a position to produce some simple kinds of fission weapons by 1978–1980. And the NPT contains an escape clause.

Whether or when that escape clause will be used, and the growing Australian option transformed into operational nuclear weapons, depends upon developments which cannot now be foreseen. It seems likely, however, that the more rigid the nuclear parity established between the Soviet Union and the United States, the more absolute the standoff between them, the more likely will be military actions at lower levels of violence by various states, not least in such areas of Australian concern as the Middle East and Southern and Eastern Asia. The more likely, also, that various other nations will build nuclear forces, albeit comparatively elementary ones, of their own. Such developments—if they occur, and they may not—would not lead to increased confidence in the military reliability of America, as distinct from her usefulness as a source of political support or technical and economic advantage. In such circumstances, Australian abstention from a nuclear weapons capability could not be guaranteed.

One point which, I hope, emerges from this brief sketch is the very great differences in the perspectives of various countries on matters of arms control and disarmament, including SALT. The whole balance of political concerns, geographic circumstances, strategic and economic ties, are entirely different for each of these states. No single set of SALT agreements is conceivable which could assuage the fears and fulfil the hopes of all these states equally. SALT may therefore somewhat change the circumstances of world politics. But it will not eliminate or even greatly slow down progress in weapons development or the evolution of the strategic patterns of the world.

We might also pause to remember that one rarely solves great international problems. One survives them. To suppose that problems always have solutions is naive. To suppose that one can foresee all the important secondary consequences of one's actions is likely to be intellectual arrogance. SALT may help to contain weapons developments at the margin. The talks may somewhat increase the degree of control of national governments over the course of events. But they will also lead to new problems for the international community, not necessarily smaller or less important than those which now confront the SALT negotiators.

9 • Arms Control and Technological Change

Freeman J. Dyson

There are two extreme points of view concerning the relation of technological change to arms control. I will call these the technocrat's and the diplomat's points of view, although I am well aware that few technocrats and few diplomats hold such oversimplified positions.

The technocrat's view is that technological facts must be decisive in assessing the feasibility or desirability of arms-control measures. Much of the public debate on arms-control issues in the United States has been conducted as if the technocrat's view were valid. For example, the discussions of a comprehensive test ban in the years 1958–63 revolved around esoteric questions of earthquake statistics and seismic instrumentation, until some of our Senators became as expert in seismology as the professors of geophysics who came to testify before them. A similar syndrome can be seen now in the public discussion of the current Strategic Arms Limitation Talks (SALT). A large part of it centers around detailed estimates of kill-ratios and cost-ratios, the feasibility of monitoring multiple warhead guidance development tests, and so forth, as if these were the only things that mattered.

In contrast, the diplomat's view is that arms control is a political problem in which technological factors in any but the broadest outline are irrelevant. Kennan was not thinking about arms control when he wrote in his *Memoirs:* "The more I see of the life of this international society the more I am convinced that it is the shadows rather than the substance of things that move the hearts, and sway the deeds, of statesmen" [p. 351]. He is too many-sided a man to hold oversimplified views about anything. Still, his words express well the essence of the diplomat's view, that arms control measures are not different in character from other political arrangements, and that the political shadows thrown by our weapon deployments are more important than their technical substance.

My main purpose here is to examine whether the technocrat's view or the diplomat's view comes closer to the truth. I shall discuss in turn three examples of arms control problems in which technological change plays an important role. I make no apology for giving part of the discussion an autobiographical flavor. A man often learns more from unimportant events in which he has been directly involved, than from important events which he sees only through books and newspapers. If you would like a more sensational title, it might be "How a Bomb-Designer Came to Believe that the Bomb Is Irrelevant." But this would also be an oversimplification.

I will begin the discussion with an episode from my own past. Once I spent a few weeks at the nuclear weapons laboratory at Livermore helping to design bombs. I was there during the bomb-test moratorium which began in August 1958 and continued until 1961. These were the only years in which our bomb designers had to do their work without nuclear tests of any kind. I worked with a small group of theoretical people who were thinking about radical improvements in weapon design. We had a number of ideas which seemed to make technical sense, and which would have had major effects on the weapons stockpile if they could have been implemented.

The result of my visit to Livermore was an article which appeared in the April 1960 issue of *Foreign Affairs* under the title "The Future Development of Nuclear Weapons." This article presents in impassioned prose the technocrat's view of arms-control problems. The main thesis of the article is that a permanent test ban would be a dangerous illusion, because future improvements in weapons technology would create irresistible pressures toward secret or open violation of any such ban. When I reread this article now, I do not know whether to be amused or ashamed. I quote now a couple of pages which will give you the flavor of it:

> I believe that radically new kinds of nuclear weapons are technically possible, that the military and political effects of such weapons would be important, and that the development of such weapons can hardly be arrested by any means less drastic than international control of all nuclear operations. . . .
>
> A fission bomb cannot explode at all unless it contains a certain quantity (the critical mass) of extremely expensive metal. . . . So the basic characteristic of all existing weapons is that it is relatively much cheaper to make a big bang than a small one. Below a certain yield of the order of a kiloton, nuclear weapons are grossly inefficient and extravagant. However, for military purposes other than wholesale annihilation, a kiloton is already an unreasonably big bang. There is a clear and acute military need for an explosive which would fill the gap between a ton and a kiloton of TNT with a cost which is proportional to the yield instead of being independent of it.
>
> There is theoretically a simple way to escape from the tyranny of the critical mass. This is to burn heavy hydrogen without a fission bomb to ignite it. A fission-free bomb, containing a small quantity of heavy hydrogen and no fissionable metal, is logically the third major step in weapon development after

> the existing fission and hydrogen bombs. Such a bomb has been occasionally mentioned in newspapers and magazines and described as a "100-percent clean bomb." It would not be 100 percent clean. It would contaminate the countryside enormously less than existing fission or hydrogen bombs, but this is not its main advantage. The decisive advantage of a fission-free bomb is that it could be built economically in small sizes. It would have no critical mass. It would provide without gross inefficiency an explosive power adapted to the needs of small-scale and local warfare. . . .
>
> Imagine a hypothetical situation in which the United States is armed with its existing weapons, while some adversary (not necessarily the Soviet Union) has a comparable supply of nuclear fuel and has learned how to ignite it fission-free. The adversary's bombs would then outnumber ours ten or a hundred to one, and theirs could be used with far greater versatility in infantry warfare. . . . Any country which renounces for itself the development of nuclear weapons, without certain knowledge that its adversaries have done the same, is likely to find itself in the position of the Polish army in 1939, fighting tanks with horses.

There is a lot more of the same kind of rhetoric. The gist of the argument is that fission-free weapons are the wave of the future, and that any political arrangement which ignores or denies their birthright is doomed to failure. This is the technocrat's view with a vengeance. It is perhaps worthwhile to analyze in some detail the mistakes in this *Foreign Affairs* article. It is now clear to me that the conclusions of the article are wrong; yet in 1960 the editors of *Foreign Affairs* thought that the arguments had enough merit to be worth publishing. If we can identify the points at which these arguments went astray, this should help us to see in other situations the ways in which a technocrat's view of arms control may be misleading.

I was wrong on three counts, technical, military, and political. Technically, I misjudged the time-scale for development of fission-free weapons. I expected that they would be a reality within less than ten years. They may yet make their appearance, but ten years have passed without any visible sign of them. If during these years there had been a spectacular technical success, I imagine that we should all have heard about it. Things of that sort do not stay secret long in the United States. So the first lesson to be learned from this episode is that, even on the technical aspects of future technology, the judgment of a scientist is not always to be trusted.

Militarily I was wrong because I believed in "tactical nuclear war" as a feasible means of employing military forces. In 1960 I was not alone in this belief. I have since taken part in some detailed studies of tactical nuclear war, and I have seen the results of some relevant war games played by professionals. I am now convinced that tactical nuclear war, conducted between any two nuclear powers, will quickly degenerate into an uncontrollable chaos that can be terminated only by an immediate cease-fire (if we are lucky) or by an escalation to strategic strikes (if we are unlucky). If either case the outcome of the war will hardly be affected by the presence of fission-free weapons in the tactical forces on one or both sides of the initial conflict. The best that one can hope for from fission-free weapons is that they may reduce the level of general devastation in a conflict that is successfully halted at a very early stage. If the conflict is not halted within a few hours, the impossibility of knowing precisely where the enemy is will compel both sides to use high-yield weapons if they were not doing so at the outset.

Politically I was wrong in saying that a test ban would necessarily be ineffective as a means of stopping development of fission-free weapons. A total test ban would certainly stop *us* from developing these weapons. If it were known that we had stopped work on them and did not consider them to be scientifically or militarily important, the incentive for any other power to put much effort into developing them would be greatly reduced. In these circumstances, a total test ban would probably be successful in discouraging the signatory nations from building fission-free weapons, even if the necessary clandestine tests would be of such low yield as to be technically undetectable. On the other hand, the one way to make certain that our adversaries would soon possess these weapons would be for us to develop and deploy them ourselves.

I now believe that we should regard fission-free nuclear weapons politically as having the same characteristics as biological weapons. There are no plausible circumstances in which we would derive any meaningful advantage from using such weapons, even if they were first used against us. They are chiefly dangerous to us because they might become cheap and relatively easy to manufacture, and because they could be extremely formidable and destructive in the hands of guerrillas or terrorists. If these weapons ever get into the hands of terrorists, it will not be because the terrorists will carry out the necessary scientific experiments, but because we will do the experiments ourselves and will be incapable of keeping the matter secret. The best way to keep such inventions out of irresponsible hands is for us to refrain from inventing them.

I would now recommend as the political solution to the problem of fission-free weapons that we formally renounce all further research on them and with due ceremony transfer to open scientific work any staff and facilities that may still be devoted to them at Livermore. We could take this step unilaterally, without waiting for a comprehensive test-ban agreement. This is the course which we have wisely adopted in connection with biological weapons. Even if I agree with nothing else that Mr. Nixon has done, I am profoundly thankful to him for that.

This is all I have to say about fission-free weapons. They are a good example to illustrate the weakness of a too technical approach to arms control. They demonstrate with particular clarity that the "irresistible march of technology" in matters of weaponry is an illusion. The march of technology easily peters out if the political tide is running against it.

The other technological arms control problem with which I have been mainly concerned is ballistic missile defense (BMD). While at the U.S. Arms Control and Disarmament Agency during 1962 and 1963 I made a study of the policy alternatives open to us at that time in dealing with BMD. The main question at issue was whether we should seek to include or to exclude BMD from the list of weapons to be prohibited or restricted in a possible arms-freeze agreement with the Soviet Union. I decided we should exclude BMD. The policy-makers at the Agency decided we should include it. The negotiations with the Soviet Union never became serious, and my policy study was buried in the Agency files and forgotten.

Now, eight years later, the SALT talks are reaching the serious stage and we are again forced to face the same old question: What should we do about BMD? I cannot here discuss all aspects of this complicated question. I will speak mainly about a narrower issue, namely, the question whether a consideration of future technological developments should influence our present negotiating positions. I do not need to remind you that I was wrong before about fission-free weapons and may be wrong again. Speculation about future technological possibilities is valuable only insofar as it is tempered with a high degree of skepticism.

Technologically speaking, there are two kinds of BMD, which I will call conventional and exotic. Conventional BMD is the kind which we and the Soviet Union have been experimenting with for the last fifteen years and are now hesitantly beginning to deploy. It consists of big interceptor rockets armed with nuclear warheads, big radars to detect and track incoming missiles, and big computers to direct the interceptors so that they can destroy attackers. Almost all the public discussion of BMD has been concerned with conventional BMD. All the systems which have been under serious development, whether designed for area or for terminal defense, for city or for hard-point defense, have been basically the same conventional BMD system. The distinctions between area and terminal, city and hard-point, are politically important but technically minor. The conventional BMD system is the only one we seriously think about building because it is the only one we know how to build.

Exotic BMD is anything that is not conventional. A great variety of exotic systems have been invented by ingenious engineers and scientists. Most of them are nonnuclear. Each of them seems to be feasible in theory but is formidable to design in detail. The two main categories of exotic BMD systems are supposed to kill missiles by direct hits of small nonnuclear interceptors (pellet systems) or by some kind of high-energy radiation (death-ray systems). The common feature of all exotic systems is that although they probably do not work at all, if by chance they do work, they may be spectacularly better than conventional systems. In particular, a nonnuclear BMD would avoid many of the political problems which conventional BMD raises, both domestically and internationally.

Four of the serious objections to conventional BMD are the following:

1. There is no politically acceptable way to find out whether or not the system works as advertised.
2. A system controlled tightly enough to eliminate the risk of a nuclear response to a false alarm will be incapable of a sufficiently rapid response to a real attack.
3. The large interceptor missiles with high-yield warheads can easily be converted into offensive weapons.
4. The development of conventional BMD is now the main

obstacle to a reduction or elimination of underground nuclear tests.

All four objections would disappear if we were dealing with exotic BMD. These political advantages of exotic BMD are to my mind more substantial than the technical advantages. It is possible that exotic BMD could be far more effective, and conceivably also cheaper, than conventional BMD, but these possibilities are necessarily remote and conjectural. The real promise of exotic BMD lies in its psychological acceptability. One can imagine a future world in which major powers protect themselves with nonnuclear BMD systems while gradually reducing offensive nuclear forces to insignificant levels.

This is a possible route to a stable international equilibrium no longer based on threats of mutual annihilation, and it is a route which most people would consider attractive if it were technically feasible. On the other hand, it is difficult to imagine reaching a stable and relaxed equilibrium with only conventional BMD systems. Even if the conventional BMD became technically capable of defending us, many of us would be unenthusiastic about relying on it as a permanent solution of our security problems.

It was probably a sound instinct that brought out the housewives of Tenafly to protest loudly when it was proposed to put a major BMD installation there as part of the Sentinel system for the defense of New York City. Though sadly misinformed about the technical details of Sentinel, the housewives made a correct political judgment that a large concentration of nuclear warheads in suburban areas, ready to be launched and detonated at a moment's notice, would not increase the security of the city's inhabitants.

The basic question which confronts decision-makers in connection with the long-range future of BMD is whether we wish to perpetuate or to nullify the supremacy of the offensive. By "supremacy of the offensive" I mean the strategic doctrine with which the United States has been living since 1945, according to which nuclear forces are so overwhelmingly strong that any defense against them is at best a palliative.

The supremacy of the offensive dictates the strategy, which the U.S. has followed since 1960 and the Soviet Union since 1965, of giving first priority to invulnerable second-strike offensive forces and relying upon deterrence rather than defense to keep us alive.

Many experts in arms control have grown so accustomed to the supremacy of the offensive that they accept it as permanent and even desirable. People who think this way consider the "balance of terror" the only feasible basis of world peace; they violently oppose population defense as a misguided and vain attempt to upset the balance. Mr. McNamara, in his pre-Sentinel days a strong exponent of this attitude, seems to have succeeded in converting the post-Khrushchev Soviet leaders to his point of view.

The SALT talks will very likely result in an agreement which solidifies the supremacy of the offensive by limiting BMD to insignificant levels while allowing the offensive forces on both sides to remain at their present enormous size. This at least is the outcome which most arms-controllers in the United States seem to desire. In the present state of the world, it may well be the best outcome that we can hope to achieve.

On the other hand, the supremacy of the offensive has grave disadvantages as a basis for any kind of stable world order. I do not need to spell out the disadvantages in detail. There is, first and never to be forgotton, the moral disadvantage of building security on the threat of indiscriminate slaughter of populations. This threat inevitably deprives our government of moral legitimacy in the eyes of many people both abroad and at home. Second, there is the inability of deterrence to stop insane or irresponsible people from attacking us. Third, there is the disproportionate size of the disaster that results if, because of some accident or misunderstanding, the strategic offensive weapons are ever used.

These three disadvantages of the present strategic situation are so overwhelming that many of us who have lived with them for twenty years have learned to turn a blind eye to them. Nevertheless they are real enough. If BMD offers any hope of breaking the supremacy of the offensive and moving us toward a world in which the major strategic forces are defensive in character, we would be wise to do all we can to keep this hope alive.

The technical arguments about BMD are mostly related to the questions whether deployment of population defenses can in the real world diminish the supremacy of the offensive. When country A deploys BMD to defend its population, country B may respond in either of two opposite ways: If country B believes that the BMD can be easily countered or saturated, then country B will presumably increase the numbers and sophistication of its offensive weapons as necessary to make sure that the effectiveness of the BMD is nullified. In this case the supremacy of the offensive is preserved or even increased as a result of deployment by country A and reaction by country B. On the other hand, if country B believes that the BMD is highly effective and that the cost of countering it with new offensive weapons is unreasonably high, the preferred response for country B may be to build an equally good population defense and leave the offensive weapons alone. In the second case BMD deployment has effectively diminished the supremacy of the offensive; the way is then open for political arrangements leading to major reductions in offensive forces and to the solidification of a strategic balance based on defense rather than deterrence.

Most of the experts today, like Mr. McNamara of old, are strongly of the opinion that BMD cannot be or look good enough to produce the second reaction. So they believe that deployment of population defense will do nothing to mitigate the supremacy of the offensive and will only lead to an intensified and useless arms race. So far as the present state of the BMD art is concerned, the experts are probably right. Mr. Nixon certainly agrees with them. He used the same argument to justify his decision to abandon the Sentinel population-defense system and to convert it into the Safeguard hard-point system.

But we should be careful not to take for granted the technical hopelessness of BMD for population defense. The present state of the art is not final. It is possible that in five or ten years the capabilities of conventional BMD will be enough improved that deployment of population defense would no longer be self-defeating. If any form of exotic BMD were to become feasible, population defense might suddenly become strategically sound as well as politically unobjectionable. So the main advice that I would give to the SALT negotiators is: "Do not do anything to permanently forbid a move to a defensively oriented world in case of a technological change that would make this possible."

There are valid technical reasons for expecting that defensive technology may advance more rapidly than offensive technology. The supremacy of offensive technology during the last twenty years has been based on two physical inventions, the hydrogen bomb and the multiple-stage rocket, which are hardly capable of further radical improvement. In contrast, defensive technology is based on sensors and computers which are still at a stage of rapid and unpredictable development.

The offense/defense battle is primarily a battle of information. If the defense can detect a target in time and know accurately where it is, it is not too difficult to destroy it. The defense can in principle win if it has complete and accurate information and the ability to process the information and to respond to it. Ultimately, it seems reasonable to expect that the defense will be able to outmaneuver and outwit the offense, simply because the defense is fighting the battle at close range and in full view, whereas the offense is fighting it blind from a command center thousands of miles away.

So I can honestly say as a scientist that the long-range prospects for a technically adequate BMD are bright. But that alone would hardly be worth saying. Much more important, to my mind, is the fact that there are compelling moral and political reasons for us to desire an adequate BMD, so that we are not condemned to live forever by threatening instant death to our neighbors and to ourselves. When moral and political imperatives create a need, and when the technological problems are not insuperable, then there is a good chance that the need will one day be filled.

The problems of fission-free weapons and of ballistic missile defense are of too recent origin to allow any reliablc judgment of their historical consequences. My third example of a technological arms-control problem is deliberately chosen for its longer history. From the perspective of 150 years one may be able to see more clearly the features of an arms-control agreement that give it durability. So I will briefly discuss the story of the Rush-Bagot Agreement limiting naval armaments on the Great Lakes of North America. I take the details from an excellent article, "Arms Control on the Great Lakes," published by James Eayrs in Volume 2 of *Disarmament and Arms Control* (Autumn 1964).

The agreement, made official in 1817 by Acting Secretary of State Richard Rush and the British Minister at Washington Sir Charles Bagot, stipulated as follows:

> The naval force to be maintained upon the American Lakes by His Majesty and the Government of the United States shall henceforth be confined to the following vessels on each side, that is—On Lake Ontario, to one vessel, not exceeding one hundred tons burden, and armed with the eighteen-pound cannon. On the Upper Lakes, to two vessels, not exceeding like burden each, and armed with like force. On the waters of Lake Champlain, to one vessel not exceeding like burden . . . .

For the full text of the agreement and for a detailed narrative of its later history I must refer you to Mr. Eayrs' account. The fleets existing on the lakes in 1817 were much larger than the agreed limit, and the individual ships were too big to be sailed down the St. Lawrence River. The agreement thus required a substantial act of disarmament, which was promptly carried out by dismantling ships on both sides. The main objective of the agreement was to avoid confrontations which might lead to a renewed outbreak of the indecisive War of 1812. This aim was achieved.

From my point of view the most instructive feature of the agreement is that it paid no attention at all to the problem of technological change. There is no sign in it that Mr. Rush and Sir Charles were disturbed by the thought that eighteen-pound cannon would not forever remain the last word in naval armament.

For a hundred years after the signing of the agreement, technological changes were constantly creating difficulties in its implementation. During these years the American-Canadian frontier was not always as peaceful as it later became. In 1841 Britain violated the agreement with two steam frigates. In 1843 the U.S. responded with a ship of 685 tons carrying two six-inch guns which could hardly have weighed less than eighteen pounds. And so it went. From the 1840s onward, there was never a time when one side or the other was not technically violating the agreement. As the political relations between the two sides gradually became less acrimonious toward the end of the nineteenth century, the magnitude of the violations increased. Each new violation was customarily greeted with vehement protests from the other side, but as time went on the protests became less public and more ritualistic. In 1920 a senior official of the Canadian navy was still writing: "It is . . . of the utmost importance that troops should be ready to immediately occupy the American shore of the St. Lawrence, that large numbers of small craft should be maintained . . ., and that a good supply of mines should be available in Canada for blocking the Straits of Mackinac, Detroit river, etc." But by that time nobody outside the military staffs was prepared to take such nightmares seriously.

The fact that the Rush-Bagot agreement was technically violated did not destroy its political usefulness. Through the worst periods of Canadian-American tensions the agreement was kept legally in force and was instrumental in holding these tensions in check. The political leaders on both sides found the agreement useful, and employed it effectively to pacify the bellicose minority on their own side of the border as well as to castigate the bellicose minority on the other side. The technical details of the agreement were important in 1817, but grew less and less important as its age and venerability increased. By the end of the nineteenth century there had developed a tacit understanding between the two governments that technical violations would be condoned provided that the "spirit of the agreement" was preserved. So now, after 150 years, the agreement is still legally in force, is still technically violated several times every year, and has passed into folklore as a symbol of enduring peace.

I cannot refrain at this point from quoting the last few sentences of Mr. Eayrs' essay:

> In 1960 there was public speculation that among proposals being considered for improving the apparatus of massive retaliation was a scheme for mounting Intercontinental Ballistic Missiles on Great Lakes missile ships. Nothing came of it. Had something come of it, the Rush-Bagot agreement would have been put to a supreme test of its malleability. Even the most seasoned manipulators of the "clausula rebus sic stantibus" might blush while pronouncing the presence of scores of weapons, each of the destructive equivalent of millions of tons of TNT, to be consistent with the spirit of an Agreement forbidding the presence of anything exceeding the normal amount of ammunition for four eighteen-pound cannon. But that is not to say they could not have done it.

Let me now try to summarize whatever lessons can be

learned from considering together these three very different episodes, the fission-free nuclear weapons that failed to disrupt a test ban, the ballistic missile defenses that are now complicating the SALT negotiations, and the Rush-Bagot agreement that succeeded in pacifying a continent by harnessing in the cause of peace the powerful forces of human inertia and hypocrisy.

What can we learn from all this? Surely the main lesson is clear in all three instances: The diplomat's view of things has proved to be more valid than the technocrat's view. In each case the feasibility and effectiveness of an arms-control agreement has depended primarily on the political advantages which it has offered to both sides. The technical arguments which loomed so large in the public discussion of the test ban and SALT negotiations were dealing only with one aspect, and not the most important aspect, of the whole situation.

The test-ban treaty of 1963 has already acquired a political solidity which technological change seems unlikely to upset. It is possible that the treaty will one day collapse, but if this happens it will probably be caused by some major political crisis rather than by the invention of some new kind of bomb. There are several indications of the growing immunity of the treaty to effects of technological change. One such indication is the readiness with which both sides have excused technical violations. Another indication is the fact that when programs of peaceful exploitation of nuclear explosives have come into conflict with the treaty it is taken for granted by everybody that the treaty shall prevail.

The Rush-Bagot agreement has shown in a spectacular way how the disturbances produced by technological change can be minimized by pretending that they do not exist. This method of handling technological problems cannot always be expected to succeed so brilliantly. Sometimes technological developments will refuse to be ignored. But it seems to me that the Rush-Bagot story teaches some lessons that apply to almost all arms-control situations. One lesson is that the value of an arms-control agreement is not automatically destroyed when the agreement is violated. The Rush-Bagot agreement has a withdrawal clause allowing either side to denounce the agreement by giving six months' notice, but this right has never been exercised even after flagrant violations. Another lesson is that the political interests which are served by a well-devised arms-control agreement and which tend to preserve the agreement are far more durable than any technological factors that may from time to time cause difficulties.

There are many examples in history of arms-control agreements that have failed. The conspicuous examples of failure have mostly occurred because one party viewed the agreement as attempting to keep him permanently in a position of political inferiority. I do not know an example of an agreement which failed primarily because of effects of technological change. If both sides have a strong and roughly equal political interest in maintaining an agreement, almost any technological change can be accommodated, either by ignoring it, in Rush-Bagot style, or, more rationally, by renegotiating it.

The SALT negotiations and the associated domestic discussions of ballistic missile defense are still at too early a stage to allow any firm conclusions to be drawn. My own judgment is that here, too, as in the other two instances, political interests will successfully override technological worries.

There are two alternative types of SALT agreement at which we can aim. One is an offensive-dominated agreement which freezes offensive deployments at about their present levels and forbids significant BMD. The technological worries in this case concern improvements in missile accuracy, MIRV, and the vulnerability of missile-carrying submarines. The other possible type of SALT agreement would give deliberate encouragement to both sides to turn gradually toward a defense-dominated posture. Such a defense-dominated agreement would freeze or reduce offensive deployments while allowing growth of BMD to continue. The main technological worry in this case is that BMD effectiveness might grow unequally on the two sides so that one side might achieve a real or imaginary strategic advantage.

I believe that if either of these types of SALT agreement were concluded, the technological worries would turn out to be unimportant. In other words, fears of technological surprise should not deter us from concluding whichever type of agreement we find politically preferable. For reasons which have little to do with technology, I think the defense-dominated agreement has greater promise as a basis for a lasting regulation of strategic power on this planet.

The defense-dominated agreement seems more likely to retain for long periods of time that political acceptability to all parties which is the only foundation for durability of such agreements. However, the prevailing climate of opinion, strongly influenced by some of my scientific colleagues, favors the offense-dominated alternative. It may be that an offense-dominated agreement will be easier to negotiate and ratify. If an offense-dominated agreement is the best we can achieve, let us sign it and be thankful. It is a great deal better than no agreement at all. But let us not delude ourselves into believing that the choice of an offense-dominated agreement is forced upon us by technology. The choice between defense and offense is a political choice, and we are free within wide limits to choose the strategic doctrines that will best serve our political interests.

If it happens that the SALT negotiations result in an offense-dominated agreement, I shall not grieve. I shall dream of some future meeting to be held 150 years from now, at which some future professor will be looking back on the history of the first 150 years of the SALT agreement. He will, if all goes well, be explaining how the technological defects of the agreement did not turn out to be fatal. He will be explaining how the clause of the agreement prohibiting the deployment of missile defense was progressively violated by each of the great powers in turn, after the first demonstration of a cheap and effective nonnuclear BMD system by the Japanese in the year 1995. And how, in spite of these violations, the agreement continued in force and was successful in dissuading each of the governments from embarking on a massive buildup of offensive weapons to counter each other's defenses. And how strategic offensive weapons gradually became obsolete toward the end of the twenty-first century and were retained only in small numbers for ceremonial purposes.

That is, if we are as wise as Rush and Bagot. And if all goes well.

APPENDIX:
The SALT Agreements and their Interpretations

Enclosure 1

Treaty
Between the United States of America
and
the Union of Soviet Socialist Republics
on the Limitation of Anti-ballistic Missile Systems

The United States of America and the Union of Soviet Socialist Republics, hereinafter referred to as the Parties,

Proceeding from the premise that nuclear war would have devastating consequences for all mankind,

Considering that effective measures to limit anti-ballistic missile systems would be a substantial factor in curbing the race in strategic offensive arms and would lead to a decrease in the risk of outbreak of war involving nuclear weapons,

Proceeding from the premise that the limitation of anti-ballistic missile systems, as well as certain agreed measures with respect to the limitation of strategic offensive arms, would contribute to the creation of more favorable conditions for further negotiations on limiting strategic arms,

Mindful of their obligations under Article VI of the Treaty on the Non-Proliferation of Nuclear Weapons,

Declaring their intention to achieve at the earliest possible date the cessation of the nuclear arms race and to take effective measures toward reductions in strategic arms, nuclear disarmament, and general and complete disarmament,

Desiring to contribute to the relaxation of international tension and the strengthening of trust between States,

Have agreed as follows:

Article I

1. Each Party undertakes to limit anit-ballistic missile (ABM) systems and to adopt other measures in accordance with the provisions of this Treaty.

2. Each Party undertakes not to deploy ABM systems for a defense of the territory of its country and not to provide a base for such a defense, and not to deploy ABM systems for defense of an individual region except as provided for in Article III of this Treaty.

Article II

1. For the purposes of this Treaty an ABM system is a system to counter strategic ballistic missiles or their elements in flight trajectory, currently consisting of:

(a) ABM interceptor missiles, which are interceptor missiles constructed and deployed for an ABM role, or of a type tested in an ABM mode;

(b) ABM launchers, which are launchers constructed and deployed for launching ABM interceptor missiles; and

(c) ABM radars, which are radars constructed and deployed for an ABM role, or of a type tested in an ABM mode.

2. The ABM system components listed in paragraph 1 of this Article include those which are:

(a) operational;

(b) under construction;

(c) undergoing testing;

(d) undergoing overhaul, repair or conversion; or

(e) mothballed.

Article III

Each Party undertakes not to deploy ABM systems or their components except that:

(a) within one ABM system deployment area having a radius of one hundred and fifty kilometers and centered on the Party's national capital, a Party may deploy: (1) no more than one hundred ABM launchers and no more than one hundred ABM interceptor missiles at launch sites, and (2) ABM radars within no more than six ABM radar complexes, the area of each complex being circular and having a diameter of no more than three kilometers; and

(b) within one ABM system deployment area having a radius of one hundred and fifty kilometers and containing ICBM silo launchers, a Party may deploy: (1) no more than one hundred ABM launchers and no more than one hundred ABM interceptor missiles at launch sites, (2) two large phased-array ABM radars comparable in potential to corresponding ABM radars operational or under construction on the date of signature of the Treaty in an ABM system deployment area containing ICBM silo launchers, and (3) no more than eighteen ABM radars each having a potential less than the potential of the smaller of the above-mentioned two large phased-array ABM radars.

Article IV

The limitations provided for in Article III shall not apply to ABM systems or their components used for development or testing, and located within current or additionally agreed test ranges. Each Party may have no more than a total of fifteen ABM launchers at test ranges.

Article V

1. Each Party undertakes not to develop, test, or deploy ABM systems or components which are sea-based, air-based, space-based, or mobile land-based.

2. Each Party undertakes not to develop, test, or deploy ABM launchers for launching more than one ABM interceptor

missile at a time from each launcher, nor to modify deployed launchers to provide them with such a capability, nor to develop, test, or deploy automatic or semi-automatic or other similar systems for rapid reload of ABM launchers.

Article VI

To enhance assurance of the effectiveness of the limitations on ABM systems and their components provided by this Treaty, each Party undertakes:

(a) not to give missiles, launchers, or radars, other than ABM interceptor missiles, ABM launchers, or ABM radars, capabilities to counter strategic ballistic missiles or their elements in flight trajcctory, and not to test them in an ABM mode; and

(b) not to deploy in the future radars for early warning of strategic ballistic missile attack except at locations along the periphery of its national territory and oriented outward.

Article VII

Subject to the provisions of this Treaty, modernization and replacement of ABM systems or their components may be carried out.

Article VIII

ABM systems or their components in excess of the numbers or outside the areas specified in this Treaty, as well as ABM systems or their components prohibited by this Treaty, shall be destroyed or dismantled under agreed procedures within the shortest possible agreed period of time.

Article IX

To assure the viability and effectiveness of this Treaty, each Party undertakes not to transfer to other States, and not to deploy outside its national territory, ABM systems or their components limited by this Treaty.

Article X

Each Party undertakes not to assume any international obligations which would conflict with this Treaty.

Article XI

The Parties undertake to continue active negotiations for limitations on strategic offensive arms.

Article XII

1. For the purpose of providing assurance of compliance with the provisions of this Treaty, each Party shall use national technical means of verification at its disposal in a manner consistent with generally recognized principles of international law.

2. Each Party undertakes not to interfere with the national technical means of verification of the other Party operating in accordance with paragraph 1 of this Article.

3. Each Party undertakes not to use deliberate concealment measures which impede verification by national technical means of compliance with the provisions of this Treaty. This obligation shall not require changes in current construction, assembly, conversion, or overhaul practices.

Article XIII

1. To promote the objectives and implementation of the provisions of this Treaty, the Parties shall establish promptly a Standing Consultative Commission, within the framework of which they will:

(a) consider questions concerning compliance with the obligations assumed and related situations which may be considered ambiguous;

(b) provide on a voluntary basis such information as either Party considers necessary to assure confidence in compliance with the obligations assumed;

(c) consider questions involving unintended interference with national technical means of verification;

(d) consider possible changes in the strategic situation which have a bearing on the provisions of this Treaty;

(e) agree upon procedures and dates for destruction or dismantling of ABM systems or their components in cases provided for by the provisions of this Treaty;

(f) consider, as appropriate, possible proposals for further increasing the viability of this Treaty, including proposals for amendments in accordance with the provisions of this Treaty;

(g) consider, as appropriate, proposals for further measures aimed at limiting strategic arms.

2. The Parties through consultation shall establish, and may amend as appropriate, Regulations for the Standing Consultative Commission governing procedures, composition and other relevant matters.

Article XIV

1. Each Party may propose amendments to this Treaty. Agreed amendments shall enter into force in accordance with the procedures governing the entry into force of this Treaty.

2. Five years after entry into force of this Treaty, and at five year intervals thereafter, the Parties shall together conduct a review of this Treaty.

Article XV

1. This Treaty shall be of unlimited duration.

2. Each Party shall, in exercising its national sovereignty, have the right to withdraw from this Treaty if it decides that extraordinary events related to the subject matter of this Treaty have jeopardized its supreme interests. It shall give notice of its decision to the other Party six months prior to withdrawal from the Treaty. Such notice shall include a statement of the extraordinary events the notifying Party regards as having jeopardized its supreme interests.

Article XVI

1. This Treaty shall be subject to ratification in accordance with the constitutional procedures of each Party. The Treaty

shall enter into force on the day of the exchange of instruments of ratification.

2. This Treaty shall be registered pursuant to Article 102 of the Charter of the United Nations.

Done at Moscow on May 26, 1972, in two copies, each in the English and Russian languages, both texts being equally authentic.

FOR THE UNITED STATES OF AMERICA:

RICHARD NIXON

President of the United States of America

FOR THE UNION OF SOVIET SOCIALIST REPUBLICS:

LEONID I. BREZHNEV

General Secretary of the Central Committee of the CPSU

Enclosure 2

Interim Agreement Between the United States of America and the Union of Soviet Socialist Republics on Certain Measures with Respect to the Limitation of Strategic Offensive Arms

The United States of America and the Union of Soviet Socialist Republics, hereinafter referred to as the Parties,

Convinced that the Treaty on the Limitation of Anti-Ballistic Missile Systems and this Interim Agreement on Certain Measures with Respect to the Limitation of Strategic Offensive Arms will contribute to the creation of more favorable conditions for active negotiations on limiting strategic arms as well as to the relaxation of international tension and the strengthening of trust between States,

Taking into account the relationship between strategic offensive and defensive arms,

Mindful of their obligations under Article VI of the Treaty on the Non-Proliferation of Nuclear Weapons,

Have agreed as follows:

Article I

The Parties undertake not to start construction of additional fixed land-based intercontinental ballistic missile (ICBM) launchers after July 1, 1972.

Article II

The Parties undertake not to convert land-based launchers for light ICBMs, or for ICBMs of older types deployed prior to 1964, into land-based launchers for heavy ICBMs of types deployed after that time.

Article III

The Parties undertake to limit submarine-launched ballistic missile (SLBM) launchers and modern ballistic missile submarines to the numbers operational and under construction on the date of signature of this Interim Agreement, and in addition to launchers and submarines constructed under procedures established by the Parties as replacements for an equal number of ICBM launchers of older types deployed prior to 1964 or for launchers on older submarines.

Article IV

Subject to the provisions of this Interim Agreement, modernization and replacement of strategic offensive ballistic missiles and launchers covered by this Interim Agreement may be undertaken.

Article V

1. For the purpose of providing assurance of compliance with the provisions of this Interim Agreement, each Party shall use national technical means of verification at its disposal in a manner consistent with generally recognized principles of international law.

2. Each Party undertakes not to interfere with the national technical means of verification of the other Party operating in accordance with paragraph 1 of this Article.

3. Each Party undertakes not to use deliberate concealment measures which impede verification by national technical means of compliance with the provisions of this Interim Agreement. This obligation shall not require changes in current construction, assembly, conversion, or overhaul practices.

Article VI

To promote the objectives and implementation of the provisions of this Interim Agreement, the Parties shall use the Standing Consultative Commission established under Article XIII of the Treaty on the Limitation of Anti-Ballistic Missile Systems in accordance with the provisions of that Article.

Article VII

The Parties undertake to continue active negotiations for limitations on strategic offensive arms. The obligations provided for in this Interim Agreement shall not prejudice the scope or terms of the limitations on strategic offensive arms which may be worked out in the course of further negotiations.

Article VIII

1. This Interim Agreement shall enter into force upon exchange of written notices of acceptance by each Party, which exchange shall take place simultaneously with the exchange of

instruments of ratification of the Treaty on the Limitation of Anti-Ballistic Missile Systems.

2. This Interim Agreement shall remain in force for a period of five years unless replaced earlier by an agreement on more complete measures limiting strategic offensive arms. It is the objective of the Parties to conduct active follow-on negotiations with the aim of concluding such an agreement as soon as possible.

3. Each Party shall, in exercising its national sovereignty, have the right to withdraw from this Interim Agreement if it decides that extraordinary events related to the subject matter of this Interim Agreement have jeopardized its supreme interests. It shall give notice of its decision to the other Party six months prior to withdrawal from this Interim Agreement. Such notice shall include a statement of the extraordinary events the notifying Party regards as having jeopardized its supreme interests.

Done at Moscow on May 26, 1972, in two copies, each in the English and Russian languages, both texts being equally authentic.

FOR THE UNITED STATES OF AMERICA:

RICHARD NIXON

President of the United States of America

FOR THE UNION OF SOVIET SOCIALIST REPUBLICS:

LEONID I. BREZHNEV

General Secretary of the Central Committee of the CPSU

Protocol

To the Interim Agreement Between the United States of America and the Union of Soviet Socialist Republics on Certain Measures with Respect to the Limitation of Strategic Offensive Arms

The United States of America and the Union of Soviet Socialist Republics, hereinafter referred to as the Parties,

Having agreed on certain limitations relating to submarine-launched ballistic missile launchers and modern ballistic missile submarines, and to replacement procedures, in the Interim Agreement,

Have agreed as follows:

The Parties understand that, under Article III of the Interim Agreement, for the period during which that Agreement remains in force:

The US may have no more than 710 ballistic missile launchers on submarines (SLBMs) and no more than 44 modern ballistic missile submarines. The Soviet Union may have no more than 950 ballistic missile launchers on submarines and no more than 62 modern ballistic missile submarines.

Additional ballistic missile launchers on submarines up to the above-mentioned levels, in the U.S.—over 656 ballistic missile launchers on nuclear-powered submarines, and in the U.S.S.R.—over 740 ballistic missile launchers on nuclear-powered submarines, operational and under construction, may become operational as replacements for equal numbers of ballistic missile launchers of older types deployed prior to 1964 or of ballistic missile launchers on older submarines.

The deployment of modern SLBMs on any submarine, regardless of type, will be counted against the total level of SLBMs permitted for the U.S. and the U.S.S.R.

This Protocol shall be considered an integral part of the Interim Agreement.

Done at Moscow this 26th day of May, 1972.

FOR THE UNITED STATES OF AMERICA

RICHARD NIXON

President of the United States of America

FOR THE UNION OF SOVIET SOCIALIST REPUBLICS

LEONID I. BREZHNEV

General Secretary of the Central Committee of the CPSU

Enclosure 3

1. Agreed Interpretations.

(a) **Initialed Statements.**

The texts of the statements set out below were agreed upon and initialed by the Heads of the Delegations on May 26, 1972.

ABM Treaty

[**A**]

The Parties understand that, in addition to the ABM radars

which may be deployed in accordance with subparagraph (a) of Article III of the Treaty, those non-phased-array ABM radars operational on the date of signature of the Treaty within the ABM system deployment area for defense of the national capital may be retained.

[**B**]

The Parties understand that the potential (the product of mean emitted power in watts and antenna area in square meters) of the smaller of the two large phased-array ABM radars referred to in subparagraph (b) of Article III of the Treaty is considered for purposes of the Treaty to be three million.

[**C**]

The Parties understand that the center of the ABM system deployment area centered on the national capital and the center of the ABM system deployment area containing ICBM silo launchers for each Party shall be separated by no less than thirteen hundred kilometers.

[**D**]

The Parties agree not to deploy phased-array radars having a potential (the product of mean emitted power in watts and antenna area in square meters) exceeding three million, except as provided for in Articles III, IV and VI of the Treaty, or except for the purposes of tracking objects in outer space or for use as national technical means of verification.

[**E**]

In order to insure fulfillment of the obligation not to deploy ABM systems and their components except as provided in Article III of the Treaty, the Parties agree that in the event ABM systems based on other physical principles and including components capable of substituting for ABM interceptor missiles, ABM launchers, or ABM radars are created in the future, specific limitations on such systems and their components would be subject to discussion in accordance with Article XIII and agreement in accordance with Article XIV of the Treaty.

[**F**]

The Parties understand that Article V of the Treaty includes obligations not to develop, test or deploy ABM interceptor missiles for the delivery by each ABM interceptor missile of more than one independently guided warhead.

[**G**]

The Parties understand that Article IX of the Treaty includes the obligation of the US and the USSR not to provide to other States technical descriptions or blueprints specially worked out for the construction of ABM systems and their components limited by the Treaty.

Interim Agreement

[**H**]

The Parties understand that land-based ICBM launchers referred to in the Interim Agreement are understood to be launchers for strategic ballistic missiles capable of ranges in excess of the shortest distance between the northeastern border of the continental U.S. and the northwestern border of the continental USSR.

[**I**]

The Parties understand that fixed land-based ICBM launchers under active construction as of the date of signature of the Interim Agreement may be completed.

[**J**]

The Parties understand that in the process of modernization and replacement the dimensions of land-based ICBM silo launchers will not be significantly increased.

[**K**]

The Parties understand that dismantling or destruction of ICBM launchers of older types deployed prior to 1964 and ballistic missile launchers on older submarines being replaced by new SLBM launchers on modern submarines will be initiated at the time of the beginning of sea trials of a replacement submarine, and will be completed in the shortest possible agreed period of time. Such dismantling or destruction, and timely notification thereof, will be accomplished under procedures to be agreed in the Standing Consultative Commission.

[**L**]

The Parties understand that during the period of the Interim Agreement there shall be no significant increase in the number of ICBM or SLBM test and training launchers, or in the number of such launchers for modern land-based heavy ICBMs. The Parties further understand that construction or conversion of ICBM launchers at test ranges shall be undertaken only for purposes of testing and training.

(b) **Common Understandings.**

Common understanding of the Parties on the following matters was reached during the negotiations:

A. *Increase in ICBM Silo Dimensions*

Ambassador Smith made the following statement on May 26, 1972: "The Parties agree that the term 'significantly increased' means that an increase will not be greater than 10–15 percent of the present dimensions of land-based ICBM silo launchers."

Minister Semenov replied that this statement corresponded to the Soviet understanding.

B. *Location of ICBM Defenses*

The U.S. Delegation made the following statement on May 26, 1972: "Article III of the ABM Treaty provides for each side one ABM system deployment area centered on its national capital and one ABM system deployment area containing ICBM silo launchers. The two sides have registered agreement on the following statement: 'The Parties understand that the center of the ABM system deployment area centered on the national capital and the center of the ABM system deployment area containing ICBM silo launchers for each Party shall be separated by no less than thirteen hundred kilometers.' In this connection, the U.S. side notes that its ABM system deployment area for defense of ICBM silo launchers, located west of the Mississippi River, will be centered in the Grand Forks ICBM silo launcher deployment area." (See Initialed Statement [C].)

C. *ABM Test Ranges*

The U.S. Delegation made the following statement on April 26, 1972: "Article IV of the ABM Treaty provides that 'the limitations provided for in Article III shall not apply to ABM systems or their components used for development or testing, and located within current or additionally agreed test ranges.' We believe it would be useful to assure that there is no misunderstanding as to current ABM test ranges. It is our understanding that ABM test ranges encompass the area within which ABM components are located for test purposes. The current U.S. ABM test ranges are at White Sands, New Mexico, and at Kwajalein Atoll, and the current Soviet ABM test range is near Sary Shagan in Kazakhstan. We consider that non-phased array radars of types used for range safety or instrumentation purposes may be located outside of ABM test ranges. We interpret the reference in Article IV to 'additionally agreed test ranges' to mean that ABM components will not be located at any other test ranges without prior agreement between our Governments that there will be such additional ABM test ranges."

On May 5, 1972, the Soviet Delegation stated that there was a common understanding on what ABM test ranges were, that the use of the types of non-ABM radars for range safety or instrumentation was not limited under the Treaty, that the reference in Article IV to "additionally agreed" test ranges was sufficiently clear, and that national means permitted identifying current test ranges.

D. *Mobile ABM Systems*

On January 28, 1972, the U.S. Delegation made the following statement: "Article V(1) of the Joint Draft Text of the ABM Treaty includes an undertaking not to develop, test, or deploy mobile land-based ABM systems and their components. On May 5, 1971, the U.S. side indicated that, in its view, a prohibition on deployment of mobile ABM systems and components would rule out the deployment of ABM launchers and radars which were not permanent fixed types. At that time, we asked for the Soviet view of this interpretation. Does the Soviet side agree with the U.S. side's interpretation put forward on May 5, 1971?"

On April 13, 1972, the Soviet Delegation said there is a general common understanding on this matter.

E. *Standing Consultative Commission*

Ambassador Smith made the following statement on May 23, 1972: "The United States proposes that the sides agree that, with regard to initial implementation of the ABM Treaty's Article XIII on the Standing Consultative Commission (SCC) and of the consultation Articles to the Interim Agreement on offensive arms and the Accidents Agreement*, agreement establishing the SCC will be worked out early in the follow-on SALT negotiations; until that is completed, the following arrangements will prevail: when SALT is in session, any consultation desired by either side under these Articles can be carried out by the two SALT Delegations; when SALT is not in session, *ad hoc* arrangements for any desired consultations under these Articles may be made through diplomatic channels."

Minister Semenov replied that, on an *ad referendum* basis, he

---

* See Article 7 of Agreement to Reduce the Risk of Outbreak of Nuclear War Between the United States of America and the Union of Soviet Socialist Republics, signed September 30, 1971.

could agree that the U.S. statement corresponded to the Soviet understanding.

F. *Standstill*

On May 6, 1972, Minister Semenov made the following statement: "In an effort to accommodate the wishes of the U.S. side, the Soviet Delegation is prepared to proceed on the basis that the two sides will in fact observe the obligations of both the Interim Agreement and the ABM Treaty beginning from the date of signature of these two documents."

In reply, the U.S. Delegation made the following statement on May 20, 1972: "The U.S. agrees in principle with the Soviet statement made on May 6 concerning observance of obligations beginning from date of signature but we would like to make clear our understanding that this means that, pending ratification and acceptance, neither side would take any action prohibited by the agreements after they had entered into force. This understanding would continue to apply in the absence of notification by either signatory of its intention not to proceed with ratification or approval."

The Soviet Delegation indicated agreement with the U.S. statement.

2. Unilateral Statements.

(a) The following noteworthy unilateral statements were made during the negotiations by the United States Delegation:—

A. *Withdrawal from the ABM Treaty*

On May 9, 1972, Ambassador Smith made the following statement: "The U.S. Delegation has stressed the importance the U.S. Government attaches to achieving agreement on more complete limitations on strategic offensive arms, following agreement on an ABM Treaty and on an Interim Agreement on certain measures with respect to the limitation of strategic offensive arms. The U.S. Delegation believes that an objective of the follow-on negotiations should be to constrain and reduce on a long-term basis threats to the survivability of our respective strategic retaliatory forces. The USSR Delegation has also indicated that the objectives of SALT would remain unfulfilled without the achievement of an agreement providing for more complete limitations on strategic offensive arms. Both sides recognize that the initial agreements would be steps toward the achievement of more complete limitations on strategic arms. If an agreement providing for more complete strategic offensive arms limitations were not achieved within five years, U.S. supreme interests could be jeopardized. Should that occur, it would constitute a basis for withdrawal from the ABM Treaty. The U.S. does not wish to see such a situation occur, nor do we believe that the USSR does. It is because we wish to prevent such a situation that we emphasize the importance the U.S. Government attaches to achievement of more complete limitations on strategic offensive arms. The U.S. Executive will inform the Congress, in connection with Congressional consideration of the ABM Treaty and the Interim Agreement of this statement of the U.S. position."

B. *Land-Mobile ICBM Launchers*

The U.S. Delegation made the following statement on May 20, 1972: "In connection with the important subject of land-mobile ICBM launchers, in the interest of concluding the Interim Agreement the U.S. Delegation now withdraws its proposal that Article I or an agreed statement explicitly prohibit the deployment of mobile land-based ICBM launchers. I have been instructed to inform you that, while agreeing to defer the question of limitation of operational land-mobile ICBM launchers to the subsequent negotiations on more complete limitations on strategic offensive arms, the U.S. would consider the deployment of operational land-mobile ICBM launchers during the period of the Interim Agreement as inconsistent with the objectives of that Agreement."

C. *Covered Facilities*

The U.S. Delegation made the following statement on May 20, 1972: "I wish to emphasize the importance that the United States attaches to the provisions of Article V, including in particular their application to fitting out or berthing submarines."

D. *"Heavy" ICBMs*

The U.S. Delegation made the following statement on May 26, 1972: "The U.S. Delegation regrets that the Soviet Delegation has not been willing to agree on a common definition of a heavy missile. Under these circumstances, the U.S. Delegation believes it necessary to state the following: The United States would consider any ICBM having a volume significantly greater than that of the largest light ICBM now operational on either side to be a heavy ICBM. The U.S. proceeds on the premise that the Soviet side will give due account to this consideration."

E. *Tested in ABM Mode*

On April 7, 1972, the U.S. Delegation made the following statement: "Article II of the Joint Draft Text uses the term 'tested in an ABM mode,' in defining ABM components, and Article VI includes certain obligations concerning such testing. We believe that the sides should have a common understanding of this phrase. First, we would note that the testing provisions of the ABM Treaty are intended to apply to testing which occurs after the date of signature of the Treaty, and not to any testing which may have occurred in the past. Next, we would amplify the remarks we have made on this subject during the previous Helsinki phase by setting forth the objectives which govern the U.S. view on the subject, namely, while prohibiting testing of non-ABM components for ABM purposes: not to prevent testing of ABM components, and not to prevent testing of non-ABM components for non-ABM purposes. To clarify our interpretation of 'tested in an ABM mode,' we note that we would consider a launcher, missile or radar to be 'tested in an ABM mode' if, for example, any of the following events occur: (1) a launcher is used to launch an ABM interceptor missile, (2) an interceptor missile is flight tested against a target vehicle which has a flight trajectory with characteristics of a strategic ballistic missile flight trajectory, or is flight tested in conjunction with the test of an ABM interceptor missile or an ABM radar at the same test range, or is flight tested to an altitude inconsistent with interception of targets against which air defenses are deployed, (3) a radar makes measurements on a cooperative target vehicle of the kind referred to in item (2) above during the reentry portion of its trajectory or makes measurements in conjunction with the test of an ABM interceptor missile or an ABM radar at the same test range. Radars used for purposes such as range safety or instrumentation would be exempt from application of these criteria."

F. *No-Transfer Article of ABM Treaty*

On April 18, 1972, the U.S. Delegation made the following statement: "In regard to this Article [IX], I have a brief and I believe self-explanatory statement to make. The U.S. side wishes to make clear that the provisions of this Article do not set a precedent for whatever provision may be considered for a Treaty on Limiting Strategic Offensive Arms. The question of transfer of strategic offensive arms is a far more complex issue, which may require a different solution."

G. *No Increase in Defense of Early Warning Radars*

On July 28, 1970, the U.S. Delegation made the following statement: "Since Hen House radars [Soviet ballistic missile early warning radars] can detect and track ballistic missile warheads at great distances, they have a significant ABM potential. Accordingly, the U.S. would regard any increase in the defenses of such radars by surface-to-air missiles as inconsistent with an agreement."

(b) The following noteworthy unilateral statement was made by the Delegation of the U.S.S.R. and is shown here with the U.S. reply:—

On May 17, 1972, Minister Semenov made the following unilateral "Statement of the Soviet Side:" "Taking into account that modern ballistic missile submarines are presently in the possession of not only the U.S., but also of its NATO allies, the Soviet Union agrees that for the period of effectiveness of the Interim 'Freeze' Agreement the U.S. and its NATO allies have up to 50 such submarines with a total of up to 800 ballistic missile launchers thereon (including 41 U.S. submarines with 656 ballistic missile launchers). However, if during the period of effectiveness of the Agreement U.S. allies in NATO should increase the number of their modern submarines to exceed the numbers of submarines they would have operational or under construction on the date of signature of the Agreement, the Soviet Union will have the right to a corresponding increase in the number of its submarines. In the opinion of the Soviet side, the solution of the question of modern ballistic missile submarines provided for in the Interim Agreement only partially compensates for the strategic imbalance in the deployment of the nuclear-powered missile submarines of the USSR and the U.S. Therefore, the Soviet side believes that this whole question, and above all the question of liquidating the American missile submarine bases outside the U.S., will be appropriately resolved in the course of follow-on negotiations."

On May 24, Ambassador Smith made the following reply to Minister Semenov: "The United States side has studied the 'statement made by the Soviet side' of May 17 concerning compensation for submarine basing and SLBM submarines belonging to third countries. The United States does not accept the validity of the considerations in that statement."

On May 26 Minister Semenov repeated the unilateral statement made on May 17. Ambassador Smith also repeated the U.S. rejection on May 26.

INDEX

N

O

P

R

S